Marketing 2000

and Beyond

Marketing 2000

and Beyond

Dr. William Lazer

Dr. Priscilla LaBarbera

Dr. James M. MacLachlan

Dr. Allen E. Smith

AMERICAN
MARKETING
ASSOCIATION

CHICAGO, ILLINOIS

Copyright©1990, American Marketing Association

President: Jeffrey Heilbrunn
Business Director: Francesca Van Gorp
Jacket Design: Frank Leone

Library of Congress Cataloging-in-Publication Data

Marketing 2000 And Beyond / William Lazer... [et al.].
    p. cm.
    Includes bibliographical references.
    ISBN 0-87757-204-6
    1. Marketing—Management—Forecasting. I. Lazer, William
(William Lazer), 1945-
    HF5415.13.M3445 1990
    658.8—dc20   89-29851
                                                         CIP

Printed in the United States of America

CONTENTS

This book is dedicated to our respective wives, families, and friends, whose generous support and encouragement throughout the years has made possible challenging pursuits such as this one.

PREFACE

This book, a product of the American Marketing Association's futures research project, Marketing 2000, is intended as a starting point toward improving the embodiment of a futures orientation on the part of academicians and business executives. The time period referred to is the "foreseeable future," about a 10 to 20 year time horizon, rather than a single future point in time.

The members of the core group who carried out the project are: Dr. William Lazer, Eminent Scholar in Business Administration, Florida Atlantic University, Director; Dr. Priscilla LaBarbera, Associate Professor, New York University, Associate Director; and Dr. James MacLachlan, Associate Professor, Rennselaer Polytechnic Institute, and Dr. Allen Smith, Associate Professor, Marketing, Florida Atlantic University, members of the Comission on Marketing in the Year 2000.

As authors, we are well aware of the unhappy thought that the events foreseen and reported may not occur at all. Generally future developments are not clearly discernable, rather only glimpses of the future and likely developments can be detected. As the project progressed, it became evident that it would not be possible to draw conclusions about future marketing developments with the same sense of certainty that marketing research studies often permitted. The normal sampling and statistical approaches they use and the search for conclusive irrefutable evidence is not possible. Futures research does not lend itself to such paradigms. A lack of certainty about future developments, however, does not negate the management benefits associated with futures projects.

No one involved with the study, whether members of the American Marketing Association's Marketing 2000 Presidential Advisory Committee, the Commission on Marketing in the Year 2000, those interviewed, nor the authors feel that they are omniscient. Rather, it is felt that even though some, or much of the information may well prove to be wide of the mark, this book can result in two major benefits.

First, the book can sensitize managers to the importance of becoming more involved with futures thinking, and to the benefits of bringing ideas about future marketing developments directly into their deliberations and decisions. Second, the perspectives developed can help managers become better apprised of some of the more likely future trends and developments along with the management implications and market opportunities they portend.

The book incorporates the following:

- Insights from visionary CEOs who were personally interviewed.

- Provocative thoughts from leading academicians and futurists.

- Perspectives on trends, changes, and challenges in marketing and their management implications.

- Insights into new directions in marketing management.

- Ideas on the future organization and deployment of marketing resources.

- An extensive review of the relevant futures literature.

The authors owe a great debt to many people who made this volume possible. Several executives of the American Marketing Association, particularly past presidents Manuel D. Plotkin and Leonard L. Berry, and both the former Executive Vice President Mr. Wayne A. Lemburg, and current President Mr. Jeffrey Heilbrunn, all lent continuous encouragement and generous support. We are most indebted to the members of the Presidential Advisory Committee, the American Marketing Association's Commission on Marketing in the Year 2000, the CEO's, and all the marketers, futurists, and academicians who generously shared their insights.

We gratefully acknowledge our very great debt to Edith Weiner, President of Weiner-Edrich-Brown, Inc.,who participated so actively as a member of the Presidential Advisory Committee, by generously sharing her thoughts and insights. She also read the entire manuscript making editorial improvements in every chapter. We offer her our deepest appreciation.

Particular recognition is due to Mrs. Jan Cooke for her contributions in preparing several drafts and the final manuscript; to Ms. Maureen Rafferty, a student assistant, for her valuable help throughout; and to Mr. Carlos Lebron, a doctoral student who contributed to the literature review process. We thank all who helped so willingly, in bringing this project to fruition.

Dr. William Lazer
Director, Marketing 2000

Dr. Priscilla LaBarbera
Associate Director, Marketing 2000

Dr. James MacLachlan
Commission on Marketing 2000

Dr. Allen Smith
Commission on Marketing 2000

INTRODUCTION

"A leader without a vision of the future is but a manager of todays affairs."

To develop a vision, you take in as many imputs as you can, often from books. The titles lining the shelves of our bookstores are full of easy answers, simplistic lists, rehashed theory, and war stories. But, there are no easy answers.

Marketing 2000 and Beyond will prepare you for today's planning of tomorrow. The book is so full of thoughtful ideas and observations, that you'll read it with highlighter in hand, and you'll refer to it for years to come. The book will stimulate your thought processes to help you develop your own unique answers.

The authors have spent several years researching and preparing this work. A separate volume, the annotated bibliography, also published by the American Marketing Association, represents the extensive secondary research that was content analyzed and distilled into the important concepts presented herein.

Combined with this analysis of the literature are in-depth interviews with leading business executives...executives like you, willing to share their visions of the future.

Being a visionary means you know where you are going; you're anticipating the changing environments of your business; and you're outlining the steps to take you to the future. **Marketing 2000 and Beyond** can help you see the future, plan for the changes, and achieve your vision.

Grab a highlighter; the future awaits you in these pages.

Jeffrey Heilbrunn
President
American Marketing Association

CHAPTER 1

WITH THE FUTURE IN MIND

"We've driving faster and faster into the future, trying to steer by using only the rear-view mirror." Marshall McLuhan

Introduction

The ability to anticipate, to be prepared, to foresee is rooted in futurity. Futurity is what this book is about. It deals with a variety of perspectives of anticipated future developments in markets and marketing as seen by insightful futurists, business executives, and academicians.

This book is the result of an American Marketing Association sponsored study, Marketing 2000, focusing on marketing in the future. The major objective is to stimulate and assist readers in developing useful insights into likely marketing developments in the foreseeable future, the next 10 to 20 years, and by so doing encourage managers to incorporate futures thinking into their decisions, strategies, and operations.

The contents present perspectives on likely marketing trends and developments, and emphasize management implications, opportunities, and challenges. Four approaches are utilized:

1. Future trends are presented and discussed in such important areas as technology, demographics, and consumer behavior, which will greatly shape and influence the future of marketing.

2. The writings and ideas of leading futurists, executives and marketing thinkers, about marketing, related business areas, and the external environments as well as likely scenarios of the future, are featured and analyzed.

3. The insights and ideas expressed, in personal interviews, by executives who are regarded as visionaries and leaders are highlighted[1].

---

[1]Two American Marketing Association appointed bodies made outstanding contributions to the direction, scope and approaches of this study. The first is the AMA's Presidential Commission that included Theodore J. Gordon, Chairman, the Futures Group; William B. Johnston, Senior Research

4. Brief idea papers prepared expressly for the book by practitioners, futurists, and marketing academicians concerned with future marketing developments are presented.

Each of these approaches provides a window onto the future. While individual windows may provide rather clouded or murky views, some of the future topography of marketing, the significant dynamic factors, and their tendencies can be discerned. Extremely valuable insights and scenarios for executive planning and decision making purposes can be developed. The results can furnish valuable information about organizing company resources for the future, and about achieving better links between businesses and the ever-changing market place.

Each window, may, of course, provide a different view. Although the landscape being scanned is the same, the perspectives vary. By examining a number of windows, and evaluating several likely perspectives, readers can gain a better understanding and appreciation of the "known" future and can better prepare to meet it. The results can provide:

- Valuable insights concerning highly attractive emerging market opportunities.

- Identification of profitable market segments.

- Information about shifts in target markets.

- Ideas about the kinds of products and services to produce and how to market them.

- Guidelines for distribution channel selection.

- Direction about positioning the firm and its products and services.

- Inputs for market communications programs and media campaigns.

- Improved packaging.

- Better understanding of supplier requisites.

- More sophisticated analyses of competition.

Fellow, the Hudson Institute; Rafael D. Pagan, Jr., Chairman, Pagan International; Florence R. Skelly, President Yankelovich, Skelly & White, Inc.; and Edith Weiner, President, Weiner-Edrich-Brown, Inc.

The second is the Commission on Marketing in the Year 2000 whose members were: Harold S. Becker, President, New Perspectives; J. Daniel Beckham, President, Health Market Inc.; Stephen J. Custer, Vice President, Marketing Services at Creswell/Munsell/Fultz and Zirbel, Inc.; Jane R. Fitzgibbon, Sr. Vice President and Director of Research Development, Ogilvy & Mather; Jeffrey Hallett, Principal, The PresentFutures Group; Ann Ives, President, The Educators Network; Dr. James MacLachlan, Associate Professor, Rensselaer Polytechnic Institute; Dr. Patrick E. Murphy, Associate Professor, University of Notre Dame; H. Paul Root, Division Director of Corporate Marketing Research, E.I. DuPont de Nemoures & Co.; and Dr. Allen E. Smith, Associate Professor of Marketing, Florida Atlantic University.

Forward Thinking

Accomplished business leaders have the ability to be immersed in present operations while at the same time keeping their eyes on the future, where success and profits ultimately reside. A futures orientation seems to differentiate the most dynamic, innovative, creative, growth, and profit-attuned organizations, from those that are not. The marketing literature is replete with examples of companies whose successful products and envied market positions were eroded, and eventually overtaken, sometimes rather abruptly, because of inadequate preparation for changing turns of future events which should have been anticipated.

Executives cannot overestimate the importance of preparing for the future. Their signal responsibility for making strategic decisions, implicitly or explicitly, involves visions and assessments of the future. In assessing threats and opportunities, executives deal rationally with the "knowable future," but are increasingly factoring "future facts," and future information, into their decisions. "Future facts" are basic inputs in such critical activities as: gaining and maintaining market position, adjusting rapidly to changing consumer wants and needs, being competitive in global markets, diversifying and spreading risks, strategic planning, and meeting investor expectations.

In making choices, executives are essentially putting their money where their vision of the future lies with expectations of successful returns. The profitability of their decisions, which are highly sensitive to unfolding future events, becomes a critical measure of their effectiveness. Yet managing today's organizations so as to be prepared for changes in tomorrow's longer-run market opportunities is becoming ever-more difficult.

That is the main reason that the American Marketing Association, the members of its Commission on Marketing 2000, and the authors, undertook a major research project culminating in this book. The project extended over four years, and included an extensive literature review, workshops with knowledgeable futures researchers, personal interviews with insightful CEOs of major corporations, and with market researchers, as well as meetings with marketing practitioners and academicians.

Concern about the future brings management face to face with broad marketing externalities outside the direct control of the company. This includes the growing importance of governmental actions and relationships with regulatory groups, the courts, federal governmental agencies, and legislatures. It emphasizes the importance of dealing with the company's many publics, including the financial community, labor, employees, and public interest groups. It means keeping abreast of many things ranging from the development and upkeep of infrastructures such as roads, ports, airports, and bridges, to the increase in health care costs related to the aging of the population, drug abuse, and AIDS.

Although no one can foresee future marketing developments with certainty, most of the forces that will shape them are already at work making themselves felt. Important dimensions of likely marketing trends and tendencies can be discerned, their implications for organizations can be set forth, and management can prepare to direct and channel resources into profitable avenues.

Caveats

In dealing with the future, executives should bear three caveats in mind. First, it is always prudent to expect the unexpected. That helps limit shocks and surprises. It is splendid preparation for dealing with some of the uncertainties of the future, and for assisting companies so that they are less likely to be caught off base.

Second, every trend may contain the seeds of a future countertrend. Those mindful of this will inject an appropriate notion of concern whenever they may be tempted to view the future largely in terms of straight line projections of the past. A greater sense of reality may be injected into future expectations with the constant reminder that the future could well bring a sharp break with the past.

Third, this book is designed to highlight an array of ideas about marketing in the future as expressed by both those who participated directly in this project and contributors to the literature. In a very real sense, the contents reflect their insights into the "state of the future." The coverage is broad, rather than narrow and deep, since an in depth discussion of future developments regarding any one of the topics could, by itself, result in a very extensive volume. What this means, of course, is that individual readers may feel that various marketing areas should have been dealt with at greater length, or that others should have been shortened.

Challenging the Conventional Wisdom

Marketing 2000 will be vastly different from marketing of the 1980s. That was one of the universal thoughts expressed in all of the personal interviews and workshops conducted, in the literature reviewed, and in the meetings and deliberations of the AMA bodies on Marketing 2000. The magnitude, rapidity, and reverberating impacts of marketing changes were themes emphasized over and over again. New demographics, vastly different consumers, rapidly changing business environments, and important technological developments were highlighted.

To gain some idea of the expected magnitude of Marketing 2000 changes, one need only reflect on the differences between marketing in 1950 and marketing today. They are worlds apart. The insights and ideas shared about marketing in the future, particularly in the interviews with CEOs, sometimes disagreed with commonly held marketing perceptions, pointing out uncommon implications, underscoring unexpected conclusions, and expounding ideas that are at variance with current marketing thought and practice.

For example, a common marketing belief is that the emergence of a global market, with newly industrialized and lesser developed countries coming on stream, will provide growing market opportunities for American companies. Several CEOs, however, suggested a much different scenario. They indicated it could mean excess industrial capacity globally with the existence of conditions of permanent oversupply for some industries, accompanied by expectations that the U.S. will fulfill its traditional role of a normal overflow market for the world. The result could be that U.S. companies will give up both market share and profits, with the future global economy possibly being detrimental to many U.S. industries.

Another changed perception relates to the unchallenged and enviable leadership position U.S. companies occupied in the past. The U.S. historically set standards of excellence for products and processes worldwide. Several participants in this study raised the pointed question, "Will U.S. business in the future be the leader in anything?" The former dominant U.S. position was perceived not only as waning in the future, but a psychological picture emerged of the U.S. as a secondary power, and certainly not as the world's premier marketer.

Some respondents noted that rather than a single nation (such as the U.S. or Japan), occupying the future leadership role in marketing or business, shared leadership positions encompassing several nations, varying by product and market area, and changing over time will evolve. There are many future implications of such a shift, including the need for American companies to commercialize the fruits of their R&D efforts more effectively. This means paying particular attention now to the development of effective future marketing programs.

The past was rooted in concepts of mass — mass manufacturing, mass middle-class markets, mass distribution of homogeneous products, and mass marketing systems linking mass production with mass consumption. This mass marketing orientation was seen by many as being tempered, and replaced, in Marketing 2000, by a relatively small-scale orientation — by an orientation focusing on heterogeneity, individualization, customization, variety, market niches, market segments, and mini-mass markets.

Thus, economies of scale, particularly those associated with mass production, may be modified and overridden by considerations of increasing customization and individualization of products, enhancing consumer satisfaction and expanding consumer choices. Productivity and efficiency may be tempered by considerations other than output maximization and cost reductions. Technology will support the economic feasibility of flexible production with smaller runs, enhanced consumer services and the practicality of servicing small niches on a global basis that, in total, will represent substantial profitable market opportunities.

The insights gathered also reflected a much different perspective on distribution channels. Distribution arrangements have customarily been portrayed as just springing up and evolving, largely in an unplanned manner, as a result of past decisions. They tended to become locked in, encased in cement. They were characterized by respondents as arrangements attuned to a bygone era, not in step with needs of the present and future. Many channel arrangements ignore the realities of the modern marketplace. By contrast, all of the Commission's input portrays distribution channel revitalization as among the most dynamic aspects of future marketing. Retrofitting and engineering of distribution channels to make them more effective was identified as a major determinant of future marketing success, and a signal ingredient of successful international marketing.

In the past, marketers have often considered consumers as groups, segments, or clusters, classified according to common demographic, social, and behavioral characteristics. But consumers remained rather hard to classify, identify, and track on an individual basis. As a result of new information technology and data bases, consumer anonymity and privacy is expected to diminish. An era of individual and small group consumer identification will emerge when information in company data banks is merged with data from sources such as credit cards, electronic fund transfers, and up-to-date purchasing records. This will be accompanied by a host of problems and issues related to privacy, encroachment, and the bombardment of consumers with targeted marketing promotions. In addition, law suits will arise out of questions of who owns the data and who may profit from it.

Competition has been the hallmark of marketing, and keener competition, on a global basis, is expected in Marketing 2000. At the same time, however, an opposing and somewhat complementary tendency is anticipated by many — the trend toward greater cooperation. New forms of marketing cooperation are expected among nations, industries, and individual businesses. Included will be orderly market agreements, harmonized trade accommodations, company consortia cutting across nations, new ownership, financing, and joint venture relationships, the use of barter and countertrade, and the encouragement of entrepreneurship through the application of new forms of cooperative enterprises in non-capitalistic environments. Marketing approaches that have been shaped by U.S. antitrust regulations will be modified, permitting, and encouraging greater cooperation among competing entities, within and outside of the U.S.

Price has been conventionally portrayed as a dominant, if not the predominant, competitive marketing variable. While it will still remain important, the competitive battleground is expected to shift significantly to include important quality and service concerns. But quality and service, in turn, will become "the ticket for admission to the marketplace," with other competitive factors being time saving, increasing convenience, ease of use, heightened user satisfaction, reduction of hassle, immediate availability, and related factors that enhance customer and consumer satisfaction.

Traditionally, service has been a significant and profitable dealer and distributor contribution to the marketing mix. The future will see a vast change, as servicing needs for many products can be drastically reduced. Increases in product quality, coupled with modularization, and smart products, will result in more trouble-free products. Consumers, dealers, and manufacturers will also be linked more directly, so that manufacturers and distributors will be able to handle consumer product problems more readily. Servicing will be supported by manufacturer service support and facilities. As a result, the profitability and functions of dealers will be changed markedly by new manufacturer/dealer relationships and responsibilities.

The recent past has heralded the era of scientific marketing, with its emphasis on the use of computers, mathematical, and statistical models, sophisticated data bases, psychographics, and physiological monitoring of subjects to support more logical, rational decisions. Suggestions have been made that even in the approaching information society, with its computer base, the future will see greater reliance on marketing management judgments, anticipations, estimates, opinions, and "gut feel." This will be augmented by far greater emphasis on the "people factor" in marketing.

In this study, those interviewed and included in our workshops rarely referred to environmental concerns. Thus, a few years ago the environment's impact on marketing in the future was not deemed to be central. By contrast, current literature is replete with information and implications about the future impact on life styles, business opportunities, and operations of such major environmental concerns as the dwindling ozone layer, the effects of pollution, deforestation, and acid rain. Among the possible implications is the likelihood that companies may not be "ready" to meet environmental realities.

The future environment could well include added threats to consumers' health and life styles, resulting in further restrictions on marketing, particularly on products, services, and marketing operations. The greenhouse effect, the results of new information about adverse impacts of chemical and pharmaceutical products, air and water pollution, and increasing poisoning of the food chain, may result in decisions mandating companies to make sudden unanticipated adjustments. Included may be such drastic actions as abruptly abandoning products and markets or significantly altering products, packages, and communications, thereby radically altering marketing operations, necessitating major business changes.

In a similar vein, the prevailing perspective of marketing control expressed by CEOs and many Commission members seems to be at odds with future reality. Control was seen largely as an internal consideration with marketing aspects being directed and shaped by internal marketing management decisions. By contrast, other comments and information gathered imply that in the future, not only will a good portion of marketing be controlled by external and extra-company forces, but the external forces will become even more important. For example, product designs and standards may well be established by international governments and world agencies, such as the units of the United Nations, as well as by global consumers and international businesses. Prices may be controlled by factors and forces existing in other nations, and the actions taken by international companies. Advertising and personal selling practices, as well as distribution arrangements, may well be shaped and structured by conditions existing in global markets. In the future, controlling marketing effort will become more of an externally-driven, and less of an internally-determined, activity.

Also in Marketing 2000, it is likely that we shall see a significant variation in future mindsets and postures of marketing managers. Some of the variations, their consequences and future impact, are discussed in detail in Chapter 8. They will certainly promote a far different marketing management emphasis than was the case in the past.

Overall, comments emphasized the anticipated dynamism and turbulence of future markets, and underscored the necessity of expecting, accepting, and creating change. Stability, or keeping things pretty much as they are now, was characterized as becoming a future anomaly, with change becoming the norm. But the comments underscored two interesting concepts.

First is the paradox that, in order to capitalize on market changes, companies will require considerable stability, particularly organizational stability, to promote the feeling of marketing management security that encourages new approaches and innovations. Second is the recognition that, in bringing about marketing changes, the easiest task will be to change future marketing mix ingredients. The harder and more critical task will be to change peoples' minds, and develop the mindsets so necessary for the effective implementation of changes.

Ever Changing Environments

The preponderance of thought about Marketing 2000 implies that business opportunities will explode. Well-established products will be displaced in the way that lasers are replacing scalpels, video recorders are displacing movies, CD's are replacing tapes and records, and word processors are replacing typewriters. Whole new industries will develop as offshoots of technological advances in such areas as computers, artificial intelligence, imaging, satellites, and genetic and bio-engineering.

According to the bulk of the evidence gathered, from both primary and secondary sources, the pace of business change will continue to accelerate, and marketing will be the company activity most directly and profoundly involved. It will feel the results of rapidly shifting markets, keen competition, technological advancements, and the emergence of new or different consumers. The time from the discovery of an invention to its commercial development as a successful product will shorten dramatically. The window of opportunity associated with new ideas will narrow, giving marketing managers less time in which to capitalize on innovation and harvest the fruits of differential advantage.

Unfolding developments will present agonizing threats as well as unheralded opportunities. Rapidly changing environments have within them inherent potential for surprises, even the power of overtaking and threatening the very well-established firms, the market leaders. Profitable survivors will be characterized by innovation, creativity, change, flexibility, the willingness to weigh and accept reasonable risks, and a readiness to actively seek new approaches.

In such a business climate, a premium will be placed on awareness of the future, on the ability to anticipate, to prepare for and capitalize on future marketing developments. Executive competence in developing insights, knowledge, and feelings about the future will become more widely sought and valued. Marketing executives will face the responsibility of translating information about indefinite market futures into definite profitable ideas, programs, and concepts for tomorrow's marketing operations.

It is sometimes possible to gain perspectives on the likely impact of marketing changes by adopting a retrospective orientation, reflecting on past developments, and thinking analogously. Such approaches, however, must be tempered by the thought that the future will differ significantly from the past, and that models of the past may well be outmoded in dealing with the future. A far different perspective, approach, and set of models may be required. (Indeed, forgetting may be a more important skill than remembering.)

To gain some perspective, we can look at recent product changes and believe that the greatest changes were in technology-intensive products such as computers, aircraft, automobiles, satellites, television, cameras, and the like. In reality, however, it is difficult to name a product class that has not been altered substantially. Material changes have occurred in every day, commodity-like products such as bread, soap, nails, and toothpaste.

Widespread agreement suggests that tomorrow's leading companies will adopt the attitude of constantly rethinking, and on occasion reconstituting, their products and services, even their highly profitable well-established products, to improve them. They will balance the inherent perceived future opportunities with the increasing risks of constantly innovating and obsoleting established profitable products. They will be involved with fine tuning to bring offerings more into line with future consumer wants and needs. The dynamics of future marketplace activities will require a philosophy of being on a continuous marketing journey, one that never ends, guided by a management that is always striving but never arriving, one that vigorously pursues adaptations and constant adjustments, managers that expect changes and strive to not only bring them about, but to market them. While no company wants to repeat the "New Coke" fiasco, future marketing managers will learn to innovate in and replace their own products and services before competitors do it for them.

Format

This book is based on a major research project sponsored by the American Marketing Association and guided by the members of a Commission on Marketing in the Year 2000. The project extended over four years, and included an extensive literature review, workshops with knowledgeable futures researchers, who served as a Presidential Advisory Committee, personal interviews with insightful CEOs of major corporations and with market researchers, as well as meetings with marketing practitioners and academicians.

This book is designed to give readers an opportunity to think more broadly and deeply about marketing futures, to develop new insights, to identify market opportunities, to reassess organizational methods and approaches, and to become part of the management group that is actively concerned with generating improvements, and involved in making things happen.

The chapters that follow provide an unusual opportunity for readers to immerse themselves in the future, broaden their horizons, sharpen their thinking, concentrate on likely developments and their business implications, and generally increase their insights about where marketing is heading.

The contents underscore the precept that while a company's future is rooted in the present, and while company well-being is being shaped continuously by current thoughts and actions, its destiny will be governed by management awareness and insights about tomorrow and the tomorrows to come.

Marketing 2000, the time horizon referred to throughout the book, is a general term used to designate marketing developments in the foreseeable future. It refers not to any specific dates, not specifically to the year 2000, but to marketing developments and changes that are expected to occur through the turn of the century, in the next 10 to 20 years.

The book is organized into 8 chapters. Chapter 1, the introductory chapter, shares some general observations about futures information and futures thinking in the management of marketing operations. It presents differences in some of the widely held notions of future marketing developments, and briefly discusses the book's objectives and approaches.

Chapters 2, 3, and 4 deal with some of the important factors that will shape and direct future marketing developments. Chapter 2 discusses several likely technological trends and their potential impact. Chapter 3 highlights important demographic trends that will reshape and influence markets. Chapter 4 focuses on likely future aspects of consumers that will be reflected in their purchases and consumption patterns. The information and ideas in these chapters dealing with important external shaping forces are intended to be illustrative rather than all inclusive. They are designed to stimulate readers to think more deeply and extensively about possible future developments that will impact on their own businesses and areas of interest.

Chapters 5, 6, and 7 focus on the insights and ideas of others about likely marketing developments over the next 10 to 20 years. These observations present several important vistas from which readers can better gauge what will likely emerge, and can help readers develop their own perspectives. Rather than establish right or wrong, they will aim to encourage futures thinking. Chapter 5 considers rather briefly some of the more important findings from our extensive search and review of the futures literature. Chapter 6 highlights the main findings of the personal interviews with CEOs. Chapter 7 shares the ideas, visions, and thinking of leading marketing academicians, practitioners, and futures researchers about Marketing 2000. The contributions are organized around broad themes and are presented in their original form.

Chapter 8, the final chapter, highlights some of the concluding comments of the authors about marketing and futurity. It focuses specifically on implications for marketing management, and marketing as a change agent.

An appendix is included for those interested in the details of the methodology used, the manner in which the study was conducted, the members of the Presidential Advisory Committee, the Commission on Marketing in the Year 2000, the CEOs interviewed, and the experts who contributed idea papers. Readers are cautioned that the materials are presented as a number of windows that permit glimpses into the unknown future. They do not cover the total range of possibilities. They are viewed more as a set of stimulating ideas and viewpoints to help and encourage readers to develop their own scenarios.

CHAPTER 2

MARKETING 2000: PERSPECTIVES ON TECHNOLOGICAL CHANGES

"Modern technology is wonderful—it enables man to gain control over everything except technology." Source unknown.

Introduction

Of all the future external marketing factors investigated in this research, technology has the potential of exerting the greatest unexpected influence. It can readily destroy or create markets, develop or obsolete industries and products, and create economic surges or rapid declines. The likely impact of future technology is among the hardest of the external marketing factors to discern.

Although the tendency exists to think of technology in terms of hi-tech products such as lasers, satellites, and computers, it is much broader in concept. Technology refers to the whole body of knowledge available to a society—knowledge that can be used to develop processes to make products, and manage them.

The literature, the ideas expressed in the interviews and the workshops suggest that Marketing 2000 will see great technological change. Distinct breaks with past technologies will occur affecting such fundamental market determinants as the way people live their lives, their home environments, the proliferation of product and service assortments, their standard of living, the quality of life, and of course, the performance of marketing management activities. A caution expressed was to expect the technologically unexpected in Marketing 2000.

Marketing Technology Interface

Marketing and technology will be more directly linked and coordinated in management's thinking than ever before, with explicit recognition given to technology's role in competition, costs, market share, advertising, product development, personal selling, distribution, and other factors shaping a company's marketing mix.

Historically, most technological change has tended to be evolutionary, representing an orderly progression from a past to a future base of knowledge. Some technological change, however, is revolutionary, leading to unexpected new directions. Some have resulted in the creation of whole new industries, opening totally new markets. Examples include telephones, automobiles, televisions, computers, satellites, atomic reactors, lasers, transistors, and superconductors.

The literature is replete with statements implying major future technological advancements:

- 90% of all the scientists who have ever lived since the recorded history of mankind are living today.

- In the next 10 to 20 years we shall double all of the knowledge that has ever accumulated throughout the history of mankind.

- Future technological changes will become ever more rapid with fundamental breakthroughs occurring regularly.

- Our society is in the midst of several technological revolutions, including an information revolution, an electronics revolution, a bio-tech revolution, a chemical revolution, a medical revolution, a transportation revolution, a computer chip revolution, a super-conducting revolution, and so on.

One might well question whether they are truly revolutions, or important continuing changes. It is interesting to observe how consumers live enjoyable lives in the midst of so many simultaneous revolutionary changes.

Future technological advancements are expected to impact more immediately and directly on markets and marketing management than was the case previously. They will shorten marketing management's reaction time with the window of opportunity remaining open for shorter intervals. New technology will greatly reshape and restructure markets by:

- Obsoleting and replacing products over shorter time frames,

- Developing substitute products/services that are vastly different, far superior in quality and performance to those currently available,

- Necessitating different marketing methods and support systems to meet consumer needs, (Felgner, 1989),

- Developing whole new industries and extending unexpected, new, profitable market opportunities,

- Shaping and influencing life styles,

- Increasing marketing efficiency, productivity, and

- Reducing costs.

Being ever mindful of technological developments will be higher on the list of marketing management responsibilities.

The blanket dominance of U.S. technology will be challenged by advances in other countries, and increasing numbers of foreign technologies will prove to be superior to those of the United States. Technological leadership will become diffused over several countries, meaning that many U.S. companies for the first time in the post-World War II era will find themselves in the unusual and uncomfortable position of losing one of their key competitive advantages, overall technological superiority. They will have to play technological catch up in Marketing 2000. Their moves to joint ventures overseas and to becoming global corporations are driven not only by access to markets and cost factors, but by considerations of technological advantages.

Technology and Marketing Management

There are wide gaps between marketing and technology. The perspectives of marketers and technologists, even within the same company, given carefully drawn strategic plans, vary widely. Marketing managers in the future will have to be informed about technology and potential market applications, and will be challenged to manage it more effectively. Technologists, in turn, will be challenged with making better use of marketing insights, knowledge, and know how.

Thus, linkages will be forged between market opportunities and technological developments. Research and development will be more market and product focused, and more basic research will be pursued with a direction well in mind.

Two thrusts are likely to emerge. First, increasing emphasis will be placed on exploring and utilizing what is known and available among current technologies. Second, there will be greater commitment to actively exploring selected new technologies that seem to have the greatest potential in solving consumer problems profitably.

In the information gathered throughout this research are implicit guidelines for dealing more effectively with the technology/marketing interface. Managers are advised to:

- Recognize technology as a major factor in the strategic marketing planning process.

- Track technology to help overcome the information and perception gaps between marketing and technological development.

- Understand and appreciate current and emerging technologies that relate directly to current markets, products/services, and customers.

- Put a formal technology scanning and technology assessment process in place.

- Generate a marketing climate and philosophy that supports and encourages technological advancements.

- Set up a priority listing of likely future technological opportunities and explore the potential in each.

- Seek to close the gap between market wants and needs and technological know-how.

- Evaluate competitors' technological capabilities and approaches, and explore their potential impact.

Global Perspective

Given the global marketplace of Marketing 2000, marketing managers will be confronted with the importance of keeping abreast of foreign technology. They can do this by:

- Scanning the relevant international literature.

- Attending professional meetings in leading countries.

- Serving on international advisory boards.

- Developing relations with international academic and research agencies.

- Engaging in cooperative research ventures.

- Acquiring, merging with, and gaining licensing agreements with innovative foreign companies.

- Visiting, observing, and researching foreign operations.

This means a major change in management attitudes. Not only will U.S. companies have to learn from competitors in other countries, and emulate them in some ways, but they will have to learn to compete effectively without the predominant technological advantages. They may have to learn to live with the psychology of being second or third best in various areas. A searching question raised by participants in this study was whether the U.S., by Marketing 2000, would be technologically superior in many things.

Computing Power

We are in the midst of an information age in which computing power has radically transformed societies. To develop a better perspective on this, consider the evolution of engine power. The first steam engines had a low power-to-weight ratio and were suitable only for stationary applications in factories and mines. As the power-to-weight ratio improved, they were used in power boats, trains, and finally automobiles. Before the invention of the steamboat, it was recognized that boats require a higher power-to-weight ratio than stationary applications, that trains require a still higher ratio, while automobiles needed a higher ratio than trains. Therefore, considering opportunities and needs, one might have forecast that improved power-to-weight ratios would see steamboats, then steam locomotives, then Stanley-Steamer-type automobiles. And, with great insight, one might have forecast air flight and finally space flight.

Examining computing power from a similar perspective, we might reach informed judgments about future computer applications. Computers, like the steam engine, provide power to get things done. In this case, power is used to store, manipulate, and transmit information rather than physical materials.

Computing power has already evolved as an affordable consumer product. Even the most basic IBM PC or Apple MacIntosh computer is capable of doing mathematics more rapidly than all residents of New York State could if they simultaneously took up pencil and paper and did the calculations. These computers are at least as capable as the IBM 360 mainframes, the mainstay of businesses in the early 1970s, which cost millions of dollars.

The Apple personal computer, in the late 1970s, used a central processing unit (CPU) chip which operated at a clock rate of one million cycles per second (1 Megahertz). In 1988, personal computers were available with clock rates of 25 megahertz, a 25 fold gain in speed, with greatly increased power, and about a 100 fold increase in performance. There continues to be a dramatic increase in CPU power per dollar, as a result of new generations of computer chips.

In addition to CPU power, the ability to store large amounts of information is important. The storage capability of magnetic media has been greatly enhanced, and the 3 1/2 inch floppy disks of the 1989 PCs can hold about 14 times as much information as the 5 1/4 inch disks of the late 1970s Apple. Hard disks are now available for personal computers which hold over 300 million alphabetic characters. Equally as important is the significantly increased ability of the new CPUs to address far more memory cells; and it appears that by the year 2000 computer power will be so cheap, powerful, and versatile that most home appliances and many important consumer products and services will be based on smart systems.

Some current consumer products depend on powerful computers built right into them and this tendency will be expanded. Compact disk players, for instance, use laser lights to read numbers from the 5-inch disks, which are then translated into music. Each second the laser reads 90,000 5-digit numbers (16 binary bits) which, if typed single-spaced onto standard typewriter paper, would occupy 112 pages. Amazingly, there are about 20,000 tracks circling the disk, with 30 tracks occupying a space the width of a human hair. Such a vast amount of information is being manipulated every second by a compact disk player that can be purchased for less than $200.

It is possible to store over 500 million characters on a single disk which, if typed single-spaced on standard size typing paper, would create a stack higher than a five-story building. One compact disk holds the full text of the Academic American Encyclopedia published by Grolier. According to Helliwell (1986):

> *The Electronic Encyclopedia* is fully searchable, allowing users to find the information they need much more quickly than they can in the printed encyclopedia. ...it makes it possible for you to find information that would be impossible to find manually using a conventional index. A key word search for information on the U.S. Civil War, for instance, would turn up not only the obvious articles on famous battles and well-known personages, but passing references in the histories of many other people and places.

Computer-Driven Products

Marketing 2000 will see the extension of computers built into more products. Computers are now an unobtrusive integral part of automobiles, that now use computer-controlled ignitions, fuel injection systems, cruise controls, and suspension systems. Currently a popular option on higher quality cars is computer-controlled, anti-lock brakes which maximize stopping power.

The future might well bring "auto-pilot cars" which will drive themselves while on controlled access highways. A precursor device is the cruise control, which automatically adjusts speed. Work is progressing on proximity-sensing devices that will alert drivers who are too close to another car or object. Combining cruise controls, a proximity sensing system, computerized automobile brakes, and a steering system responsive to cable buried in the lanes of controlled access highways, would result in an auto-pilot car. Other computer-driven future automobile features may include a drowsiness monitor, sideways parking, and keyless locks and ignition systems (The Futurist, 1986a). The key to such applications is the availability of affordable high-power computers.

A few of the computer-based future product applications that have been suggested (and already developed) are:

- Heating systems that adapt to homeowner life styles by turning down the heat automatically when people are not at home, lowering the heat in infrequently used rooms, but heating them quickly when the presence of a person is detected (Mason and Jennings, 1982).

- "Child Finders" that will enable parents to monitor where their children are electronically. This could provide general peace of mind as well as protection against child abduction. The device would be an extension of the technology which now gives police stations the capability of monitoring the whereabouts of prisoners under house arrest who are wearing electronic leg-cuffs.

- Security devices that make a home burglar proof via installed "brains," using motion or heat sensors that can detect intruders prior to break-in, and can directly contact authorities (Mason and Jennings, 1982). Tomorrow's computers will be able to discriminate among residents, friends, strangers, pets, and children, selecting out those whose sound and mass measurements are coded into the computer (Atlas, 1988).

- "Scavenging floor cleaners" that will slowly roam around the home cleaning all floors, much as a snail cleans the glass of an aquarium (Cornish, 1988).

- "Auto-pilot lawn mowers" which will automatically mow the lawn in an even pattern guided by buried wires. Such devices are already available in industry for movement of materials to production line locations.

- Computer-monitored and controlled homes in which a central-ized computer system would control everything from climate to entertainment to household chores (Mason and Jennings, 1982).

- Self-monitoring, modular-designed, consumer-durable prod-ucts in which warning lights would signal consumers to replace a module that is about to fail.

- Room lights with proximity sensors that will automatically turn themselves on and off when people enter into or exit a room.

- Electronic instruments that will be able to duplicate almost perfectly the sound of any instrument including large pipe organs.

- Systems that recycle and conserve water used in the home.

- Temperature controlled clothing that will keep consumers comfortable indoors or outdoors.

These products are mainly "smart" versions of present products. Some of them require high levels of computer power. For example, creating an electronic instrument capable of duplicating the sound of any other instrument requires tremendous computing power, nevertheless, it is expected to be available to consumers at reasonable prices within ten years.

In the long run, electronics and computers may result in quantum leaps in many products, processes, and areas, such as medicine, well beyond the exceptional improvements that have already been made. By the year 2000, for example, it may be possible to manipulate living organisms via cell-sized computers that will flow through the blood stream and repair injured cells. Bloodless laser surgery, the use of soundwaves, imaging, and electronic medicine will replace some of the current, less effective, and more invasive diagnostic and treatment techniques.

Computing power is expected to "duplicate man," simulating the human thinking, feeling, and manipulative processes. The development of artificial intelligence will progress dramatically as a result. Other tech-nological developments, based on new insights and information, are expected to extend and increase the experience and enjoyment of life. They will add to longevity, overcome barriers of space and time, height-en and improve the reach of the senses, and literally shape life styles and the meaning of living.

Some undesirable consequences will accrue as well. We will likely see the results of information pollution as consumers are deluged with data, electronic telephone messages, electronic mail, advertising, fax materials, and the like. Information overload seems likely to occur, with consumers reaching the limits of their abilities and desire to process and absorb information. The merging of media will provide advertisers with new ways to handle sound and video, and will encourage more direct and constant consumer communications contacts. That could spur adverse consumer reactions, such as seeking relief in the form of regulatory restrictions.

Other undesirable consequences that have received attention relate to the nature of our fragile ecological system and the dangers of new technology. Sometimes marketing approaches are cited for wasting physical resources, and adding significantly to air, water, and ground pollution. Regardless of some CEO opinions to the contrary, it seems that environmentally-concerned groups in Marketing 2000 will exert much greater influence in shaping future marketing/technology connections. The results will be reflected in product design and development, product costs, packaging, the application and adoption of new inventions, and pricing, advertising, and distribution channel policies.

Environmental groups are already confronting such activities as biogenetic testing, animal and human tests, the release of biogenetically-derived organisms, waste of scarce resources and pollution of various kinds. They will likely continue to oppose such technology-driven activities as nuclear energy, various forms of waste disposal, off-shore oil exploration, and chemical sprays and processes, pressing technologists to solve the current problems and find future alternatives. They will likely be joined by other groups in heading off technological advances that not only affect environments, but displace and relocate workers.

The advancement of technology will have many backers, some unrealistically seeking quick technological fixes for environmental, health, hunger, cost, and competitive problems. Future technological developments will result in new and improved products and services, and will lower costs, extend lives, and increase the quality of life, but at a price. Moreover, the price may not be known until well after the technology is actually in place.

Technological risk, with all its legal implications, will become a major concern in developing and marketing products. The risks may be too great for any one company to absorb, and several companies, as well as the government, may be directly involved. For example, a company with a new superior fire extinguisher may hesitate to install it in tankers hauling explosive materials for fear that a faulty extinguisher could cause a tanker explosion in a harbor, which although very unlikely, could devastate part of a city. Such risks are staggering with a total company being bet on the application of a superior technology. Who can assume the risk? This suggests that changes in our product liability laws need to be brought on if we are to capitalize on research, develop and adopt new technologies, and better deal with their attendant risks.

Home Information Systems

Electronic networks will span the earth, and the use of remote control computer capabilities, along with the ability to bridge media electronically, will bring the world to the consumer's doorstep. Electronic advances will alter homes and their roles in our lives. Homes will serve as libraries and information centers because computers and compact discs can make unbelievable stores of customized information readily available. Homes will become work stations, permitting many people to eliminate commuting in favor of the convenience and efficiency of working at home. Home entertainment centers will provide customized entertainment that combines music, information, live pictures and graphics, delivering theatre-quality sight and sound events at the time and place desired. Consumers will be able to bring live entertainment events directly onto their individual screens, with relative ease, and prepare their own recordings, books, magazines and newspapers both electronically and in hard copy.

Changes of great magnitude will occur because of the tremendous increase in computational power that will be readily available for much lower costs. A revolution in converting sounds, images, and words into computer data will facilitate the manipulation and reformulation of information, along with the ability to transmit it instantly all over the globe.

Market communications will see many changes as media becomes more integrated, resulting in more effective communications systems. For example, as print media becomes more electronic, and as computers, televisions, phones, and data bases are linked, the scope and potential for improved and tailored market communications, globally, are enhanced greatly.

Electronics and home computers will provide the capability of printing custom catalogs, books, newspapers, and magazines. Consumers will be able to squeeze massive amounts of audio and visual data onto very small discs. They will have the ability to make sophisticated recordings in their own homes by manipulating electronic equipment and using various media.

In France, "Minitel," an example of Videotex, allows users to bank, shop, read the morning paper, and maintain anonymous friendships. The system is an interactive, mass communication medium that delivers text and visual information directly to consumers through a telephone line, fiber optic cable or personal computer network. The terminals are connected via the phone system, and the total connect time already exceeds 13 million hours. There are more than 3,000 Videotex services being offered (Oren, 1988).

The Prodigy Videotex Service

In the U.S., IBM and Sears began a $450 million venture, the introduction of a Videotex service called *Prodigy*, in May of 1988, the forerunner of things to come. As of early 1989, this service offers consumers home shopping information, news and message capabilities via home computer in Los Angeles, Sacramento, Santa Barbara, San Francisco, San Diego, Hartford, Fairfield County Connecticut, and Atlanta. It is expected to cover 20 markets by the end of 1989 (Graham, 1988).

The use of *Prodigy* requires an IBM PC-compatible personal computer, equipped with a modem. The type on the bright orange box containing the kit promises that: membership lets up to six people in a household explore a constantly growing selection of useful information and helpful services. One can, for example,

- See the latest news and sports,
- Check local, regional and national weather,
- Book airline reservations through EAASY SABRE,
- Order groceries delivered to one's home (in some areas),
- Get advice from nationally known experts,
- Shop from dozens of different merchants,
- Get stock quotes from *Dow Jones News/Retrieval,*
- Buy and sell stocks from a discount broker,
- Send and receive electronic mail,
- Tune in to the latest entertainment news,
- Learn from many educational features,
- Play challenging and fun games, and
- Look up product information in *Consumer Reports,*

According to their literature, the *Prodigy* service is for people who want to get things done, and want to do them smarter, faster, and easier!

Exploring The Prodigy System

Since our research confirms that *Prodigy*, and systems like it, may be a harbinger of things to come in electronic shopping and information systems, we subscribed to the system as it is now being implemented in Atlanta to experience various features. By actually using the system for about 20 hours, the following preliminary views concerning the strengths and weaknesses of it, and a sense of where this general technology is heading, were developed. A detailed account of a few initial experiences is given below.

Getting the News

It took us less than 15 minutes to install the software on our computer and sign-on. The first screen displayed gives news headlines and permits selection of stories people wish to read. *Prodigy* was more up-to-date than the conventional morning newspaper. News stories appeared that had occurred a few hours earlier. On the other hand, the *Prodigy* news stories were not as extensive as those in the conventional morning papers.

Planning a Vacation

To facilitate planning a vacation to Europe we moved to the travel section. The British Railway System presented details about railway passes. The screen displayed a map of England and when pairs of cities were selected, the system showed the frequency of rail service between them. Information was displayed on the screen within about 5 seconds.

The British Railway System had many free brochures to offer, and those desired were indicated by typing an X in the appropriate boxes. The system responded by showing the address given when signing-on to the system, and asked if that was where the brochures were to be sent. Rail tickets can be ordered by typing appropriate information on the screen. Tickets are charged to credit cards and mailed directly. In similar fashion, subscribers can avail themselves of information presented by the British Tourist Authority.

The Air France offerings were also explored. In addition to presenting on-screen information and offering brochures, Air France offered to send several videotapes which could have been sent to us and billed to credit cards. When the videotapes have been viewed, they can be mailed back and the credit card will be credited for the full charge. Flight reservations and purchases of Air France tickets (or tickets from virtually any airlines) can be made by using the on-line travel agency service.

Buying Cars and Appliances

If subscribers are considering replacing an automobile, they can browse through the *Consumer Reports* pages for information. The information includes both ratings and repair data. Some manufacturers offer special information sections which can be read leisurely. Also, some gather information, such as the Buick screen which requested that a marketing research survey be completed. The questionnaire was quite brief, seeking information about demographics, automobile preferences, and our attitudes toward Buick. A small gift is sent to all who fill out the questionnaire.

Shopping electronically for a house humidifier, one can read the *Consumer Reports* information, including the extensive section concerning the three different kinds of humidifiers with the strengths and weaknesses of each. Information about maintenance requirements and operating costs are also included, as are ratings of many different models. It is possible to order all of the products listed in Sears catalogs via *Prodigy*.

Entertainment

This section is extensive, featuring "an encyclopedia of over 25,000 movies." Ratings for each movie appear along with very brief information about the plot (Dvorak, 1989). Concerning television, the latest Nielsen ratings are posted for the top 20 and bottom 10 television shows.

Investments

The status of an investment portfolio can be checked easily. A listing of stocks can be keyed into *Prodigy*, either by ticker symbol or corporate name, and that list will be placed in computer memory. Any time people wish, they can get current (delayed 15-minutes) quotes on all stocks in the list. The list can be accessed without keying in the stock names again. If desired, stocks can be ordered or sold directly from the screen via a discount broker. If the subscriber has a printer connected to the computer, then printouts of all transactions are available. On-line banking is possible with Manufacturers Hanover Trust and Key Bank.

Bulletin Board

Like a newspaper, *Prodigy* also has columnists on such matters as finance and sports. Users are encouraged to use *Prodigy's* electronic mail facility to send questions or comments to the columnists. The more interesting questions are then addressed on a public bulletin board which is easily accessed by *Prodigy* users. It is also possible for any *Prodigy* subscriber to send electronic mail to any other *Prodigy* subscriber, and a directory listing the mailbox numbers of all subscribers is available on-line.

In addition, readers can post bulletins on public bulletin boards within the *Prodigy* system. For example, one person posted a bulletin saying that he needed help in selecting a certain type of software and several *Prodigy* subscribers responded. Any subscriber can read the questions and responses on the public bulletin boards.

Advertising on Prodigy

The bottom 1/5th of the television screen in *Prodigy* is devoted to an advertisement. The consumer can see a larger version of that advertisement by pressing the letter "L" for "look." Research on reading from CRTs has demonstrated that reading and proofreading speeds are essentially the same for both CRTs and papers when fully formed characters are used on the CRT (Gould, Alfara, Finn, Haupt, and Minuto, 1987). Advertising messages can be read as quickly and comprehended as well from CRTs as from paper when equivalent type styles are used (MacLachlan, Newsome, and Shattuck, 1989).

Many of the advertisements continue for several pages, and in some cases consumers may be offered an opportunity to branch to specific pages of a mini-catalog ad. Advertisers can keep track of which pages are being viewed, as well as what is being bought, and it is expected that advertising testing through the equivalent of split-runs will be possible.

Advertising charges are based on how often the ads are viewed, with an extra fee when an item is ordered on-line from an advertisement (Hughes, 1989). As is the case with newspapers and magazines, the majority of the revenue from such a system may eventually come from advertisers. This may be a reason why *Prodigy*, unlike earlier teletext systems which have been implemented in the United States, is able to operate with no hourly charge.

To gain an inkling of possible consumer reactions to systems like *Prodigy*, the system was demonstrated to students at a major university. Some students used the system while others watched the action on a large projected screen. Students then shared their first impressions and a mini focus group session was held among actual student users. The following observations emerged:

- They considered the system very easy to learn and use.

- They wished that more lines of text had been presented on the screen.

- They wished for more detailed stories and better indexing of the current news.

- They wanted to be able to look at past news stories, which is not currently possible.

- They wanted to be able to store information on computer disks, and that is not currently possible.

- They wanted to be able to print out any material they wished. Currently the system will only allow a computer user to print transaction receipts, such as stock or merchandise purchases.

- They wanted faster screen response times. Having to wait four seconds for the next page in a story was considered too long.

The overall impression of *Prodigy* was favorable and, assuming "reasonable" charges, a majority of the students indicated that they would either definitely or probably buy the system. There is a big leap, of course, between such findings and widespread consumer acceptance in the market place.

Although the future thrust of such systems seems to be established, the diffusion of *Prodigy* may be fairly slow. Users must have an IBM PC or compatible computer, with at least 512K of memory, equipped with a high speed modem, that is capable of operating at least 1200 baud. The modem alone can cost several hundred dollars. Over time, however, computer modems will be less costly and more generally available, so that this will be less of a barrier.

If *Prodigy* is successful, Sears will control an important advertising medium. They will be able to research the effectiveness of their advertising in the medium vs. their competitors. They will have access to very valuable consumer information. Furthermore, the usage of their Discover Card could be increased and their market outreach extended.

Consumer Information

Not surprisingly, *Prodigy* already has a competitor. *PC-Link* service is now available nationwide. *PC-Link* has a similar pricing structure, but the standard price provides access only during evenings and weekends. It overcomes the response time problem experienced with *Prodigy* and produces down-loadable files so that information can be saved on computer disk files and printed on paper if desired.

A great deal of effort is currently being expended in the development of electronic news services (Antonoff, 1989), and they will probably emerge as major competitors to newspapers and magazines by the year 2000. According to Reilly (1989):

> Publishers attending the 103rd annual meeting of the American Newspaper Publishers Association voiced concern about whether the nation's seven regional telephone companies would usurp newspapers' roles as generators of information and news in the burgeoning area of electronic publishing... AT&T Company asked the U.S. District Court for the District of Columbia to let expire a ban that prevents the company from entering electronic publishing. ...(They) the seven regional phone companies, formed after the 1982 breakup of AT&T, also seek the right to compete with newspapers by generating information that can be transmitted over phone lines to customers with either push-button phones or home computers. If the ban is lifted, phone companies could be the creators — not just the carriers — of information.

There is also the possibility that newspapers, in the future, will work in cooperation with the phone companies, with the newspapers supplying the news and the phone company supplying the teletext delivery system. In the Houston area, Southwestern Bell is involved in a year-long test in which it has distributed 6,000 small computer terminals to homes. Residents will receive Videotex services provided by various sources, including Hearst Corporation's *Houston Chronicle*.

The potential advantages of future on-line home information systems include:

- Up-to-date news.

- Great breadth and depth of information.

- Easy information retrieval.

- Facilitation of transactions such as banking, purchasing stocks, getting airline information and tickets, making reservations for hotels and rental cars, and shopping.

Although all products will not lend themselves to computer shopping, to the extent that products such as groceries, meat, and vegetables can be standardized as to quality, accurately described, and precisely measured, so that consumer confidence is built-up in grading systems, home shopping will expand.

It is less likely that consumers will choose to use an on-line information system to order goods such as ladies' clothing or major durables such as furniture. However, as video images are combined with text, advertising messages can show and demonstrate products, such as those depicting adjustable-contour beds. While this may not always result in computer ordering, it could at least allow consumers to narrow their choices to an "evoked set" of products to be investigated in in-store shopping.

The future will see home information systems expanded as the present capacity constraints, caused by bandwidth limitations of conventional telephone lines, are overcome by fiber optics. Fiber optic telephone lines, in which a single cable can carry thousands of telephone calls, are now being installed directly into homes in a few geographic areas. As more homes are connected to such high capacity channels, teletext can be used to transmit television as well as text information. According to Bulkeley (1988):

> "... a select handful of people in this (Cerritos) upper-middle-class suburb of Los Angeles (are moving) into the video world of the future... They will be able to have the movie of their choice transmitted right into their TV sets. They also will be able to connect their telephones with their video cameras and television sets to create picture phones. They will be able to set up video cameras to monitor a sleeping infant from a neighbor's house. And within a few years, they will be able to video-shop from a Sears, Roebuck & Company catalog... due to an experiment by GTE Corporation. GTE is wiring Cerritos with an optical-fiber cable-TV system that can carry almost unlimited amounts of information right to a television set."

Fiber optics can provide an efficient means of transmitting high definition television images that will be available well before the year 2000. High definition television brings the sharpness and clarity of image of theater movies, which can be accompanied by stunning digital sound.

Fiber optic technology, such as is being tested in Cerritos, will also make telecomputing a practical reality by the year 2000. The ability to communicate high quality video images, as well as "faxes" of documents and computer-edited text, will mean that tele-conferencing between home and office will be practical for many persons whose work primarily involves the handling of information (Clemons, 1986; *Communication News*, 1985; Zemke, 1987). Tele-conferences can be videotaped for later reference if desired. There is, of course, a potential security problem as sensitive company information is communicated back and forth. Corporate information security will be a growth industry in Marketing 2000.

Some of the Essentials

There is no dearth of predictions about essential products of the future emanating from anticipated technological advancements. To illustrate some of the expected developments, a few of the predictions about clothing and energy are presented. They are suggestive only, indicating the magnitude of changes that are anticipated.

The New Clothing

The so called "miracle fibers," nylon, dacron, polyester, and orlon, have made possible attractive, easy-care clothing at reasonable prices. Compared with natural fibers, however, the fabrics lack the feel and look, and do not "breathe" as well. They are not as comfortable in the summer as natural fibers such as cotton, but these and similar deficiencies will likely be overcome by the year 2000.

Furthermore, fabrics will be made that automatically increase their bulk when in cold weather, much in the manner of cats who are able to tolerate cold winter temperatures, while remaining comfortable inside a heated home. Cats' fur fluffs out when it is cold, creating a large dead-air mass, an excellent insulator around an animal. A similar effect can be achieved by using fibers made of two materials, laminated together, with one having a higher co-efficient of expansion than the other. Artificial furs will be made that fluff out in the cold.

Clothing will also be available which has heating wires woven into fabrics that are connected to a small, rechargeable battery pack. Sony is working on rechargeable battery packs that will hold charges several times longer than present nickel cadmium packs do.

Wrist watches are now available with built-in digital thermometer features that could be combined with an appropriate control circuit to provide a personal thermostat to control clothing temperatures.

Clothes of the future will be attractive, yet comfortable. Similar to shoes, they will be durable and easy to care for, and will adjust and adapt to individual needs, with many customized features such as maintaining a personal comfort zone around the body.

Energy

There is widespread concern among many futurists, and among some of the respondents in our research, that energy will, once again, become an important concern for marketers by the year 2000. Despite the decline in oil prices during the mid-1980s, which gave the world a respite from the energy crisis of the 1970s, petroleum stocks are definitely dwindling. Some have forecast long lines at gasoline stations once again. Serious efforts need to be made to conserve energy and develop alternative sources. Such efforts, in the future, will spur the development of energy-saving products and increase promotional programs to bring alternate sources of energy on stream. Coal, shale, synthetic, and nuclear alternatives will be considered. Among the likely ways in which major new sources of energy will become available, three are noted:

- Superconductivity, which is being explored in laboratories around the world, involves the discovery, development, and application of "perfectly" conducting materials that lose no heat or energy from source to end use.

- Electricity-producing solar cells that could become cheap enough to shingle the roof.[1]

- Laser fusion that may offer a path to clean atomic power. Advances show that there is great potential in this area and Japanese scientists expect to begin building a prototype fusion reactor to test its feasibility for commercial use in 1992 (Johnstone, 1987).[2]

There is also the possibility that totally new sources of energy will be found.

> Two chemists who claimed last week to have triggered nuclear fusion in a jar of water have ignited a major uproar in the scientific world. At a news conference Thursday, Dr. B. Stanley Pons of the University of Utah, and Dr. Martin Fleischmann of the University of Southampton, announced that they had not only achieved hydrogen fusion in a simple electrolytic cell, but had obtained a substantial yield of energy. (Browne, 1989).

This process might provide small scale, clean sources of power which could be used in the home by the year 2000. However, the scientific community has expressed a great deal of skepticism, although a few researchers, such as an Italian group, report having replicated part of the claim (Simons, 1989).

At this time no one knows whether scientists will actually find a route to clean and cheap nuclear power. To the extent that research continues,

---

[1]Westinghouse's pioneering work with dendritic cells indicates that silicon cells for power production can be grown as crystals using a continuous production, extrusion-like process which greatly reduces costs.

[2]Batteries which are cheap and electronically efficient, but low in volumetric efficiency, could probably be produced by drilling a hole in the ground, lining it with a corrosion resistant material, filling it with an acid to serve as an electrolyte, and then suspending pipes of proper metals to serve as electrodes. With today's solid state technology, converting the low voltages from such a battery to household voltages would not be difficult.

the probability will increase. Fusion is a much cleaner process than the fission process currently used in atomic power plants, and future developments may overcome the radioactivity problem associated with nuclear power generation and waste.

The above technological advances present but a few exciting portrayals of an evolving technologically-enchriched future that will see advances in materials, communications, biogenetic engineering, and medical science. They will not only present new opportunities for marketers, governments, and society, and challenge current products and services, but will force marketers to re-evaluate many of their precepts and methods of operation.

REFERENCES

Antonoff, Michael (1989), "The *Prodigy* Promise," *Personal Computing*, (May), 67-78.

Atlas, Randall (1988), "Secure Homes: The Future of Anti-Crime Technology," *The Futurist*, (March-April), 25-28.

Browne, Malcolm W. (1989), "Fusion in a Jar: Announcement by 2 Chemists Ignites Uproar," *New York Times*, (March 28), Cl.

Bulkeley, William M. (1988) "GTE Test Offers View of Video Future," *The Wall Street Journal*, (December 29), Bl.

Clemons, Eric K. and Warren McFarland (1986), "Telecom: Hook Up or Lose Out," *Harvard Business Review*, (July-August), 91-97.

Communication News (1985), "The 1990's will be the Tele-conferencing Age According to a University of Wisconsin Study," 22 (May), 46.

Cornish, Edward (1988), "Dream Houses of the Future," *The Futurist* (Nov.-Dec.), 21-24.

Dvorak, John C. (1989) "Inside Track," *PC Magazine*, Vol. 8, No. 4 (February 28), 73.

Felgner, Brent H. (1989) "Retailers Grab Power, Control Marketplace," *Marketing News*, (January 16), 1-2.

The Futurist (1986a), "You Auto See it! The Car of Tomorrow," (May/June), 56.

Gould, John D., Lizette Alfaro, Rich Finn, Brian Haupt, and Angela Minuto (1987), "Reading from CRT Displays Can Be as Fast as Reading from Paper." *Human Factors*, 29, 5 (October), 497-517.

Graham, Judith (1988), "Linkup: IBM, Sears Set Ads for Videotex Venture." *Advertising Age*, 59, 22 (May 23), 1, 93.

Helliwell, John (1986), "Optical Overview: What's Coming in CD-ROMs and WORMs." *PC Magazine*, 5, 17 (October 14), 149-164.

Hughes, Kathleen A. (1989), "IBM-Sears Computer-Services Venture Shows Promise, but a Lot of Kinks Remain." *Wall Street Journal*, (February 8): B1.

Johnstone, Robert (1987), "Japan's Rising Man-Made Sun," *New Scientist*, (February), 53-57.

MacLachlan, James, Sandra L. Newsome and Lawrence G. Shattuck (1989), "Evaluating a New Medium: Text on CRT Displays," *Rensselaer Polytechnic Institute*, School of Management Working Paper #89-1, Troy, NY 12181.

Mason, Roy and Lane Jennings (1982), "The Computer Home: Will Tomorrow's Housing Come Alive?" *The Futurist*, (February), 35-43.

Oren, Haim (1988), "The Impact of Videotex on the Direct Marketing Industry: A Clear Trend or Just a Fad?" *Marketing Review*, 43, 9 (June), 17-18, 24.

Reilly, Patrick (1989), "Newspapers Eye Electronic Future," *Advertising Age*, (May 1), 4.

Schlender, Breton R. (1988), "Circuit Advance Made by Texas Instruments, Inc.," *Wall Street Journal*, (Thursday, December 15), Section B: 1, 5.

Simons, Marlise (1989), "Italian Researchers Report Achieving Nuclear Fusion," *New York Times*, (April 19).

Zemke, Ron (1987), "Training in the 90's," *Training: The Magazine of Human Resource Development*, 24 (January), 40-53.

CHAPTER 3

SPOTLIGHT ON CONSUMERS OF TOMORROW

"If we could first know where we are and wither we are tending, we could then better judge what to do and how to do it." Abraham Lincoln

Introduction

Every information source we covered — the literature, members of the Commission, the Presidential Advisory Committee, CEOs, and marketing researchers — noted directly or by implication that businesses will track and study consumers much more carefully in the future. They pointed out that more insightful and actionable data about consumers would be available. All indications are that in Marketing 2000 such information will play a significant role in guiding and shaping business actions, and that marketing will be challenged to bring consumer perspectives into the forefront of management deliberations.

That consumers of the future will differ from their cohorts of yesteryear in important purchase dimensions is certain. Factors shaping their market responses and determining their life styles will be far different. The future will see a new consumer emerging, a consumer who is much better informed, more discerning, less fettered economically and socially, and more willing to act independently, in his/her own best interest. Consumers in Marketing 2000 will be more likely to make themselves heard and their feelings known, to act in their own behalf, to become involved in directing business and in making markets work better.

Economic Shifts[1]

Many economic shifts and trends will affect consumers and market-

[1]These materials and those on shaping factors and lifestyles are based on William Lazer (1987), "The New Consumers," Chapter 9, *Handbook of Demographics for Marketing and Advertising.*

place behavior over the next ten to twenty years. Not listed in any order of importance, the following are examples of some of these shifts:

- From an emphasis on production to consumption utility, which highlights such dimensions as user-friendliness, quality, service, modules, guarantees, and product modifications.

- From mass to mini-mass, with the emphasis on niches, segments, product customization, individualization, and flexible production.

- From individual accumulation to greater sharing, meaning more cooperation, mutuality of interests, networking, interconnectedness, and personal involvement.

- From the flow of materials and products to the flow of information, featuring data banks, marketing intelligence systems, communications, and knowledge.

- From consumption and immediate gratification to conservation, with its emphasis on efficient utilization of resources, preserving environments, abating pollution, downsizing, recycling, and securing the world of tomorrow.

- From the national and regional perspective to the global interconnectedness of economies, with multinational businesses, world trade, global networks, and worldism.

- From smokestack to high-tech industries that are information rich, adaptive, R&D oriented, and robotics driven.

- From labor and power driven to education driven businesses, featuring highly educated labor/management inputs, research, software, and computers.

- From individual business entities to total systems that emphasize efficiency and consumer satisfaction through loose alliances as well as formal organizations.

- From great centralization to decentralization, with its emphasis on getting closer to consumers.

- From a perspective of scarcity to one of abundance within limits, recognizing the need to make good use of resources and the possibility of superabundant life styles.

- From a total emphasis on the bottom line, sales, profits, and production figures, to a more balanced concern for consumer satisfaction.

- From standardization and homogeneity of products to individualization, customization, and differentiation.

Economic trends such as the above are among those that will have great impact on how future consumers behave, their purchasing reactions, the variety and assortment of products and services available to future consumers, and how they are marketed.

Shaping Factors

Factors affecting future 25-34 year olds (including the future young marrieds) or those 65 and over (the future senior citizens) will differ greatly from those of their predecessors. Indeed, all generations in the future will differ markedly from their predecessors because of the changed world in which they do and will live. As a result, purchase behavior, expectations, attitudes, and orientation will also differ. Some of the major shaping factors affecting the behavior of consumers in Marketing 2000 are shown in Table 1 and are briefly noted.

Tomorrow's affluent consumers, unlike their predecessors, will not have felt the ravages of a major depression or war. They will tend to be less cautious and concerned about spending their incomes and will be less conservative consumers. They will be less likely than their parents to save for a "rainy day" and more likely to adopt the feeling of live and enjoy.

Table 1
SOME FACTORS SHAPING FUTURE CONSUMER BEHAVIOR

- No major wars
- No extended depression
- More affluence
- More highly educated workforce
- Working women
- More first births
- Smaller-sized families
- Longer and healthier lives
- Cultured and cosmopolitan outlook
- More information-seeking activities
- Leisure-oriented perspective
- Mobile populations
- Increased restlessness and seeking the new
- Multiple household types
- Polarization and fragmentation of the marketplace
- Overchoice from product/service proliferation

Overall, they will also be the highest educated consumers in our history. Education is associated with the appreciation and purchase of different kinds of products and services such as books, art objects, wines, and classical CDs. Future consumers will be the most affluent consumers ever, many with working spouses and fewer children, two factors which contribute to family affluence. Accompanying many working spouses are two pensions and more complete insurance coverage, which might further encourage them to spend more freely. Consumers will be more likely to enjoy today when they feel that they have provided for tomorrow.

Families of the future will be smaller in size reflecting the decrease in the birth rate. This means that dual-income families will have the opportunity to spend more time and money on their individual offspring. Smaller-sized families are also more portable and mobile, affecting travel, recreational, educational, and leisure opportunities.

Future families will also have more first-born babies, both absolutely and proportionately, which will be reflected in purchasing patterns. Studies indicate that more is lavished on a first born child, sometimes twice as much, as on succeeding children. When a child enters a family, many expenditure patterns are changed, including housing, transportation, clothing, pharmaceuticals, household help, and so on. When these first-borns grow up, they will likely be more successful, more demanding, and more informed.

New consumers will be better traveled. They will be more mobile having a world, rather than a local or regional, perspective. They will take more frequent vacations of shorter duration, but longer in distance. They will live longer and healthier lives, being more active throughout their older years, truly marking the appearance of younger olders. They will be more cultured, the cosmopolites, having been exposed to a wider range of educational and cultural experiences, and will be more appreciative and supportive of the arts. They will be more demanding of good design, good taste, and pleasing environments.

As compared with their forefathers, many new consumers will have higher expectations. They will expect the future to be better than today. Their outlook will be for an ever increasing standard of living, for an expansion of "the good life" that will be considered a birth right. They will expect businesses and government to provide this.

New consumers will be information seeking and the technology will exist to satisfy them. Many will have the resources to be very well informed and, as a result, will expect those servicing them, such as doctors and retailers, to be up-to-date. They will be leisure-oriented, for

Americans take their leisure seriously.

Many business opportunities will be spawned as a result of leisure activities, and limitations on a large proportion of consumer expenditures will more likely be the scarcity of time rather than of money.

Many new consumers will continue to be restless and seek change. They will be interested in what is new, in the latest fads, fashions, and tendencies. But they will be more discerning, and less likely to be subject to manufacturers' dictates. They are also less likely to succumb to societal dictates, as more and more will go on embracing a multiplicity of household types — being in any of several combinations of married or single, with or without children, living with some or other sex partner out of wedlock, moving back in with parents, living cooperatively, divorced once or many times. Marketers have endless opportunities as a result of the diversity.

However, along with the upscale consumers, we must recognize the growing numbers of people who now and likely into the future represent lower income segments. Heavily dominated by the young and female-heads of households, these people will also constitute major markets that shrewd marketers will understand and be responsive to.

Lifestyle Influences

Consideration of future lifestyle directions and tendencies can furnish insights about how people will likely live their lives in Marketing 2000, the kinds of values that will be maintained, and the potential future prod-

---

TABLE 2
SOME FUTURE LIFESTYLE ORIENTATIONS
- Living my life my way
- Enhancing psychological self
- Enhancing physical self
- Being cosmopolitan
- Seeking security and avoiding risk
- Expressing restlessness and impermanence
- Valuing leisure and discretionary time
- Changing perspectives of work
- Escaping from it all
- Wanting convenience and immediate gratification
- Becoming more product dependent and dominant
- Expecting secure living spaces

---

uct and service opportunities they suggest. Table 2 presents the results of deliberations about the likely lifestyle trends of Marketing 2000.

Living my life my way emphasizes that future consumers will be more likely to do the things that please them in work, in social activities, in their homes to enjoy their life styles, and to do more of what they want, rather than what society wishes. It is a selfish orientation, a "me" outlook, but not to the exclusion of others, particularly those who are among the poor or the underclass. My life my way, can also have a strong social orientation.

Enhancing psychological self refers to the desires of consumers to improve their psychological dimensions, orientations, outlooks, images, and perceptions of self. Many products, symbols, and programs exist to accomplish this. Included are designer symbols on shoes, belts, handbags, and ties, self-improvement tapes and programs, adult education classes, memberships in exclusive clubs...a host of outlets for recognition and feeling good about one's self.

Enhancing physical self is the complement of the above. Numerous products and services reflect the challenge, including vitamins, facials, cosmetic surgery, diets, exercise salons, hair coloring products, grooming, and clothing services. Remaining "young," a widely sought-after goal, provides enormous present and future market opportunities.

Cosmopolitanism refers to the cultured good taste of future consumers. Since they are better educated, more traveled and affluent, future consumers will more likely be cosmopolites — they will have cosmopolitan tastes from around the world. They will seek out homes, clothing, food, and furnishings that reflect these preferences. Consumers will be style and color-coordinated, making their kitchens and bathrooms more integrally related to the design of the rest of their living quarters. Their wardrobes, including cosmetics and fragrances, will be varied to reflect disparate cultures, moods, and sensibilities. Paintings, art, sculpture, good music, and other aesthetically desirable products and services will be sought. Marketing 2000 may even see a return to the widespread fashionability of reading a "good" book.

In the midst of the ever-imposing complexities of society, with crime, drugs, AIDS, man-made and natural disasters, technological foul-ups, and employment uncertainties, consumers will seek security and risk avoidance. The need for safety nets provided by governments, insurance, and savings programs of various types, and products and services that will make consumers feel more secure, will be accentuated. All kinds of home, office, and community safety features will be valued, as will medical breakthroughs in disease detection and cure.

Consumers of the future will be even more restless and desirous of change. They will desire new products, be willing to throw products away before they are worn out and actively seek that which is new and different. Impermanence will be a characteristic of future purchases, reflecting a basic consumer restlessness and the resources to indulge them. However, environmental concerns will impact upon this frivolity, and the ability to recycle throw-aways will be a consideration at the time of purchase. Manufacturers that capitalize on this will do very well indeed.

Future consumers will have more leisure time, and more discretionary time, which is not the same as having time available to do nothing. Rather, they will not spend as much time on the job or time necessary to earn a basic living. While their discretionary time will actually increase, at the same time they will be more programmed, their schedules will be full and their leisure will be tightly scheduled. This will reflect more hectic life styles, with a wider assortment of attractive leisure activities competing for consumer time and dollars.

The new consumer will have a different philosophy of work. Previous generations had more of the philosophy of living to work, while the modern consumer works to live. Future consumers will continue to view work as a means to more enjoyable ends, and not as the most important of life's goals. The result is that they will demand more from employers and expect to realize themselves on their jobs and enjoy their life styles. If not, they will readily change jobs. This will be true even at lower levels of opportunity. With lowered unemployment rates, even entry-level workers will be more demanding.

The complexities of society and its ills, coupled with the pressures of daily tasks will cause consumers to seek opportunities to get away from it all. This may mean a summer home, a family farm, travel, more vacations, and so on. It can mean a home that shuts out the outside via secure, peaceful, inner-home environments. This could involve escape from beepers, fax machines, and computer link-ups. It may mean clubs, time-share arrangements, working at home, and regular psychological sessions.

Convenience and immediate gratification refers to the fact that consumers will want to do things conveniently and at the time and place of their choosing. They will want products and services readily available to them, 24 hours a day, in their homes, cars, hotel rooms or wherever they happen to be around the world. They will purchase products that permit them to perform activities conveniently. One need only consider the host of household products such as washers, dryers, microwave ovens, and other appliances, as well as the home-delivered products and services, and the computer-driven and automated products, to sense the potential. Consumers in Marketing 2000 will be willing to pay much for immediate gratification; they will be more impatient and less willing to wait.

The future will find consumers that are more product-dependent and dominated. Consider what happens when automobiles, air conditioners, telephones, or computers break down. Life is disrupted and plans change in a hurry, causing great problems. As homes, offices, factories, and retail stores are automated, machines tend to dominate, with consumers becoming more dependent. Quality, self-monitoring devices, modularization, and immediate service become important considerations in product purchases.

Wanting secure living space is related to seeking security and risk avoidance, except that it highlights the home as a universal theme of future consumers. In the future, consumers will consider secure living spaces to be a necessity, rather than a privilege, to be obtained through a combination of public and private initiatives. Rich and poor alike will represent great opportunities for marketers of homes, appliances, health care, transportation, communications, banking, and shopping services and products that have protection, security and safety as inherent features.

New Product Affects

New products shape and change the way consumers live. They alter behavior significantly and will do so in the future. To gain perspective we might look back upon this century and see that many of the forces discussed, demographic and technological, gave consumers new options and changed life styles markedly. Innovations have altered how consumers spend their time.

Suppose consumers were told a century ago, "an appliance will be placed in homes, and every time that appliance signals, people will stop whatever they may be doing and attend to it." Consumers would have thought it ridiculous that an innate appliance could exert that kind of influence. Nevertheless, when the telephone rings, most of us will stop what we are doing immediately and hurry to attend to it. Indeed the telephone has taken on many roles including a social role, for some people spend hours on the telephone visiting every day.

Even more remarkable has been the impact of television and the automobile. Television has altered the way consumer time is spent and lives are lived. It affects consumption patterns and purchases, as well as dreams and aspirations. Nielsen studies have shown that in the average American home, the television set is on over 40 hours per week and a typical individual spends over 25 hours a week watching it. The 1989 Super Bowl Game was watched by 43.5% of the U.S. homes. It would have been hard for a person in the 1940s to imagine that a new product would consume so much time from that many households.

The automobile has made suburbia and shopping centers the pervasive reality they are today. It has given consumers independence and extended their range of possible activities. Vacations have been greatly influenced by automobiles, and who can deny that how and where we spend our leisure time has been substantially impacted. Sexual mores were reshaped by the availability of the "back seat." Driver's licenses became a means of general identification. And world economies were reshaped by the dominance of the auto-related industries (including steel and rubber), and the role of the Middle East as suppliers of fuel. What future products may have the same impact on our society? Certainly telecommunications is beginning to show signs of similar impact, revising whole industries, and effecting many of the ways we shop, live, behave, and think. But even something focused, like a cure for cancer, could have enormous impact.

Daily Discretionary Living

Major social changes have occurred in recent years, in such areas as education, higher education for women and minorities, marriage, divorce, household arrangements, pre-marital sex, and the employment of women. Social trends, it should be noted, also set into motion countertrends (Kahle, Beaty, and Homer, 1986; McCann and Reibstein, 1985; Wells, 1985). Therefore, considerations about future day-to-day life must take into account the likelihood of opposing trends emerging. We have organized the information gathered so we can explore the following aspects of life: education; shopping; food selection and preparation; housing; social relationships; leisure, entertainment, and recreation; and health care.

Education

In Marketing 2000, higher education will become the norm, rather than the province of the gifted, the wealthy or academically inclined. People who have only a high school diploma will have discovered that their educational preparation is marginal (Magnet, 1988), and the jobs open to them are close to minimum wage. Still, the escalating cost of private and public colleges is of concern to many parents and future students. This will prompt more targeted savings programs, as well as greater prevalence of part-time working students.

A college degree is now held by less than 1/4 of those 25 and over, and these graduates lead more economically rewarding lives. In the future, more extensive schooling in professional fields will be requisites of an enjoyable lifestyle.

Consumers will be more educated and better trained than ever. Many with college degrees will realize a need for further education and updating to achieve their goals. Education will be viewed as a life-long, continuing experience. Advanced degrees will be available through programs specially tailored to build on non-academically acquired abilities.

In Marketing 2000, an educated populous, geared to meeting the changing environments, will be among the nation's most valuable assets. More attention will be paid to the poor performance of elementary and adolescent education. Professionals will continue their education, pursuing several careers in a lifetime. People will view current jobs as temporary. They will view periods of being "in and out of work" as normal, with supporting income and education programs to tide them over. They will seek education to successfully change. Business executives will be lent to governments, universities, and other non-profit institutions. Education and training will be considered more in a different context than is now the case.

Universities will fulfill two important functions in these rapidly shifting environments.

1. They will make leading edge knowledge available through sponsored research, and disseminate that knowledge rapidly to the appropriate individuals and institutions; and

2. They will accredit people by certifying that they have mastered materials and achieved specified levels of competency.

The future will see some "unbundling" of these two functions. Universities will use alternative instruction methods and delivery systems, including computer-aided instruction, tele-conferencing, television, interactive video, videotapes, and other technologies to bring realism and meaning into the classroom. Laser disk video, which enables a computer to locate any frame on a video disk and then start a video playback, while currently expensive, will be widely available by 2000, at least in libraries. This will foster interactive learning centers and greatly extend ready access to relevant information.

Shopping

In the chapter on technology, brief reference was made to future shopping developments including alternative shopping approaches. Communications technology will enable consumers to make purchases via interactive video systems, computer networks, and telephones. For those consumers who wish to view or feel their selections in person, retail shopping will be the method of choice. Retailers will differentiate themselves increasingly on such features as merchandise specialization, guarantees, quality, value, service, image, and store atmosphere. Supermarkets will become more modern, stream-lined and even fashion conscious, and display foods in boutique-style settings (*The Futurist*, 1986b). They will stock more gourmet and ethnic foods, have fast-food counters, increase the non-food items, provide faster check-out, offer cash machines, mini-banks, and various services for the convenience of their patrons.

Wide usage of teletext may replace more expensive print media advertising. By pressing a few buttons consumers will be able to select those ads they wish to see. This will affect all current forms of advertising. Unlike videotex, teletext does not require a telephone line or fiber optic cable for transmission, but piggybacks text on standard television programming, adds little to broadcast cost and uses special TV set computers that are able to recognize and display the text which otherwise is invisible.

Companies, such as Sears, have applied for numerous licenses to operate low-power television stations (LP-TV) which can broadcast advertising messages to a market within a 25 mile radius. Retailers in the future will recognize the powerful potential of broadcast teletext and use it for future advertising and direct marketing strategies (Edwards, 1982).

By the year 2000, direct marketers will send "direct messages" to consumers on laser disks that will contain catalogs and offerings by many different firms. Efficient software will enable consumers to search quickly all offerings in product categories from accordions to zithers. Facsimile machines and faxes are becoming a business necessity and along with them has come "junk fax," streams of ads moving over phone lines to tout the latest products and services. By the year 2000, homes will be equipped with computers that can print on laser disks, thereby being able to store vast amounts of information temporarily on reusable media (Hudson, 1986).

A laser-equipped computer could receive an electronic newspaper, plus various magazines and catalogs during the course of a day, which could be perused at the consumers' leisure using existing teletext technology.

Manufacturer Brands vs. Store Brands

Manufacturers' brands and national brands are giving way to retailers' brands and private labels. Consumer brand loyalty appears to be waning in the face of increasing emphasis by manufacturers on price and promotions — they are buying volume and price discounting, rather than relying on advertising to generate sales. Within the past decade an increasing share of marketing budgets has gone into price-oriented promotions vs. advertising (Ogilvy, 1983). But the domination of one over the other is not yet guaranteed:

> "Yet, in the long run, the manufacturer who dedicates his advertising to building the most sharply defined image for his product gets the largest share of the market."

The Advertising Research Foundation Conference on *Advertising 2010: The Next 25 Years* (Ogilvy 1986), raised questions about the existence of brands and brand loyalty in the future. The preference for house brands and private labels attests to diminished loyalty to manufacturer's brands, which results in retailers rather than manufacturers "owning" customers.

Consumers have always felt a need for reassurance and risk reduction, particularly when purchasing expensive items and technically complex products. Manufacturers who guaranteed and stood behind their brand of products have traditionally provided an important means for consumer risk reduction. Indeed, a single brand name, such as Yamaha, can reduce risk across a wide range of products: pianos, sound systems, motorcycles, and sports equipment. As retail chains expand in the future, they will have the resources and advertising economies of scale to apply store brands over a wide variety of products. In Marketing 2000, retailers' brand names may well be as important to the consumers as manufacturers' brands.

Current newspaper retail advertising, devoted largely to listing products and prices rather than describing products, depends on pre-selling a product usually by other advertising so that the retailers only need inform customers of availability at reasonable prices. The news media of the future will allow retailers to use informative, persuasive copy without heavy expenses. By the year 2000, advertising could be less intrusive than present media, since consumers would select it and the cost per word for advertising copy distributed via compact laser disk could be about 1/1000th the cost of print.[2]

Currently, direct marketers are pleased that more sophisticated computer data bases enable them to target their mailings more precisely to households which are likely to buy. By the year 2000, direct marketers will be able to band together to send laser disks, containing as many as 100 catalogs, to virtually every laser/computer-equipped home. Consumers will select which ones to be perused —thus — in a sense, consumers will be self-targeting. Homeowners will then be able to use their software to select clothing from specific merchants such as Brooks Brothers, Land's End or L.L. Bean. Consumers will be able to specify the type of product and price range, and view the total range of offerings from those merchants who are on the laser disk.

Foods in the Year 2000

There are a number of opposing tendencies in our food purchase behavior. Included are: meals at home vs. meals in restaurants; fast foods vs. gourmet foods; eating healthy vs. pigging-out; family meal scenes vs. grazing; eating at prescribed times vs. eating on demand. One fact seems clear. Markets for foods will appropriately be characterized as studies of opposites.

A revolution is occurring in foods. In the future, more attention will be directed to good nutrition as society ages, becomes informed, and increasingly more health conscious. More attention will be given to and much more will be known about the effect on humans of food additives, chemicals used in producing foods, sodium, fat, calories, and cholesterol content. The emphasis generally is changing from assuring enough to eat, to preventing overeating. Our society will see a swing to more natural food — foods without preservatives, that use natural fertilizers and bio-genetic engineering to develop disease-resistant strains of food.

Major manufacturers, such as Proctor & Gamble, are developing food oils that will pass through the body largely unabsorbed. The technology involved may be extended to bond other molecules, such as starches, into forms that are less likely to be absorbed by the body. The net result may be new categories of foods that are eaten more for enjoyment with little impact on nutrition. There will be changes in packaging and in storage,

---

[2]Consider that a five-inch compact laser disk can hold an entire encyclopedia and can be produced currently for about $2 per incremental copy.

with an increase in the use of radiation treatments that allow foods to maintain freshness without using chemical preservatives. Foods in the future will also be better tasting and more convenient.

Foods reflect an ever-present conflict between what consumers ought to do for their own good, for the purposes of health and desired physical images vs. what consumers prefer and really like to do. Both sets of forces will be present in the future categories, and both will represent enticing future market opportunities that exist side-by-side.

For example, consumers have become extremely diet conscious. Thinness is associated with being happy, healthy, attractive, and productive. In a relatively short period of time we have seen a proliferation of new products and services for dieters, including low calorie foods, beverages and lean meats, sugar substitutes, Weight Watchers and other weight-loss organizations, exercise classes, diet camps, appetite suppressants, spas, exercise videotapes and diet-related, best-selling books, magazines, newsletters, and television and radio programs. At the same time, there exists markets for good tasting foods that are high in calorie content. The future seems bright for them as well — witness premium ice creams with high fat content, rich chocolates, and fattening, delicious pastries.

There will be a further deterioration of the family-dominated meal scene. It has already given way to individual family members exercising their own food choices to meet their own time schedules and tastes. Sit-down meals, particularly family meals, have given way to grazing — as snacks and sampling become more popular (*The Futurist*, 1986c).

Future consumers will confront the dilemma of their desire to be thin, on the one hand, with high-calorie, gourmet, food snacks, and a wide variety of world delicacies on the other. Some consumers will feel trapped by this dilemma and develop eating disorders, such as anorexia nervosa and bulimia. Others will continue to select foods with little regard for weight and size consequences. The U.S. population is generally considered to be overweight, and children are no exception.

Marketers will be challenged to respond by offering a wide variety of products and services that will assist consumers in making difficult food trade-offs. For consumers who have accepted their fuller figures and food enjoyment, there will be designer clothes in larger sizes, and fashion consultants specializing in attractive presentations of larger persons. For consumers who seek to remain thin, there will be increasing availability of gourmet frozen dinners, nouvelle cuisine restaurants, and medical operations that remove fat from bodies, put balloons in stomachs or cut out part of the stomach. Starch blockers preventing the absorption of carbohydrates, offered a few years ago but removed from the market due to alleged side effects, may be perfected. There will be opportunities for the development of diets for making fat indigestible, so that consumers can eat to their heart's content without suffering ill effects.

Marketers will continue to be challenged with the development of low calorie snacks and delicious gourmet foods. As a result, by the year 2000 consumers may focus less on food as representing nutrition, nourishment, and fuel, and more on food as a reward and a diversion. The role of food as a social facilitator will be expanded when food no longer carries the calorie penalty. Numerous other food trends will persist, including an increase in the usage of paper bottles, pouches, and other packages that protect freshness and are lighter (*The Futurist*, 1985), as well as being more environmentally safe.

Home Environments

It seems that individual, free-standing housing, in the future, will give ground to multiple dwellings, townhouses, condominiums, and high rises to maximize the use of land and keep housing costs in check. Greater reliance will be placed on solar energy with housing being clustered to maximize the use of efficient, active solar collectors, and conserving heat by having fewer exposed walls. Furthermore, architects will capitalize on new materials to make optimal use of winds, sunlight variations, and temperature-conserving characteristics (Mason and Jennings, 1982). Although new materials will make possible exciting, futuristic designs, it is likely that consumers in Marketing 2000 will show a preference for the traditional look. Homes and furnishing style preferences will likely change slightly overall over the next decade because, in an age of rapid change and uncertainty, consumers tend to seek the known and traditional.

The price of housing has risen rapidly, to spectacular levels in many areas. During the early 1980s, the West and South experienced explosive growth, and despite overbuilding and a collapse of prices in several of the markets (e.g., Houston) others remain strong (e.g., San Francisco). Still, despite the fact that prices have stopped escalating and, indeed, are now experiencing downward pressure as a result of a smaller market following the baby boom, housing remains a critical issue. There will be increasing pressure on many suburban communities and communities in the sunbelt areas to relax zoning requirements to allow housing configurations of greater density. Other communities, on the other hand, will exhibit a counter-tendency to limit and even prohibit growth in housing.

Consumers will seek perceptions of more spacious and luxurious housing, partly reflecting the proliferation of goods they will own, their status in life, and the high costs per square foot. Ways of utilizing space more effectively will be sought — creating increased demand for customizing closets, improving room layouts, developing furniture that is flexible and serves multiple purposes, and making available computer entertainment, social, and athletic environments.

In the houses of Marketing 2000, consumers will be able to change the color and look of appliances via custom panels. They will have flexible wall and room treatments. Houses will be self-monitoring for purposes of security and safety, as well as preventing breakdowns. More efficient use will be made of resource usage such as water and energy. Households will have communications centers as a result of some of the global computer network and television advances discussed in Chapter 2 on technology.

Homes of tomorrow may be so designed as to shut out the outside world — by the use of inner courts, walls, security gates — to permit people to escape from it all. Many people will chose to live vertically in well-protected, high-rise apartments. The basic design for safe and secure homes and communities will present great future product/service opportunities.

Consumers in Marketing 2000 will change homes readily. They will be able to select from an array of configurations to better fit their household type, e.g., bachelor, suburbanite, divorcee, retiree, or step-family. Family homes that formerly remained in the family for generations will be considered temporary, and the farm or vacation house may be the one that remains in the family for generations.

Social Relationships

Consumers in the year 2000 will be more informed, better traveled, and worldly. They will be more willing to act independently and express their opinions. They will rely less on families and relatives than has been the case, and more on extended relationships and groups sharing common interests. Some children will leave home at an earlier age, establish their own households, move into their educational endeavors and careers, and out of family domination. Others will stay home longer or return home later into adulthood as a result of high housing and living costs. As a result of travel and electronic networks, consumers in Marketing 2000 will be more globally-oriented. They will be much more sensitive to the other nations and cultures, and will bring products and services of the world to their homes.

Over the next 10 to 20 years, not only will the concept of the family relationship change, but laws will enable alternative family formations to gain recognition and legitimacy. We will have moved from a nation which defined family as being a husband/wife with two children, to single-parent families, singles living together, serial divorce, and remarriages with their own or step children, single-child families, childless couples, multi-generational households, etc. We shall witness the first time in history in which family members may be able to know personally four or even five generations (Lazer, 1987).

Because consumers are becoming increasingly fearful of their environments and of strangers, it will become commonplace to purchase background checks on others by the year 2000 prior to engaging in social interaction or making business commitments.

There will be more emphasis on electronic mate-matching services such as computer dating and video match-making. The former will use computer algorithms to permit one to specify many pre-screening criteria while the latter will allow interested singles to personally assess their potential partners prior to arranging a first meeting.

Privacy Fences

Consumers in the future will continue erecting barriers to preserve their safety and privacy in an increasingly complex, intrusive, and hostile environment. They will feel the need to protect themselves and to escape from drugs, crime, AIDS, and the like that threaten their personal safety and property. Also, some consumers will feel they are being bombarded by aggressive and intrusive sales efforts. Recent laws limiting telemarketing, such as the Florida "asterisk law," which prohibits unsolicited commercial telephone calls to numbers in the telephone directory that are marked with an asterisk, are the precursor of things to come in Marketing 2000.

People will continue building privacy fences in the future by limiting access to themselves in various ways. They are obtaining unlisted phone numbers (50% do this in some cities), they are not answering telephones or doorbells, answering machines are used as pre-screening devices before speaking to someone or opening their doors. Television screens in apartment lobbies, one-way mirrors, key cards, and special combinations and codes are used for protection and privacy. Consumers on the street avoid eye contact or speaking with people they don't know. This will be heightened by Marketing 2000 with electronic hedges being erected.

Nevertheless, people have social needs and are gregarious by nature. Consumers will continue to feel comfortable having casual interactions with strangers in selected situations, such as at charity and major social events, clubs, and singles weekends all of which present many future marketing opportunities. Because of their ability to allow people to get to know each other over time, the workplace and volunteer activities will become even more important sources of social interaction.

Leisure, Recreation and Entertainment

In the future, American consumers will take their leisure even more seriously — they will work at it. Leisure spawns a host of industries. Consumers in Marketing 2000 will treat air travel as more of a commodity rather than as a special item. They will have a global perspective of shopping, vacationing, second homes, culture, medical treatment, and so on. For example, we can expect that fashion and cost-conscious consumers will visit the shopping cities of the world, such as Singapore and Hong Kong, for additions to wardrobes, as well as for electronics, shoes, and eyeglasses. They will fly to vacation spots of the world where their currency is strong, commanding better values. Second homes will be built where labor is inexpensive and middle income people can afford a more luxurious lifestyle. Consumers will fly to different parts of the world for a few days to experience cultural events and entertainment. Charter flights to England or Vienna for groups wanting to see a Shakespearean play or take in a concert will be quite common. Ease of air travel will permit the proliferation of dream vacations in which "experience brokers" will custom design trips to cater to the fantasies and desires of the individual traveler (Kotler, 1984).

At least one hospital is already offering free air transportation to anyone with insurance who wishes to receive medical treatment at its facilities. By the year 2000 this will be common as hospitals specialize in offering package deals for procedures, such as open heart surgery, colon cancer treatment or prostrate surgery. Jet-setting will no longer be limited to the highest income groups. Internationally usable, smart cards will enable anything to be purchased, at any time, anywhere and from any source.

Affinity groups for leisure enjoyment of such things as square dancing, hiking, cross country skiing, playing bridge, and archeology will absorb an increasing amount of leisure time. Activities that combine moderately active exercise with an opportunity for meeting people in safe and pleasant settings will have great appeal. This will have growing commercial implications for such ventures as activity-specific videotapes, magazines, retail outlets, and catalogs.

Health Care

Given the increasing proportion of elderly consumers in Marketing 2000 who absorb a major portion of health care services, and account for a larger proportion of costs, there will be great emphasis on the delivery of adequate health care and on cost containment. There will be trends toward more efficient, less expensive health care facilities, such as HMOs. Nutrition will be emphasized as one means of promoting wellness (*The Futurist*, 1986a). Communications technology will make possible access to the opinions of expert physicians regarding illness and treatment (Bezold, 1982).

Consumers in the future will think of health care as an ongoing process of body maintenance rather than as emergency disaster control. They will deem access to good health care a right, and not a privilege of only those who can afford it. But universal access to all forms of health care and treatment might be constrained by rapidly rising costs. We may see, by Marketing 2000, a rise in the application of health care rationing (for open heart surgery, dialysis, and transplants for people over 70, for example), with the attendant opportunities for private coverage to supplement these targeted areas. Consumers will be able to obtain extensive preventative, maintenance style diagnostic checks along with recommendations concerning diet, exercise, control of stress, vitamins, and needed medical procedures.

Society/Technology

Evidence also suggests that in the future, society will likely be more aware of the health risks posed by substances such as drugs, alcohol, and cigarettes. Perhaps through education, their use will decline, but overall, that does not seem likely before the year 2000. Crime, which is highly dependent on the employment opportunities, particularly for the less educated and younger minorities, is a difficult factor to forecast. Also the spread of dreaded communicable diseases such as AIDS, which are difficult to forecast, could greatly affect and disrupt society.

We have already discussed some of the ways that technology can impact on society. The reverse, the impact of society on technology, will also occur. As social problems grow, technology emerges to deliver solutions. For example, if crime problems, such as property crimes, continue to become more serious as appears likely, there will be extensive development of technologically, sophisticated, property-protection equipment.

An interesting technological solution has been proposed for the problem of street crime, drug trade, and counterfeiting. Each person would be given a number similar to a credit card number which would be implanted under the skin with a special laser device. When a person wishes to buy or sell, the number can be scanned from the hand or forehead. As with a credit card, money would be immediately charged or credited to individual bank accounts. This would put a stop to most thefts, for if money were not used, then a thief's goods could not be fenced. Also, individuals could not be robbed for cash and credit cards (Smith, 1977). Crime probably will continue to be with us and prompt technological solutions and opportunities.

Another example of the impact of society on technology is the sexual revolution. Because it had become so ingrained, it not only spawned singles-housing markets, clubs, clothing fashions, dating services, and unwed parenthood, but also sexually transmitted diseases. Scientists are now challenged to find cures for herpes and AIDS, find new drugs for antibiotic-resistant syphilis, make better screening programs for dating services, prevent unwanted pregnancies with more successful contraceptive devices, and find evidence to support contentions on both sides of the abortion debate.

So it is clear that while technology often creates social change, social change also creates enormous challenge and opportunity for technological innovation, application, and marketing. The moral and ethical issues, however, become more and more complicated, and that provides more than enough material for yet another book.

REFERENCES

Bezold, Clement (1982), "Health Care in the U.S.: Four Alternative Futures," *The Futurist*, (August), 21-24.

Edwards, Kenneth (1982), "Broadcast Teletext: The Next Mass Medium," *The Futurist*, (October), 21-24.

The Futurist (1985), "More Convenience in Food Packaging," (April), 60.

The Futurist (1986a), "Rx for Doctors: Learn More About Nutrition," (March/April), 42.

The Futurist (1986b), "Tomorrow's Supermarkets," (September/October), 49.

The Futurist (1986c), "Snacks Replace Meals," (March/April), 50.

Hudson, Richard L. (1986), "Erasable Optical Disk Comes Closer, But Problems Remain," *The Wall Street Journal*, (Sept. 5, 1986), 21.

Kahle, Lynn R., Sharon E. Beaty and Pamela Homer (1986), "Alternative Measurement Approaches to Consumer Values: The List of Values (LOV) and

Values and Life Styles (VALS)," *Journal of Consumer Research*, 13 No. 3 (December), 405-409.

Kotler, Philip (1984), "Dream Vacations, the Booming Market for Designer Experiences," *The Futurist*, (October), 7-13.

Lazer, William (1987), *Handbook of Demographics for Marketing and Advertising*, Boston, MA: Lexington Books.

Magnet, Myron (1988), "How to Smarten Up the Schools," *Fortune*, 117 No. 3 (February 1), 86-94.

Mason, Roy and Lane Jennings (1982), "The Computer Home: Will Tomorrow's Housing Come Alive?" *The Futurist*, (February), 35-43.

McCann, John M. and David J. Reibstein (1985), "Forecasting the Impact of Socio-economic and Demographic Change on Product Demand," *Journal of Marketing Research*, 22 (November), 415-423.

Ogilvy, David (1983), *Ogilvy on Advertising*, New York, NY: Vintage Books, Division of Random House, 169.

Ogilvy, David (1986), "Sound an Alarm!" *Proceedings, Advertising 2010: The Next 25 Years*, Advertising Research Foundation, New York, 97-104.

Smith, Chuck (1977), *What the World is Coming To*, Costa Mesa, California: Maranatha House Publishers.

Wells, William D. (1985), "Attitudes and Behavior: Lessons From the Needham Life Style Study," *Journal of Advertising Research*, 25 No. 1 (February/March), 40-44.

CHAPTER 4

THE DEMOGRAPHIC VISION

"Demographics: Again, 'dull'. Again, crucial. Again, the basic frame for all subsequent analysis." Daniel Bell

Introduction

No single set of forces will impact more on marketing strategies and operations than changing demographic factors. In the future, there will be more turbulence and greater change in demographic segments of U.S. markets than has occurred since the taking of the first census in 1790. The people underpinnings of future U.S. markets, which are now veering in new directions from those of the 1960s, 1970s, and 1980s, will create vastly different market opportunities between now and 2010. Whereas past markets in the U.S. were dominated by babies, teenagers or young adults, its future markets will be driven by middle agers and mature consumers, new types of households will become increasingly important and the rapidly aging, greying and coloring of U.S. markets will be felt.

Market Focus

The general market focus of each of the decades from the 1950s on is characterized in Figure 1. The 1950s, overlapping with the 1960s, was characterized by a baby and teenage orientation. The 1960s and 1970s represented a thriving teenage and young adult market. The 1970s and 1980s marked the years of young adults and young marrieds. The 1980s overlapping with the 1990s will be the decades of young marrieds and middle agers; first, the younger middle agers and then the older middle agers. As for the future, the 2000-2010 decade will be indeed a time of the mature consumers, with those 55 and over leading the thrust, and the 65 and older group becoming far more important.

FIGURE 1
MARKET FOCUS BY DECADES*

Decade	Market Focus
1950 & 1960	Babies
1960 & 1970	Teenagers
1970 & 1980	Young adults and young marrieds
1980 & 1990	Early middle agers
1990 & 2000	Late middle agers
2000+	Mature consumers

* Adapted from Lazer, William (1987). *Handbook of Demographics for Marketing and Advertising.* Boston, MA: Lexington Books.

The aging and greying of America will redirect marketing thinking and business activities. Slower population growth, the proportion and number of working women, continuing migrations to the West and South, slowing of birth rates, new family structures and living arrangements, different life styles and shifting age distribution will bring about marketing changes. They are among the most important considerations and, as Drucker noted, demographic shifts "will challenge widely held beliefs regarding the structure and segmentation of consumer markets...(they) will stand on their heads some of the most cherished beliefs and habits of business" (Drucker, 1980).

Although key to marketing, the impending demographic changes were surprisingly neglected by almost all of the top executives interviewed during the course of this study. They were hardly mentioned; their implications were rarely discussed. Little appreciation and understanding of the nature and scope of future demographic tendencies was expressed. Perhaps these senior executives regarded demographic considerations as specialized, technical concerns, that are handled by others in the organization. Or perhaps the demographic developments were assumed and just taken for granted as something that would command attention. Possibly, demographic factors were perceived as being somewhat less important than they will be. Regardless, a realistic grasp of future company market, product and service opportunities, whether consumer or industrial, requires an appreciation at the top for future demographic developments.

In this chapter we can deal with a small proportion of available relevant marketing/demographic data. The materials that have been selected from the vast array of socio-economic government statistics are illustrative and suggestive. The topics include: population growth, immigration, births, deaths, projected age distribution, population shifts by cities and states, the changing racial mosaic, working women and mature consumers and their life styles.

Population Change

Overall population growth, one of the fundamental factors governing future market opportunities, is a function of two variables: net immigration and net internal growth. The latter, net internal growth, refers to the surplus of births over deaths. The former, net immigration, comprises both legal and illegal immigrants.

In the future, America will feel ever-increasing pressure from people around the world seeking entry into the U.S. New legislation will likely set forth different ground rules affecting immigration limits. Legal immigration has remained for decades in the 400,000 to 425,000 annual range, but there are pressures to increase it. Illegal immigration, in the form of undocumented aliens, has risen to unprecedented heights. In the near future their numbers could well rival those of legal immigration. Total annual immigration, legal and illegal, is now officially estimated to be in the 600,000 range, but some observers have placed it as high as 1.5 million in any one year.

While accurate data for illegal immigration are impossible to obtain, official estimates for the 1970-80 decade often vary from 2-1/2 to 5 million. Estimates of total immigration for the 20-year period, 1985 to 2005, are for an addition of about 10 million legal immigrants and perhaps 6 to 8 million illegals. Projected totals of 16-18 million immigrants means they could well account for 50% of our population growth over the next 2 decades. This, in turn, could mean the greatest melting-pot adjustment ever in the history of the U.S., particularly among Hispanics, Blacks, Asians, and working-class and rural whites. Regrettably, it could generate hostility among ethnic groups of the lower economic classes. It will result in the further coloring of America, signaling changes in the American mosaic and heralding greater diversity in life styles.

Increasing immigration, besides adding to our population base, shapes our tastes, life styles, marketing methods and future market opportunities. The surface impact is evidenced by the widespread acceptance of foods such as pizzas, bagels, tacos, croissants, pitas and sushi; and new tastes in furniture, furnishings, automobiles, art, music, and clothing styles. "Foreign objects" will be further integrated into the ever-changing

FIGURE 2
LIVE BIRTHS

Year	Births (000's)
1940	2,570
1950	3,645
1960	4,307
1970	3,725
1975	3,144
1980	3,413
1982	3,600
1985	3,761
1990 (est.)	3,900
2000 (est.)	3,700

Source: U. S. Bureau of the Census 1986. *Statistical Abstract of the United States, 1986.* 106th edition and authors' estimates.

American bloodstream. Life style changes will be even more dramatic, as a variety of global life styles are accepted and merge. Immigrants, in the year 2000 and beyond, will continue to shape basic values affecting such fundamentals as work, education, families, homes, religious institutions, laws and communities.

Birth Expectations

American births will remain relatively low with rates continuing below our zero population growth rate of 2.1 births per woman. Data on live births from 1940 to 2000 are given in Figure 2.

The following facts indicate the likelihood of slow future population growth. The current total fertility rate for all women is just over 1.8, down from the relatively high 3.4 in the 1960-64 period and the 2.1 rate in the 1970-74 period. The birthrate among women aged 18-24 has remained low for over ten years, averaging about 1.9 births per woman. For women 18-34 the average number of lifetime births is now a relatively low 2.02 births. When this is coupled with the fact that the number of women of child-bearing age, those 15-44, will actually decrease between 1990 and 2010, the outlook for births is gloomy.

Women, particularly married women, expect to have about two children over their lifetime, one of each gender, a sort of "matched set." The childless family has received considerable attention in recent years, far more than it deserves. In reality, surveys have always indicated that the childless family is totally atypical. Fewer than 5% of the wives now say that they expect to have no children. By contrast, twice as many expect 4 or more children, a fact that is rarely mentioned. Regardless, there has been a great departure from the large-sized families of 6, 8, 10 or 12 children, of the 1920s, 1930s and 1940s.

Lower birthrates and fewer children will be a hallmark of Twenty First Century family demographics. The result will be an era of smaller-sized, more mobile and portable families which will impact directly on life styles, living standards, market opportunities, and product and service demands.

Population Growth

Population data for 1900-2050 are given in Figure 3. In 1988, the total U.S. population reached 245 million. While the rate of population growth has been slowing steadily, our total population will continue to

---

FIGURE 3
U.S. POPULATION GROWTH
1990 - 2050 (000's)

Year	Number (000'S)
1900	76,303
1930	122,755
1940	132,594
1950	152,271
1960	180,671
1970	205,052
1980	227,704
1990	249,657
2000	267,955
2010	283,238
2020	296,597
2030	304,807
2040	308,559
2050	309,488

Source U. S. Bureau of the Census 1984b. *Projections of the Population of the United States by Age, Sex and Race: 1983-2080.* Series P-25, No. 952.

increase for several decades. About 23 million people, almost the equivalent of Canada, were added to the U.S. over the decade of the 1970s. A similar increase of about 22-24 million, including legal immigration, is expected over the decade of the 1980s, albeit on a larger population base. The expected population growth over the 1990s, by contrast, is only estimated at 18 million, a 22% decrease in growth from the 1980s. This is well below the 29 million increase in the 1950s, which, it should be remembered, occurred on a population base of only 150 million.

Total U.S. population in the year 2000 is estimated at about 268 million, well below the 300 million figure that marketers commonly projected in the 1950s. The U.S., throughout the Twenty First Century, will continue to be a slower population growth country, with expectations of a low rate of increase of less than 1% per year. Beyond the year 2000, while our total population will still increase, it will do so at an even slower rate. The population is projected to grow by only 16 million during the 2000 to 2010 decade, and 13 million between 2010 and 2020. Strikingly, *the total population growth over the 50 year period from 2030 to 2080 is expected to be less than 6 million.* That represents a radical change from the past as the data in Figure 3 indicates.

Most of the population growth over the next century will, in fact, occur by the year 2030. After that, around 2038, our population is expected to reach zero population growth. The growth rates will slow noticeably. The annual percentage change in population from 1950-60 was in the 1.7 range, but declined to the 1.05 range from 1970-80. By contrast, it is only expected to be in the low .7 range between 1990 and 2000, with a continuing decline for the next 100 years, through 2080. This represents a major shift of fundamental import.

Evidence indicates that businesses in the past have been propelled by growing populations, as was the case in the golden years of the late 1950s and early 1960s. The so-called "soaring sixties" were energized by "the baby boomers." In the future, however, businesses will have to base their marketing plans and strategies on the realities of much lower population growth rates.

The U.S. is now in the throes of a transformation to a slow population growth nation. This will require far greater marketing skill and acumen than ever before. In the past, the burgeoning population growth compensated for many marketing miscalculations and provided marketing management with a degree of slack and latitude that will not exist in the future. Emphasis on improving marketing productivity, increasing marketing efficiency and maintaining competitiveness will become even more vital for future business success. Growing populations, so characteristic of the past, will not be there to provide a future market cushion.

Impact of Babies

As marketers well know, the addition of a baby to a household, particularly a first-born child, can have profound effects on how life is lived, on household activities and routines and on purchasing decisions and patterns. Both birthing order and the actual number of live births power demand for a wide variety of products and services.

The baby boom, after the end of World War II, propelled the high economic growth years of the 1960s. Birthrates rose, and a large number of live births occurred between 1954 and 1964, averaging more than 4 million per year. *The total hit a peak of 4.4 million in 1957, which has not been matched since, and will not likely be in the next 100 years, even on our higher population base. This total compares with 3.8 million live births in 1988.*

Trends in actual births are shown in Figure 4. In the 1970s the number of live births tapered off and fell, although they have been picking up a

---

FIGURE 4
BIRTHS AND DEATHS: NUMBER AND RATE
1910-1985

Year	Number (1,000)		Rate per 1,000 Pop.	
	Births	Deaths	Births	Deaths
1910	2,777	697	30.1	14.7
1920	2,950	1,118	27.7	13.0
1930	2,618	1,327	21.3	11.3
1940	2,559	1,417	19.4	10.8
1950	3,632	1,452	24.1	9.6
1960	4,258	1,712	23.7	9.5
1970	3,731	1,921	18.4	9.5
1980	3,612	1,990	15.9	8.8
1985	3,749	2,084	15.7	8.7

Source: U. S. Bureau of the Census 1984b. *Projections of the Population of the United States by Age, Sex, and Race: 1983 to 2080.* Series P-25, No. 952.

little recently, and have increased a little every year since 1975. Total births are expected to reach a peak of 3.9 million by 1990, and then continue a slow, long-run, downward trend. The estimate for 2000 is in the 3.6 to 3.7 million range.

An interesting shift that will affect future purchase behavior is occurring among the proportion of first births. When the first baby enters a family, the proud parents (or parent) are much more amenable to spending freely and generously, showering the newest family member with products and services. Less is spent on succeeding children and they become the recipients of "hand-me-downs." Traditionally, first-born babies represented about 25% of all the births. By 1982 that increased to 38% — a 50% jump. In the 2000 era, first-born babies will likely be upwards of 40% of total births. Since families spend far more on them than on succeeding children (estimates for some products are over twice as much), the market impact of future births is expected to be more substantial than the total alone would suggest.

The introduction of the first child into the household can also render some products and services less desirable or even obsolete. Examples are sports cars, which give way to sedans and station wagons; conveniently located bachelor pads and small metropolitan apartments, which are exchanged for larger apartments and houses in the suburbs; laundromat visits which decline as a result of the purchase of washers and dryers; and so on.

A significant change in the future age of birthing will also occur. More women will continue to postpone having babies until later in life, but will still choose to become mothers. In the 1960s and 1970s women regarded 30 years of age as the "now or never age," an automatic cutoff for having their first child. A major change in thought and action has occurred with more women delaying having their first child until their middle and late 30s and even early 40s. In the future, a growing proportion of first children will be born to women older than 30, representing a permanent change in patterns and mores. This will result partly from medical advances that can handle previously feared birth complications and partly from women's life style changes, particularly the attitude towards careers and gainful employment.

Marketing 2000 will likely see the emergence of a larger number of much older, more experienced, informed and worldly mothers. They will represent some of the better educated and better paid women. Their families will be able to afford better homes than was the case previously. With smaller-sized families, parents will have the opportunity of directing more individual attention to each child, and to increase the quality of time spent with them. Such trends augur well for the demand for baby-related products and services. They underscore future needs for daycare centers, preschool nurseries, flexible work time and a host of products promoting the automation of household chores and the easing of the burden of child care. A premium will be placed on products and services that effectively assist the more mature, working mothers with the responsibilities and activities involved in caring for small children.

On the other end of the spectrum will be the continued high rates of out-of-wedlock births to teens, especially in minority communities. Educators and training programs will be in increasing demand, as will health care for teens and infants. Because these children will be the focus of social reform in the next decade, the private sectors will be encouraged to play a more active role in their lives. Marketing tie-ins with all sorts of products and services aimed at aiding low-income children and communities will become more commonplace. Furthermore, given the growth in childhood poverty, upscale families will not be as comfortable flaunting their wealth as they were in the 70s and 80s.

Deaths

In addition to births, deaths are the other component of the internal growth equation. As we have noted, the actual number of live births per

FIGURE 5
DEATHS 1950 - 2050

Year	Number
1950	1,452,500
1960	1,712,000
1970	1,921,000
1980	1,986,000
1990	2,164,700
2000	2,363,100
2010	2,634,800
2030	3,434,400
2050	3,957,000

Source: U. S. Bureau of the Census 1984b. *Projections of the Population of the United States by Age, Sex, and Race: 1983 to 2080.* Series P-25, No. 952.

year has decreased as compared with the 1960s and, over the same time, the number of deaths has increased steadily. This is shown in Figure 5.

The total number of deaths in 1985 was 2,084,000. 1983 marked the first year of more than 2,000,000 deaths and in the future there will not likely be a year with any less. As our population ages, deaths are expected to increase, reaching an estimated 2.4 million by 2000 and 3.8 million by 2040, an increase of about 60%. The continuing increase in demand for death-associated products and services is evident. Already the boomers are becoming an active market for cemetery plots.

Changing Age Distribution

Some future population dynamics are shown in Figure 6, which deals with changes in the age composition of the population from 1980 to 2020. There will be a rapid and dramatic aging of our population, with the median age rising rapidly from 30.3 years in 1980 to 36.3 years in the year 2000 and 40.9 years in 2020. The data reflect the growing importance of the over 35 age segments.

FIGURE 6
U.S. POPULATION BY AGE 1980-2020
(in thousands)

AGE	1980	1990	2000	2010	2020
Under 5	16,298	19,198	17,626	17,924	18,357
5-14	34,940	35,384	38,277	35,554	36,896
15-19	21,178	16,968	18,943	19,114	17,158
20-24	21,294	18,580	17,145	19,857	18,308
25-34	37,181	43,529	36,415	36,978	39,834
35-44	25,638	37,847	43,743	36,772	37,343
45-54	22,732	25,402	37,119	42,946	36,180
55-64	21,786	21,051	23,767	34,848	40,298
65-74	15,590	18,035	17,677	20,318	29,855
75-84	7,715	10,349	12,318	12,326	14,486
85+	2,193	3,313	4,926	6,551	7,081
TOTALS	226,546	249,656	267,956	276,687	296,596
Median Age	30.0	33.0	36.3	38.4	40.9

Source: U. S. Bureau of the Census 1984b. *Projections of the Population of the United States by Age, Sex, and Race: 1983 to 2080.* Series P-25, No. 952.

In 2010 the 55 and over age group, the mature consumers, will have grown significantly both numerically and proportionately. The 44 and under categories will show little or no growth. Future decades will underscore the growth of middle aged and elderly consumers who will total about 60 million in 2000 and 90 million in 2020.

The 35-44 year olds will make up the largest age concentration in the year 2000. As they age, the bulge moves to the 45-54 year old band in 2010 and the 55-64 year old band in 2020. By then, an amazing total of 51 million people, about one sixth of the total population, will be over 65 years old. On the average, they will be relatively well off, can look forward to living another 15 years, will enjoy better health than any previous senior cohorts, and will comprise a vital, active market segment. Interestingly, over 21 million of them will be over 75 years of age, and the 100-and-over age category is projected to include 233 thousand people.

Population shifts, for the 1980-2030 period are shown in Figure 7. Proportionately, the trend will be an increase in both the 45-64 and 65-and-over groups. The under 25 age categories will realize continuing declines while the 35-44 age group will increase as a percent of the population until 2000 and then decline.

Figure 8, the population pyramid, highlights the striking changes in age and sex distributions from 1982 to the year 2080. While the 1982

FIGURE 7
PERCENT DISTRIBUTION OF THE POPULATION, BY AGE:
1950 to 2080

Age (years)

Year	Total Population	Under 5	5-13	14-17	18-24	25-34	35-44	45-64	65 & Over
1980	100.00	7.2	13.6	7.1	13.3	16.5	11.4	19.5	11.3
1985	100.00	7.7	12.4	6.2	12.0	17.5	13.4	18.7	12.0
1990	100.00	7.7	12.9	5.2	10.3	17.4	15.2	18.6	12.7
1995	100.00	7.2	13.3	5.4	9.1	15.6	16.2	20.2	13.1
2000	100.00	6.6	12.8	5.7	9.2	13.6	16.3	22.7	13.0
2010	100.00	6.3	11.3	5.3	9.8	13.1	13.2	27.5	13.8
2030	100.00	5.8	10.8	5.0	8.6	12.2	13.2	23.2	21.2

Source: U. S. Bureau of the Census 1984b. *Projections of the Population of the United States by Age, Sex, and Race: 1983 to 2080.* Series P-25, No. 952.

FIGURE 8
PERCENTAGE DISTRIBUTION OF THE U.S. POPULATION
BY AGE AND SEX

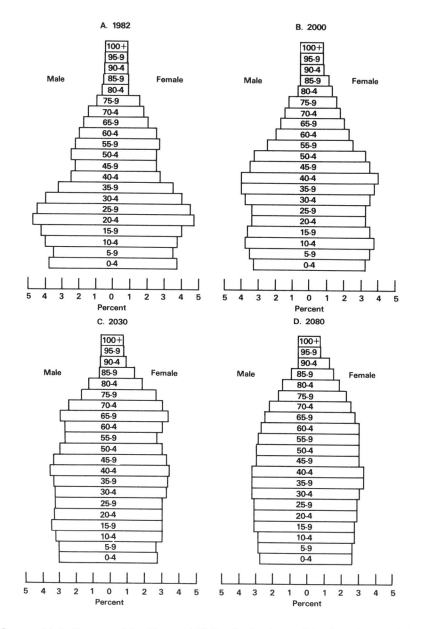

Source: U. S. Bureau of the Census 1984b. *Projections of the Population of the United States by Age, Sex, and Race: 1983 to 2080.* Series P-25, No. 952.

median age of 30.6 years was an all-time high, never again is our population projected to be so young. From 36.6 years in the year 2000, the median is expected to increase continuously to a high of 42.8 years in 2080. The population pyramid shows the diminishing concentrations in the lower age classes.

These adult and more mature consumers will likely be more interested in maintaining and enhancing their households, families and positions, than in radically changing the social and economic order. They are expected to become more conservative in values, outlooks and actions, and more interested in gracious living and comfortable life styles. They will tend to be more conformist than rebellious, resulting in a fairly stable future society, and a furtherance of traditional values.

Geographic Shifts

Since 1790, the geographic center of our population, which was located in Maryland, has moved steadily toward the West and South. It is now in the Eastern sector of Missouri, as shown in Figure 9.

The geographic trends and population shifts of the 1960s, 1970s and 1980s tend to mirror each other. Expectations are that in the future the South and West will continue to grow the most, both absolutely and relatively, although not as rapidly as in the late 70s and early 80s. The Northeastern states will realize either stability or some decline with some selected areas experiencing healthy growth. The North Central states will either grow slowly or remain stable.

As in the last three decades, the same three states, California, Florida and Texas, are expected to account for over 50% of the population growth from 1980 to 2000. The population additions anticipated are: Florida 7.7 million, California 7 million and Texas 6 million. *This represents an astonishing 21 million people of a total growth of 41 million.*

By 2000 the West will account for almost one fourth of our population, about 23%. The South will total over one third, 37%. This reflects the continuing growth of the Sunbelt, which shortly after 2000 could contain seven of the ten largest cities. Texas alone will have 3 of the 10 largest cities. Many newer cities have more efficient infrastructures and greater socio-economic appeal than do former leading cities of the North and East.

Figures 10 and 11 indicate the fastest and slowest growing states on a percentage basis between 1980 and 1990, and 1990 and 2000. Other than Florida, the fastest growing states all have relatively low population totals. Thus, relatively small total increases signal large proportionate gains. The states that are the biggest losers, or the slowest gainers, are

FIGURE 9
CENTER OF POPULATION:
1790 TO 1980

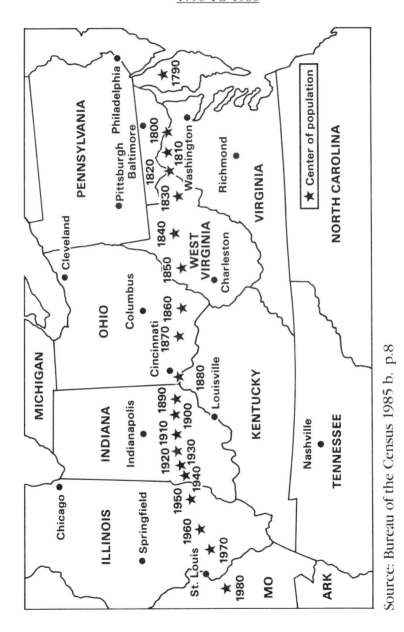

Source: U. S. Bureau of the Census 1986. *Statistical Abstract of the United States: 1986*, 106th edition, p. 8.

shown in Figure 11. Iowa, West Virginia and Pennsylvania are projected
to be substantial losers in both decades.

Rural America is still undergoing major transition as the U.S. continues its transformation into a more highly concentrated, urban society. At
the same time, "rurbania," the combination of urban amenities and con-
veniences with the attractiveness of uncrowded rural environments and
values, will have even greater appeal. Much of the future geographic
growth, and the fastest rate of growth, will occur in smaller towns of
rural areas that are contiguous to large urban areas. The preponderance
of urban growth will occur outside the cores of cities, resulting in a pronounced doughnut pattern, with a hole in the center and expansion
around the periphery.

Agriculture will continue as one of our most productive sectors, with
relatively fewer farmers being able to feed not only the 245 million peo-

---

FIGURE 10
FASTEST GROWING STATES

1980-1990		1990-2000	
Alaska	43%	Arizona	23%
Arizona	38%	Nevada	21%
Nevada	35%	New Mexico	21%
Florida	32%	Florida	20%
New Mexico	25%	Georgia	19%

Source: Adapted from *Wall Street Journal*, Thursday, November 17, 1988, B1.

FIGURE 11
SLOWEST GROWING STATES

1980-1990		1990-2000	
Iowa	5.4%	Iowa	7.6%
W. Virginia	4.8%	W. Virginia	7.3%
Pennsylvania	0.3%	N. Dakota	4.7%
Ohio	0.1%	Pennsylvania	2.7%
Michigan	+ 0.3%	Wyoming	2.6%

Source: Adapted from *Wall Street Journal*, Thursday, November 17, 1988, B1.

ple in the U.S., but untold millions abroad. *The farm population, which was one-fourth of the total population in 1930, declined to 2.2% by 1985.* Currently, in the U.S., there are a little over 5 million people, as compared with 16 million people in 1960, living on fewer farms than ever before and supporting our growing population. Much of our farmland is rapidly being transformed into suburban residential areas, towns, cities and shopping centers, which, of course, will have direct market impact. Those living on or near farms will have life styles that from many marketing perspectives, will be similar to those of urban America. They will have access to all manner of shopping, satellite dishes will grace their lawns, their gardens and fields will include exotic and designer fruits and vegetables for sale to niche markets in nearby cities, and increasing numbers of their neighbors will be part-timers who have bought vacation homes in farm country away from city life.

Where Will We Live?

Figure 12 traces the annual rate of population growth by region giving the rate for each decade and the overall rate for the U.S. The heavily shaded areas indicate where the U.S. population is concentrated. Our future population will continue to be concentrated in a rather small proportion of our land mass, certainly in less than 5%. One can almost follow the water to develop a clear picture of population thrust. The pattern will continue along a strip down the Eastern seaboard, from Maine through the east coast of Florida then up the west side of Florida and through the Gulf states to Texas. In the North, the population will cluster along the eastern extremities of the Great Lakes through Cleveland, Detroit and Chicago, up the west side of Lake Michigan, and then form a crescent from Chicago through the St. Louis area. On the West coast the clustering will start well above San Francisco and continue down to the Mexican border.

Vast unpopulated areas of the U.S. will continue to exist, as visitors from crowded countries around the world, such as Japan, readily note. The United States is, indeed, a large land mass compared with that of many European and Asian countries. The fact that it is spread over thousands of square miles results in more demanding, costly, and time-consuming marketing activities, such as distribution and communications. It permits "nations" to exist within the United States. Geographic diversity, an American characteristic, will endure.

FIGURE 12
GROWTH IN POPULATION, BY REGION
1980-2000

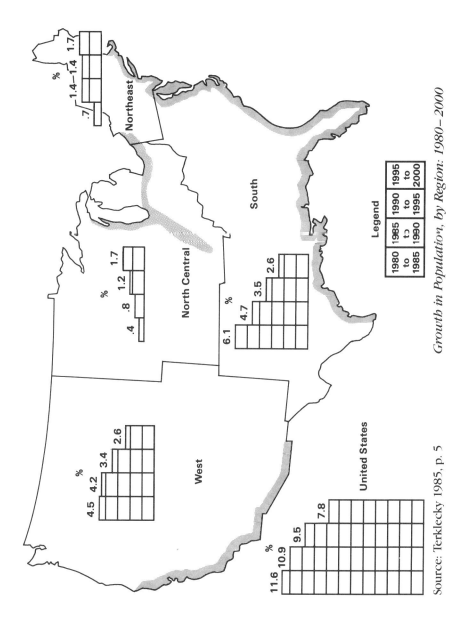

Based on: Terkleckyj, Nestor E. 1985. *Regional Growth in the United States.*
NPA Data Services, Inc. Report No. 85-R-1.

Future Diversity

As a nation within nations, the U.S. comprises a mosaic of people from around the world. Marketers in 2000 will have to focus on the more pronounced diversity. Black, Hispanic, Asian, European and other populations will be of sufficient total numbers that special segments will receive increasing attention. In 1980 minorities made up the majority of the population in 25 U.S. cities of 100,000 or more. Population projections for Blacks and Hispanics are given in Figure 13. Blacks, our largest minority, will grow faster both proportionally and absolutely than the population at large, reaching 35,795,000 in 2000 or 13.4% of the population.

Hard data on the actual number of Hispanics, as well as future projections, are difficult to get. Furthermore, the Hispanic population is composed of a wide variety of different nationalities such as Cuban, Mexican, Puerto Rican, and people from Central and South America. Each has its own culture, language pattern, belief systems and community affiliations. Estimates are that in 1985 there were 17.3 million Hispanics, and about 18.8 million in 1987. When the totals are coupled with estimates of undocumented aliens, those of Hispanic origin could well begin to rival Blacks as the largest minority in the next 20 years. They could account for one-fourth of the nation's growth between 1990 and 2010.

FIGURE 13
PROJECTIONS OF THE POPULATION,
BY RACE AND SPANISH ORIGIN:
1982 TO 2080

(in millions)

Population group	1982	1990	2000	2010	2020	2030	2040	2050	2080
TOTAL	232.1	249.7	268.0	283.2	296.6	304.8	308.6	309.5	310.8
Spanish origin	15.8	19.9	25.2	30.8	36.5	41.9	46.7	50.8	59.6
White non-Hispanic	183.5	192.0	198.9	202.6	204.5	202.4	197.2	190.8	176.0
Black	27.7	31.4	35.8	40.	44.2	47.6	50.3	52.3	55.7
Other races	5.9	7.5	9.5	11.7	13.7	15.6	17.3	18.9	23.4

Source: U. S. Bureau of the Census, *Projections of the Hispanic Population: 1983 to 2080*, Population Estimates and Projections, Series P-25, No. 995, p. 10.

The Hispanic population is projected to double within 30 years and triple in 60. Most of the growth will occur in the 35-and-over group, with the 65-and-over category quadrupling by 2015. By about 2015, Hispanics will be our major minority, and by 2020 they will be 12% of the population, growing proportionately to 16% by 2050. Data projecting the growth of the Hispanic population from 1982-2080 is shown in Figure 14.

Working Women

The growing proportion of working women, particularly wives and mothers, marks the most dramatic of all the socio-economic changes. It will continue to transform families, households, living arrangements, employment practices, shopping patterns, markets, products, services and other fundamentals of our future lifestyles. It will affect both the standard of living and the quality of life.

Gainfully employed women, who grew from less than 30% of the labor force in 1950 to over 43% in 1988, are heading toward 50% by the

---

FIGURE 14

HISPANIC POPULATION: 1982 TO 2080

(in millions)

Year	Lowes Series	Middle Series	Highest Series
1982	15.8	15.8	15.8
1985	17.1	17.3	18.0
1990	19.1	19.9	22.1
1995	21.1	22.6	26.5
2000	23.1	25.2	31.2
2010	26.8	30.8	41.9
2020	30.1	36.5	54.3
2030	32.7	41.9	67.7
2040	34.5	46.7	81.9
2050	35.4	50.8	96.1
2060	35.6	54.2	110.6
2070	35.3	57.2	125.6
2080	34.6	59.6	140.7

Source: U. S. Bureau of the Census. *Projections of the Hispanic Population: 1983 to 2080*, Population Estimates and Projections, Series P-25, No. 995, p.2.

year 2000. The majority of the new jobs created in the 1970s and 80s, as well as those projected for the 1990s and the turn of the century, will be taken by women. The labor force participation rate for women in 1970, which was 43.3% vs. 79.7% for men, grew to 54.5% by 1985. In contrast, labor force participation for men actually declined to 76.3%. That trend is projected to continue with the differences between the sexes narrowing further.

Furthermore, these data do not tell the whole story. Hoist Stipp, Director of Research of NBC, says research demonstrates among women aged 18-49, about 90% have participated in the labor force, even if only temporarily or part time. Psychologically, and when responding to research, about 9 in 10 of all women in these important market target ages consider themselves to be "working women," even if not currently employed full time. In over half of all married-couple families, both husband and wife are in the labor force full time. The majority of mothers with children under 6 (56.9%), and with children under one (52.6%), are in the labor force. These trends are expected to continue and such shifts will further amplify the already high demand for child care services such as public and private nursery schools, pre-school care, both all-day and part-day family daycare centers and after school care.

Marketing 2000 will see working women participating in a broader base of occupations. Their compensation will more nearly approximate those of their male counterparts, and a larger proportion of them will shift from part to full time. Many changes will be made in employment policies and practices to accommodate their special needs. Future education levels of women, particularly minority women, will continue to rise. The high correlation between educational attainment and the proportion of working women suggests further increases in the future number and proportion of working women, particularly professional women. Whether this will result in the establishment of a "Mommy Track" in business is open to question.

Working women tend to be more independent, and are more likely to form and manage their own households. They will continue to have great impact on future life styles. They will face a poverty of time to pursue activities and will seek products and services that expand time, reduce chores, diminish hassles, and provide rewards for getting through another day, or another year. Their economic contributions will alter their own future life style expectations, ranging from the kind of retirement living two persons might buy to remaining active and employed beyond widowhood.

The Mature Market

Marketing 2000 will see the aging and greying segments of our markets becoming increasingly important, both absolutely and proportionately. The older population has been described by a variety of terms including senior, mature, silver, retired, elderly and so on. Mature consumers, those 55-and-over, are often divided into 4 age groups: the olders, 55-64; the elders, 65-74; the aged, 75-84; and the very old, 85-and-over. In the year 2000, they will total almost 59 million, or about 22% of the population. The expected totals for each age sector is shown in Figure 15.

The mature market is among the least intensively researched and understood of all our age segments. Their numbers will continue to grow through 2050. The 65-and-over segment alone will be over 35 million by the year 2000, and will reach 51 million by 2020. *Then about 19 million will be in the 75-and-over segment.*

Regardless of the terminology used to describe them and the classifications adopted, two points will become even more evident about mature consumers in the future. *First, the mature market, from the point of view of market and purchase behavior, will not be homogeneous, but will be comprised of several vastly different segments.* There will likely be more intra-segment differentiation among older consumers than inter-segment differentiation. For example, the 75-and-over group will comprise very diverse sets of consumers, some of whom are vigorous, active and young, while others will be infirmed and incapacitated.

Second, mature market segments will be much different in their consumption orientations and financial resources. The attitudes, outlooks and lifestyles of future mature consumers will be far younger and more youthful than ever. Previously, those surpassing retirement age were

---

FIGURE 15
MATURE CONSUMERS IN THE YEAR 2000

Age	Total
55-64	23,767,000
65-74	17,677,000
75-84	12,318,000
85 +	4,926,000

Source: U. S. Bureau of the Census 1982. "Projections of the Population of the United States: 1982 to 2080." *Current Population Reports.* Series P-25, No. 922 (November).

often depicted as being inactive, incapacitated and living in poverty. In the future, however, the older age groups will be among the most prominent, active and productive participants in many activities, such as cultural events, the arts, voting, the procurement of fine foods and wines, patronage of gourmet restaurants and deluxe hotels, and luxury travel.

Tomorrow's 55 year olds will be more like the 35 or 40 year olds of previous generations than their 55 year old counterparts of yesteryear. Physically and psychologically, they will feel and act significantly younger than their chronological age suggests. They will enjoy longer and more potentially rewarding lives. They will invite marketers to appeal to the younger person existing inside their older exteriors. They will alter perceptions, images and stereotypes of older consumers.

Projections Regarding the Mature Consumer

Over the last 80 years the life expectancy at birth of Americans has jumped strikingly, for a variety of reasons, from an average of only 49 years in 1900, to 70 years in 1954 and an amazing 74 years in 1981. This is a 50% increase in 80 years. Future average life expectancy is expected to continue increasing, but not as rapidly, reaching 76.7 years in 2000 and almost 80 years by 2030.

Currently, the life expectancy at birth of women exceeds that of men by about 8 years. It is roughly 70 years for men compared to 78 years for women. But the life expectancy for males who reached age 65 in 1978 was a striking 14 years. For females it was 18.4 years. When this fact is coupled with the marriage practice of men marrying women about two years their junior, it reflects a large increase in the elderly single women sectors of our markets. This too will impact greatly on the demand for a wide variety of products and services such as cosmetics, cosmetic surgery, clothing and beauty aids, and savings and annuity plans.

Figures 16 and 17 present data on the younger olders, middles, seniors and very old segments from the present to the year 2050. The number of younger olders, those 55 to 64, is expected to grow only slowly to the year 2000, and then will increase by over 80% by 2020. The 65 and over segments will grow more rapidly, totaling over 21% of the population in 2020 and doubling in number by 2030. The 75-84 group will double between 1990 and 2030 becoming about 7% of the population. The fastest growth will occur among the very old, those 85 and over, the true elderly of our society. They will more than double in number between 1980-2000, and will increase eight-fold by 2050, when they will comprise an amazing 16 million people.

FIGURE 16

Growth of the Older Population, Actual and Projected: 1900-2050

(thousands and %)

Year	Total Population, All Ages	55-64 Number	%	65-74 Number	%	75-84 Number	%	85+ Number	%	65+ Number	%
1900	76,303	4,009	5.3	2,189	2.9	772	1.0	123	0.2	3,084	4.0
1910	91,972	5,054	5.5	2,793	3.0	989	1.1	167	0.2	3,950	4.3
1920	105,711	6,532	6.2	3,464	3.3	1,259	1.2	210	0.2	4,933	4.7
1930	122,775	8,397	6.8	4,721	3.8	1,641	1.3	272	0.2	6,634	5.4
1940	131,669	10,572	8.0	6,375	4.8	2,278	1.7	365	0.3	9,019	6.8
1950	150,697	13,295	8.8	8,415	5.6	3,278	2.2	577	0.4	12,270	8.1
1960	179,323	15,572	8.7	10,997	6.1	4,633	2.6	929	0.5	16,560	9.2
1970	203,302	18,608	9.2	12,447	6.1	6,124	3.0	1,409	0.7	19,980	9.8
1980	226,505	21,700	9.6	15,578	6.9	7,727	3.4	2,240	1.0	25,544	11.3
1990	249,731	21,090	8.4	18,054	7.2	10,284	4.1	3,461	1.4	31,799	12.7
2000	267,990	23,779	8.9	17,693	6.6	12,207	4.6	5,136	1.9	35,036	13.1
2010	283,141	34,828	12.3	20,279	7.2	12,172	4.3	6,818	2.4	39,269	13.9
2020	296,339	40,243	13.6	29,769	10.0	14,280	4.8	7,337	2.5	51,386	17.3
2030	304,330	33,965	11.2	34,416	11.3	21,128	6.9	8,801	2.9	64,345	21.1
2040	307,952	34,664	11.3	29,168	9.5	24,529	8.0	12,946	4.2	66,643	21.6
2050	308,856	37,276	12.1	30,022	9.7	20,976	6.8	16,063	5.2	67,061	21.7

Source: U. S. Bureau of the Census 1982. "Projections of the Population of the United States: 1982 to 2080." *Current Population Reports.* Series P-25, No. 922 (November).

The mature market overall will continue to grow for the next 50 years at a rate exceeding that of the population as a whole. The most rapid increases will occur between 2010 and 2030. By 2010 almost 75 million people, about one fourth of the total population, will be at least 55 years old. Then 34.3 million, or one seventh of all Americans, will be 65 and over. The shift in marketing focus away from a continuing emphasis on the young and youth will represent a real and pervasive transformation.

As was noted previously, the median age of our population will increase significantly and steadily from 30.0 years in 1980 to 40.8 years in 2030. Our aging population will result in important social and economic changes.

The ratio of the working age population, those 18-64, to the retirement age population will soon begin an unprecedented and continuing decline. In 1982 there were 5.3 people of working age for every person 65 or older, but the ratio is projected to decline to 4.7 in 2000, 2.7 in 2030, and a very low 2.4 in 2080. This suggests a gloomy picture for current social

FIGURE 17

POPULATION 55 YEARS AND OVER: 1900-2050

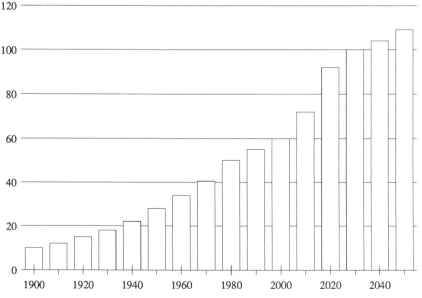

Source: U. S. Bureau of the Census 1982. "Projections of the Population of the United States: 1982 to 2080." *Current Population Reports.* Series P-25, No. 922 (November).

programs, with increasing pressure on public and private retirement plans, medical programs and tax bases supported by a proportionately declining working population. These developments have the potential for generating unprecedented inter-generation conflicts.

The other part of the aging picture is the relative and absolute decline of the younger adults, the 18-24 year olds. They provided the engine for growth during the late 1960s and during the 1970s. Now they are at an all time high of 30 million, but, by 1995, they will experience a sharp drop to about 23 million, at the very same time that the older population will grow. Beyond 2000, the younger adults, the 18-24 year olds, will realize slow growth to 24.5 million in 2000 and only 28 million in 2010.

Mature Consumer Activities

Going forward, the older markets will continue to bode well for a wide variety of products and services ranging from cosmetic surgery, vitamins, diets, health foods, sports and exercise equipment, to clothing and personal services. Seniors will think younger than their previous counterparts and will lead far more active lives. They will have more of an orientation toward working to live rather than adopting their parents' orientation toward living to work. Many will be financially constrained because of job hoping, career switching, single parenthood and divorce. But for those who remained in two-earner households for much of their adulthood, there will be less likelihood of their denying themselves immediate gratification and comfort in order to hope for greater satisfaction later on. They will be more interested in pursuing a pleasurable existence and in enjoying their remaining years.

Increasing numbers of our future work force will take earlier retirement, thereby exercising more control over their own lives and time usage. Data indicates that retirement age, particularly for men, has been decreasing steadily. Retirees do not automatically enter the ranks of the poor. Rather, on a per capita basis, they will have the greatest discretionary income of all age segments.

Furthermore, in Marketing 2000, we may see more seniors returning to work full or part time on a discretionary basis to augment incomes, fill in time or remain socially and intellectually connected. This will be encouraged by the private sector because of labor shortages and the public sector because of the costs of social insurance programs for retirees.

Thus, retirement will not mean that people will become inactive, do nothing and abandon all work. Rather, retirement will come to mean moving on to other activities, doing something else, such as working at hobbies, accepting new part-time jobs, doing things that people always wanted to do. It will embody actualizing wishes and dreams, moving into totally new careers and pursuing activities that bring feelings of accomplishment and well-being. Mature consumers will become even more oriented to personal maintenance and support products and services. Included will be lighter and healthier foods; skin care products and services; pharmaceutical products; and a broad variety of products that ease pain and promote the ready performance of everyday physical activities.

A greater proportion of the services formerly handled by mature consumers themselves, within their homes, will be performed by others. Included are lawn care, car care, home maintenance, snow removal, repairs of all kinds, cooking and meal preparation and the broad spectrum of household chores. Appliances and machines will be developed to automate undesirable household tasks. The trend will be to reduce household responsibilities and, to the extent possible, create a "hassle-free" life space.

Health eventually becomes a problem for all mature consumers and tomorrow's are no exception. Mobility becomes more limited. Although many mature consumers will have substantial assets, and will be relatively well off financially, physical and psychological security, will remain a pervasive concern. The extensive aging of future populations will foster more extensive health care services and special care facilities. The savings and insurance mechanisms to pay for these will begin to find ready and lucrative markets today, as people become more aware of their own future scenario.

The growth of the 85-and-over age group, the frail elderly of our society, suggests that many will be in the unique position of knowing 4 or even 5 generations of their offspring. Some will have had working lives that spanned 50-60 years or more. They will likely be much different in their purchase decisions and behavior from other sectors of the mature market segments. This is partly because most will not be as independent as other mature consumers, often requiring a variety of support services, special health care or regular medical and hospital care. Also, many will lack mobility and the capability of getting around.

The frail elderly portend a vast and growing future market for many new products and services, and for the adaptation of existing market offerings, such as vans that take them to shopping centers or shopping aids in the home. They will grow almost five-fold as a market from about 2.5 million in 1980 to over 13 million in 2040. Their wants and needs are not at all well understood.

Concluding Comments

The future demographic makeup of the U.S. will change dramatically over the next few decades. Markets of the year 2000 and beyond will differ greatly from those of the immediate past. This will reshape marketing opportunities and force marketing managers to rethink some of their basic precepts.

Many dimensions of the future population are quite well established and can be predicted with considerable certainty. Included are: the aging and greying of the population, slower population growth, increasing proportions of first-born babies, population movements to the West and South, the growth of rurbania, increasing pressures of both legal and illegal immigration, the coloring of the U.S. market, smaller-sized families and changing household structures.

The growing importance of the 35-54 year old age group and the 65-and-over population will greatly influence marketing activities. The previous emphasis on the young and young marrieds will shift as the U.S. rapidly becomes a middle aged society. Increasingly, attention will be directed to the needs and desires of more mature consumers.

Demographic factors have not received the attention they should from marketers concerned with delineating future opportunities, developing strategic marketing plans and arriving at effective marketing mix decisions. Viewing the future through a demographic lens can help readers develop a more realistic perspective of business futures.

Lesser Developed Countries

This chapter has been directed to demographic trends in the U.S. pointing up potential marketing opportunities among relatively affluent, future U.S. consumers, thereby highlighting upscale offerings. We have not discussed demographic developments abroad. It would be shortsighted for marketers to overlook them and the opportunities that exist in markets of lesser developed and newly industrializing countries. They will also afford profitable opportunities. For example, the findings of a United Nations study suggests that in the year 2000, "79% of the world's population will live in countries that U.S. companies do not yet consider important consumer markets" (Walsh 1983). While most of these markets may not support large volumes of luxury products, they nevertheless, represent a sizable and growing demand for basic products and services.

Looking ahead to emerging foreign markets, it is also worthwhile noting that the population of both Chinas will be added to that of Asia, a continent where the population is already about 2.5 billion. By 2025, Africa will gain over one billion people; and Latin America will grow by about 500 million (Walsh 1983). When trends such as these are coupled with the current push toward market economies among the communist/socialist countries, and this in turn is reflected in the growth of joint ventures and strategic alliances, the potential for rapidly changing, exciting market opportunities become readily apparent.

In the future, targeting of lesser developed and developing country markets, marketing executives will be cautioned to:

- recognize the existence of various degrees of economic, demographic and market sophistication among countries.

- think in terms reflecting more than the current tendency to force on the dichotomy of "developed/ lesser developed" countries.

- think of a spectrum of countries and market opportunities and delineate the market potential of those countries that are likely to move ahead of or behind the pack.

- distinguish among foreign countries with youthful populations, such as Mexico, Brazil and Indonesia and those with maturing and aging populations.

- determine the purchasing potential of various segments within emerging countries to establish the appropriate mix of upscale and basic products/services.

REFERENCES

Drucker, Peter F. (1980) *Managing in Turbulent Times*, New York: Harper and Row, 76.

Lazer, William (1987), *Handbook of Demographics for Marketing and Advertising*. Boston, MA: Lexington Books.

Terkleckyj, Nestor E. (1985) *Regional Growth in the United States*.NPA Data Services, Inc. Report No. 85-R-1.

U.S. Bureau of the Census (1982), "Projections of the Population of the United States: 1982 to 2080." *Current Population Reports*. Series P-25, No. 922 (November).

U.S. Bureau of the Census (1983a), *1980 Census of Population: General Population Characteristics*, Vol. 1.

U.S. Bureau of the Census (1984a), *Fertility of American Women: June 1983*, Series P-20, No. 386.

U.S. Bureau of the Census (1984b), *Projections of the Population of the United States by Age, Sex and Race: 1983 to 2080*, Series P-25, No. 952.

U.S. Bureau of the Census (1984c), *Fertility of Women: June 1983, Population Characteristics*, Series P-20, No. 386.

U.S. Bureau of the Census (1984d), *Fertility of American Women: June 1982*, Current Population Reports, Series P-20, No. 387.

U.S. Bureau of the Census (1985a), *Estimates of the Population of the United States by Age, Sex and Race: 1980 to 1990*, Series P-25, No. 965.

U.S. Bureau of the Census (1985b), *Estimates of the Population of the United States by Age, Sex and Race, 1980 to 1983*, Series P-25, No. 949.

U.S. Bureau of the Census (1986), *Statistical Abstract of the United States: 1986*. 106th Edition, pg. 8.

U.S. Bureau of the Census, *Projections of the Hispanic Population: 1983 to 2080*, Population Estimates and Projections, Series P-25, No. 995, p. 10, Table P.

U.S. Bureau of the Census, *Projections of the Hispanic Population: 1983 to 2080*, Population Estimates and Projections, Series P-25, No. 995, p. 2, Table B.

Wall Street Journal (1988), Thursday, November 17, B1.

Walsh, Doris (1983), "World Futures," *American Demographics*, 5 No. 8 (August), 38-39.

CHAPTER 5

AND SO THEY SAY: INSIGHTS FROM THE LITERATURE

"It is our ignorance of the future and our persuasion that ignorance is absolutely incurable that alone gives the past its enormous predominance in our thoughts." H.G. Wells

Introduction

In the past 30 years a considerable body of literature has been developed dealing with the future. A substantial part of it contains meaningful insights and implications for marketing management perspectives and insights into future marketing developments.

The bulk of the literature characterizes future environments as being unstable and complex, creating difficult challenges for business leaders. Environmental turbulence is seen as making planning more difficult and decision making more risky[1]. Executives are advised to:

- Gather wider perspectives of possible developments over long-range periods;[2]

- Develop and use new approaches and methods for portraying, assessing, and planning for likely future environments;[3]

- Formulate more complete strategic plans;[4]

---

[1]Brown and Weiner 1984; Drucker 1980; Kotler 1988; Michman 1984; Naisbitt 1982; Ross and Silverblatt 1987; Silverblatt and Korgaonkar 1987; Toffler 1970 and 1985; Weiner 1976.

[2]Enzer 1984; Fowles 1978; Keane 1987; Michman 1984; Wack 1985; Weiner 1976.

[3]Ayres 1984; Carbone and Makridakis 1986; Garde and Patel 1985; Gilbreath 1987; Leemhuis 1985; Maddox, Anthony and Wheatly 1987; McCann 1985; Renfro 1987; Saunders 1986; Stubbart 1985; Weiner 1976.

[4]Silverblatt and Korgaonkar 1987.

- Make strategic adjustments;[5]
- Employ, in certain instances, pro-active marketing, and public relations efforts.[6]

Executives and leaders are also charged with finding and assessing new opportunities, developing strategic options for their organizations, and sustaining their competitive advantages.[7] They are challenged to deal with alternative possibilities and choices in ways that guide rather than immobilize future strategic action, and to find future opportunities while avoiding disasters in tomorrow's shifting environments.[8] It is not surprising, therefore, to find that the literature depicts the study of future environments as a management and marketing imperative for industry, government, social, religious, and academic leaders, alike.[9]

Marketers, however, have just recently begun[10] to orient futures research to such marketing activities as strategic market planning, assessing organizational structures and cultures, restructuring distribution strategies, upgrading R&D, and investing in management and personnel development.[11]

This chapter summarizes and highlights the main lines of thought expressed in the futures literature relevant to marketing. It has four objectives:

- To trace the development of strategic marketing planning, the use of futures research, and approaches to longer range planning in marketing.

- To identify the contributions and limitations of futures research methods.

- To portray visions of strategic marketing landscapes of the future.

- To develop a compendium of marketing directives for success in the future, as presented in the literature.

---

[5]Aaker 1988; Enzer 1984; Gilbreath 1987; Michman 1984.

[6]Zeithaml and Zeithaml 1984.

[7]Cravens 1986; Kotler 1988; Porter 1979.

[8]Brown and Weiner 1984; Enzer 1984; Gilbreath 1987; Keane 1987.

[9]Kahn and Wiener 1967; Lazer and Culley 1983; McHale 1978; Meadows, Meadows, Randers and Behrens 1972; Richardson 1984; Taylor 1984; Toffler 1970; Weiner 1976.

[10]Fahey, King and Narayanan 1981; Keane 1987; Michman 1984.

[11]Achrol and Stern 1988; Beasley and Johnson 1984; Cravens 1986; Deshpande and Webster 1989; Kotler 1988; Zemke 1987.

Futures Research
and Strategic Marketing Planning

Futures Research Evolution

Futures research is largely the creation of U.S. corporate executives.[12] It began in earnest during the immediate post-World War II period in the defense industry (e.g., Rand Corporation) during a time when, according to Masini (1978):

> Mankind sought to tackle the ever quicker and more interrelated transformations taking place, and to identify the future consequences of present actions and thereby avoid being overcome or taken unawares by events.

Futures research often focuses on environmental changes, highlights attention to their importance and enables executives to gain insights about the relevance of shifting external factors.[13] Thus, it can help executives make the needed transition from an internal business operations focus to that of a strategic marketing planning and decision making orientation.

Corporate planning assumed a central role in the long-term planning orientation of corporations in the 1960s.[14] It focused mainly on financial, budgetary, capital, and physical capacity and facilities aspects of planning. It largely ignored shifts in relevant external environments and markets.[15] These omissions became glaring as environmental turbulence increased, resulting in less effective, more costly, and often futile crisis management.[16]

Executives, in the early 1970s, realized the need to link long-term planning efforts to significant changes in the firm's relevant and unstable marketing environments.[17] Too many corporate plans were rendered obsolete by unanticipated changes that might have been foreseen had current and future environments been researched.[18] Corporate long-term planning orientations, in response, evolved from narrow-focused corporate planning to strategic planning, including marketing planning.

---

[12]Masini 1978.

[13]Fowles 1978.

[14]Aaker 1988; Taylor 1984.

[15]Aaker 1988; Taylor 1984; Webster 1988.

[16]Weiner 1976.

[17]Aaker 1988; Kotler 1988; Weiner 1976.

[18]Taylor 1984; Wack 1985; Weiner 1976.

At the outset, executives began to embrace strategic marketing planning as a key management activity allowing companies to react and adjust to shifts in external environments, which were initially described as uncontrollable.[19] (Executives who came later in the 1980s were prodded to try to control and create environments that were more favorable to both their firms and society.)[20] Strategic marketing planning was a direct result of turbulent marketing environments.[21] Unstable environments were cast from such factors as: increasing foreign competition, material shortages, demographic shifts, rapidly advancing technology, inflation, stagflation, intensified government regulation, the growing demand for social responsibility, deteriorating physical environments, and the energy crises.[22]

The "Energy Crisis of 1974" has been recognized widely as the watershed. It marks the end of a period of relative economic stability and U.S. dominance of world business, and the beginning of turbulent marketing times.[23]

In the course of the development of strategic planning, executives began to question the predictive accuracy of traditional forecasting practices, which were largely based on extrapolation or on a simple jury of executive opinion.[24] They soon recognized that strategic adjustments are often predicated on discontinuities or unexpected changes.[25]

Discontinuity is either impossible, or difficult, to forecast[26] because of difficulties in factoring it into models,[27] and because of the limitations of mathematical models in approaching reality.[28] Discontinuities are far more puzzling to forecast than are changes resulting from variable but more continuous trends, such as population, income, and various legal developments.[29]

The Appeal of Futures Research as a Planning Tool

Executives in the 1970s began to turn to futures research to capture a

---

[19]McCarthy 1978.

[20]Stubbart 1985; Taylor 1984; Zeithaml and Zeithaml 1984.

[21]Drucker 1980; Kotler 1988; Taylor 1984.

[22]Barney 1980; Kotler 1988; Lazer and Culley 1983; Meadows et al., 1972; Shama 1978; Young 1985.

[23]*Challenge* 1977; Kotler 1988; Taylor 1984; Young 1985.

[24]Armstrong 1985; Taylor 1984; Weiner 1976.

[25]Amara 1978; Enzer 1984; Taylor 1984.

[26]Amara 1978; Fowles 1978; Kahn and Wiener 1967; Taylor 1984; Wildawsky 1973.

[27]Wack 1985.

[28]Ayres 1984.

[29]Beasley and Johnson 1984.

wider array of developments that might affect their companies and society.[30] One result was a spate of experiments utilizing futures research methods to forecast emerging future environments.[31] The development and use of "future scanning" was a breakthrough for managers searching for new ways to deal with the pace and magnitude of the environmental changes. It refers to an organized and systematic process of literature scanning carried out by experts to identify and interpret the plausible strategic impact of emerging ideas, knowledge, and events on a business.[32]

The adoption of such futures research methods and scanning techniques was reinforced by growing concern about the quality of future environments,[33] the future quality of life,[34] and social responsibility in marketing.[35] Greater concern developed about the impact of business and marketing decisions on future well-being, particularly during the last two decades of this century.[36]

These concerns, which were heightened by the oil crisis, were reinforced through the years by such external crises as the recent Alaskan oil spill, the Chernobyl and Three Mile Island nuclear accidents, Tylenol tampering, the Bhopal disaster, acid rain, ozone depletion, and the international boycott of Nestlé.[37] These occurrences and the resulting reactions affect both marketing and strategic marketing planning. They generate new constraints and challenges, and make marketing planning more difficult.[38]

The result of such occurrences was that the study of the future gained popularity.[39] One authority assessed futures research and stated that it now, "...absorbs a considerable proportion of the energies invested in our major social institutions."[40]

In the 1970s and 1980s, professional marketing organizations gave future environments more attention. The American Marketing Associa-

---

[30]Fowles 1978; McHale 1978; Taylor 1984; Wack 1985.

[31]Fowles 1978; Garde and Patel 1985; Hankinson 1986; Martino 1972; Meadows et al., 1972; Michman 1984; Richardson 1984; Taylor 1984; Wack 1985.

[32]Weiner 1976.

[33]Barney 1980; Meadows et al., 1972; Mesarovic and Pestel 1974.

[34]Behrman 1986; Verwayen 1984.

[35]Galbraith 1968; Lazer 1969; Patterson 1966.

[36]Aaker 1988; Taylor 1984.

[37]*Columbia Journal of World Business* 1987-b.

[38]Brown and Davis 1983; Garrett 1987; *Petroleum Economist* 1986; Post 1985; Sethi, Etemad and Luther 1986; Shama 1978; Stambler 1986.

[39]Fowles 1978.

[40]McHale 1978, p.5.

tion devoted a special issue of the *Journal of Marketing* (1970) to the future and also published the output of a workshop on the future of marketing. Likely future environments were the focus of its special 50th Anniversary World Marketing Conference and Exhibition in Montreal in 1987. The *Marketing News* regularly projects future trends and likely developments in a variety of important areas.

Similarly, advertising associations expressed growing interest in the future. The American Association of Advertising Agencies, American Advertising Federation, and Association of National Advertisers combined efforts and presented a portrayal of advertising in the year 2000 to the Federal Trade Commission. The National Association of Broadcasters, the Newspaper Advertising Bureau, the International Advertising Association,[41] Marketing Science Institute, and the Conference Board all participate in future studies.[42]

The widespread use of professional trend spotting firms, such as Weiner-Edrich-Brown, Inc., the Naisbitt Group, and Yankelovich, Skelly and White, to analyze developments, within and outside an industry, that might affect business futures is evidence of the growth of interest in the future. Their reports and related services, have become integral components of early warning systems.[43]

Several books portraying possible future environments, and/or strategies for dealing with them, became classics in the field. Examples are: *Uncertain Futures* (Ayres 1979), *Silent Spring* (Carson 1962), *Managing in Turbulent Times* (Drucker 1980), *Handbook of Futures Research* (Fowles 1978), *The Year 2000: A Framework for Speculation on the Next Thirty-Three Years* (Kahn and Wiener 1967), *Limits to Growth: Report of the Club of Rome's Project on the Predicament of Mankind* (Meadows et al., 1972), *Mankind at the Turning Point* (Mesarovic and Pestel 1974), *Megatrends: Ten Directions Transforming Our Lives* (Naisbitt 1982), *Future Shock* (Toffler 1970), and *The Third Wave* (Toffler 1981). These works have raised mankind's consciousness about the future.

Integrating Strategic Planning and Futures Research

The growing needs to improve strategic planning and to integrate futures research into strategic planning, are major and interrelated themes

---

[41]Association of National Advertisers 1984; Boddewyn 1982; Bogart 1973 and 1985; *Broadcasting* 1985 and 1986-a; *Marketing and the Future* 1981.

[42]Gordon 1974; Sutton 1986; Webster 1981.

[43]Magnet 1985; Weiner 1976.

in the contemporary marketing literature. Strategic planners are challenged to improve their effectiveness. Recommendations involve directives, such as:[44]

- Conduct more thorough investigations of relevant environments.

- Employ several forecasting methods to generate wider perspectives and to point up additional discontinuities.

- Factor into strategic planning basic marketing concerns, such as channel analysis, positioning, market analysis, and the like.

- Extend planning horizons.

Some of the strategic planning literature prods executives to use futures research to improve strategic marketing. Marketing professionals are being told that futures research employs extended time horizons, recognizes the importance of uncovering discontinuities, and generates wider perspectives on relevant topics.[45]

The moment appears right to forge a more constructive partnership between strategic marketing planning and futures research, given an apparent blending between their once polarized planning horizons.[46] Futures researchers appear to be decreasing their planning horizons,[47] while strategic marketing planners are urged to extend their horizons beyond the short-term.[48] Advances in such areas as electronic computing, expert systems, artificial intelligence, mathematical modeling, and the emergence of a number of new quantitative methods may well make futures research more feasible and meaningful.[49]

Integrating strategic planning with futures research is seen as an important corporate development as companies are challenged to become change sensors, change agents, and change controllers.[50] To meet that challenge, planning practices, planning systems, and personnel decisions will be affected.[51]

---

[44]Richardson 1984; Keane 1987; Michman 1984; Stubbart 1985; Wack 1985; Webster 1986 and 1988.

[45]Keane 1987; Michman 1984; Morris 1987; Stubbart 1985; Wack 1985.

[46]Keane 1987; Michman 1984; Richardson 1984.

[47]Richardson 1984.

[48]Fahey, King and Narayanan 1981; Keane 1987; Michman 1984.

[49]Ayres 1984; Carbone and Makridakis 1986; Cole 1987; Kahle, Beaty and Homer 1986; Maddox, Anthony and Wheatly 1987; Meadows 1985; Mockler and Dologite 1988; Renfro 1987; Wilson and Ticer 1985.

[50]Keane 1987.

[51]Fahey, King and Narayanan 1981; Keane 1987; Lutz 1986; Stubbart 1985; Van-Dam 1977; Webster 1988.

Strategic planning practices may be modified somewhat to reflect such evolving tendencies as:

- Extending planning horizons;[52]

- Attending to marketing issues[53] and human resources aspects when formulating strategic plans;[54]

- Using multi-disciplinary approaches and considering opposing views and conflicting scenarios;[55]

- Selecting carefully the appropriate strategic planning mode;[56]

- Moving from a strategic planning orientation to more integrated strategic management.[57]

In the future, company information systems will likely be upgraded[58] to include knowledge-based systems.[59] Rank promotions will likely go to strategic planning system managers who value wide perspectives and combine a strong set of business, social, and technical skills.[60] A better understanding of the purpose, contributions, limitations, and methodological advances of futures research also appears needed.[61]

As mentioned earlier, time horizons have traditionally been used to categorize types of planning activities. Futurists, for example, indicate that five to ten-year periods are characteristic of long-range planning, whereas futures research usually focuses on twenty or thirty-year periods or beyond.[62] Futures research has also been characterized by periods of from five to five hundred years.[63] By contrast, the typical focus of strategic planning is periods of no more than three years, with up to five-year horizons being the exception.[64] Long-range planning generally employs time frames of from two to ten years.[65]

---

[52]Fahey, King and Narayanan 1981; Mockler and Dologite 1988.

[53]Cravens 1986; Webster 1988.

[54]Metz 1984.

[55]Van-Dam 1977.

[56]Taylor 1984.

[57]Ross and Silverblatt 1987.

[58]Lederer and Mendelow 1988; Lutz 1986.

[59]Mockler and Dologite 1988.

[60]Lutz 1986; Stubbart 1985.

[61]Michman 1984; Richardson 1984.

[62]McHale 1978.

[63]Richardson 1984; Tonn 1986.

[64]Keane 1987; Michman 1984.

[65]Aaker 1988.

The bulk of investigations of marketing in the future fall into five to ten-year time horizons.[66] Some futures studies use time horizons extending beyond ten years,[67] but most marketing studies dealing with future environments tend to focus on current or "immediate future periods" — a time frame of from one to four years.[68]

Methods or techniques are also used to distinguish among planning activities. Corporate planning relies on such methods as executive opinion and a variety of budgeting techniques.[69] Long-range planning relies more on historical forecasts,[70] although planners are urged to use some of the newer techniques to account for increasing turbulence.[71] Futures research uses techniques such as Delphi studies,[72] cross-impact analysis,[73] scenarios,[74] future histories,[75] global models, and simulation.[76] Strategic planning has traditionally relied on extrapolation which is generally based on rational, mathematical data manipulations.[77] The contemporary strategic planning literature, however, encourages borrowing techniques from futures research[78] because this may well detect unpatterned changes that are often missed by extrapolations.[79]

Current approaches to futures research involve descriptive, exploratory, and prescriptive dimensions. Six objectives of futures research that have direct relevance to marketing managers are:[80]

1. To identify alternative futures.

2. To characterize the degree of uncertainty.

3. To identify precursors or early warnings of particular futures.

---

[66]Distribution Research and Education Foundation 1983; Gallup 1988; Knee 1986; Laczniak and Lusch 1987; Laczniak, Lusch and Udel 1977.

[67]Association of National Advertisers 1984; Bogart 1973 and 1985; *Broadcasting* 1985; *Chain Store Age Executive* 1987; Fuerst 1985; Hiller 1983; Whittemore 1986.

[68]Bennett, Donegan and Sullivan 1987; Cardozo and Shipp 1987; *Harvard Business Review* 1987; Marcus and Kaufman 1988; *Progressive Grocer* 1987; *Research Management* 1986.

[69]Taylor 1984.

[70]Aaker 1988.

[71]Michman 1984.

[72]Bogart 1973 and 1985; North and Pyke 1969.

[73]Beasley and Johnson 1984.

[74]Hankinson 1986; Leemhuis 1985; Wack 1985.

[75]Renfro 1987.

[76]Cole 1987; Fowles 1978; Meadows 1985.

[77]Maddox, Anthony, and Wheatly 1987.

[78]Keane 1987; Maddox, Anthony and Wheatly 1987; Michman 1984; Taylor 1984; Wack 1985.

[79]Keane 1987; Michman 1984; Taylor 1984; Wack 1985.

[80]Amara 1978; McHale 1978.

4. To examine "if...then" sequences.

5. To better understand the underlying processes of change.

6. To sharpen knowledge and understanding of preferences.

The politics of strategic planning and futures research are critical. Strategic marketing planning can facilitate vertical and horizontal communication as well as coordination in organizations.[81] Futurists see a growing need to do a better job of communicating and coordinating planning activities.[82] National planning has been depicted as requiring a political power base in order to wield knowledge effectively in society, maintain the preeminence of future objectives in the present, and guide decisions. Implications for corporate planning are direct and important, for corporate planning provides a central steering mechanism that ties together each strategic business unit of the corporation and each specialized, functional area.[83] Planning is very concerned with supply and demand estimations, and these are the focus of much marketing effort.[84] The politics of supply and demand, and of getting estimates accepted by planners, are always tricky.

Executives and corporate planners, especially those in marketing, have often been slow to recognize the value of futures research because it usually avoids point or single estimates. Instead, futures research focuses on portraying a range of possible conditions.[85] Futurists argue that broadranging portrayals can help marketing executives prepare for the future, since point estimates are rarely accurate.[86] Debate exists among executives whether the main contributions of futures research in marketing lie in the accuracy of its projections or in the ability to generate plausible portrayals of alternative futures.

Methodological Issues in Futures Research

A review of the literature indicates that a large majority of futures studies are based on the opinions of a relatively small number of industry or activity experts, or even a single expert. Portrayals of marketing futures, in fact, are most frequently generated by judgmental methods.

---

[81]Aaker 1988; Yip 1985.

[82]Ayres 1984; Meadows 1985; Richardson 1984; Wildawsky 1973.

[83]McHale 1978.

[84]Taylor 1984.

[85]Amara 1978; Michman 1984.

[86]Fowles 1978.

Ideas and opinions of experts are valued for different reasons. Some have gained unique insights as a result of their experience and research. Others have the influence and authority to make decisions and shift resources that impact on the future.[87] However, some recognized weaknesses are associated with the use of experts and various judgmental methods. Included are: a narrow talent pool from which to draw; no sampling procedure by which to select experts; the inability to apply statistical sampling theory; poor predictive validity and inbreeding.[88] Inbreeding, which results in the repeated selection of a small number of experts, may limit the chance of getting a variety of values and perspectives.[89]

Under the guise of futures forecasting, advertising and corporate executives tend to make overly optimistic projections and often ignore major problems and hazards in the environment. They often appear reluctant to confront the consequences of larger or negative trends affecting their industry. This is because executives become too entrenched in their own industry to see larger developments, and as a result may become poor forecasters. "Illusionary expertise" is the term applied to this phenomenon.[90]

Regardless, advertising executives are still turned to for analyses of the future of advertising;[91] distribution managers for assessments of the future of distribution;[92] retail executives for reports on the future of retailing;[93] and vice-presidents of marketing for projections of the future marketing environment.[94] Exploratory phases of many formal futures studies in marketing also conform to this seeking of functional expertise — extracting opinions from those experts directly involved in the area on a day-to-day basis.[95] Wider ranges of expertise are only sought in a minority of cases.[96]

The major methodologies used in futures research are cross-impact analysis, Delphi technique, scenario writing, social indicators and social

---

[87]Bogart 1985; Laczniak and Lusch 1987.

[88]Fowles 1978; Kahn and Wiener 1967; Laczniak, Lusch and Udel 1977; Larreche and Moinpour 1983; Linstone 1978; Miles 1978.

[89]Linstone 1978.

[90]Bogart 1985; Carson 1978; Linstone 1978.

[91]Association of National Advertisers 1984; *Broadcasting* 1985.

[92]Berkwitt 1986; Fuerst 1985.

[93]Bennett, Donegan and Sullivan 1987; *Chain Store Age Executive* 1987;Laczniak and Lusch 1987.

[94]Laczniak and Lusch 1987.

[95]Bogart 1985.

[96]Barney 1980.

forecasting, technological forecasting, trend extrapolation, barometric forecasts, simulation modeling, and gaming and global models.[97]   Each method has a unique set of advantages, but readers should be aware of such specific disadvantages or limitations as the following:[98]

Cross-impact analysis is limited in application not only because it is difficult to operationalize out, but it generally deals with events, and most systems cannot be described fully by events.[99]

Delphi techniques require iterations that take precious time, tend to be low in temporal stability, and force a consensus that typically averages out meaningful, maverick ideas.[100]

Scenario writing is limited since scenario writers may not select the best items or present the true flow of action. Regardless of the number of scenarios written, no scenario is likely to become reality because of unforeseen events and responses. The precise combination of events selected for a scenario is highly unlikely to develop in the real environment. A central problem with scenario analysis is its interface with the CEO, who tends to trust personal judgment over scenario planning, citing its lack of "definiteness" and its presentation of alternative futures. These futures are often deemed uncontrollable and vague.[101]

Trend extrapolation is criticized in some cases for: overlooking discontinuity; lacking relevant time series data; projecting trends that, in reality, are highly unstable; and lacking causal explanations, since extrapolation is descriptive and does not identify external forces at work.[102]

Simulation modeling and gaming-based forecasts suffer limitations derived from their very nature and the data used.[103] The problems of the future are not as well organized and concrete. A wide variety of causal relationships must be considered under several different conceptualizations, each of which should be developed according to con-

---

[97]Fowles 1978; Michman 1984.

[98]Fowles 1978.

[99]Stover and Gordon 1978.

[100]Linstone 1978.

[101]Wack 1985; Wilson 1978.

[102]Hill 1978; Keane 1987.

[103]McLean 1978.

trasting viewpoints. Most simulation models have been built on the basis of a single conception and modelers are reluctant to re-evaluate or change it. Attempts at building complexity into models are often self-defeating.

A major complication in futures research is the large number of variables and their interactions. But as models become more detailed and explicit, futures research can begin to identify a greater number of key marketing and marketing-related variables, and their inter-relationships.[104] Recent advances have, in fact, resulted in new approaches and methods for investigating future marketing environments. We now have better methods for:

- Global forecasting,[105]

- Developing computer population images,[106]

- Measuring consumer values[107] and images,[108]

- Estimating the impact of socio-economic and demographic change on demand,[109] and other factors.[110]

Strategic Landscape of the Future

Futures research is being used in more ways related to marketing interests. Future marketing environments are receiving much greater attention in the literature.[111] The physical environment affecting marketing is usually depicted as being fragile and in need of greater attention.[112] The need for greater social expenditures will continue to exist, exacerbated

---

[104]Achrol and Stern 1988; Cravens 1986; McCann and Reibstein 1985; Metz 1984; Webster 1988.

[105]Cole 1987.

[106]Fox 1988.

[107]Kahle, Beaty and Homer 1986.

[108]Maddox, Anthony and Wheatly 1987.

[109]McCann and Reibstein 1985.

[110]Carbone and Makridakis 1986; Dowling and Walsh 1985; Mockler and Dologite 1988; Renfro 1987.

[111]More literature information regarding the future of marketing and its environments is published in an annotated bibliography, *Marketing 2000: Future Perspectives on Marketing, An Annotated Bibliography of Articles*, which summarizes and categorizes well over three-hundred articles, and which was developed as part of the AMA's Marketing 2000 project. American Marketing Association 250 S. Wacker Drive, Chicago, Illinois 60606. For a listing of other sources of information about the future, see Richardson, John M. (1984), "The State of Futures Research - Personal Reflections," *Futures*, 16 (August) 382-395, and *The Futurist Bookstore*, a publication of the World Futures Society 4916 St. Elmo Avenue, Bethesda, Maryland 20814.

[112]Aldred 1987; Barney 1980; Brown, Flavin and Wolf 1988; Rice 1988-a; Rowland 1987; Schwartz 1988; Smart, Smith, Vogel, Brown, Wolman, Brandt, Mitchell, DeGeorge and Fins 1987; Stambler 1986; Tokarski 1988.

by inadequate budgets, affecting supply, and demand equations. The literature suggests that divided opinions on social spending may capture most of the political and legal attention in the future.[113] Concern about America's competitiveness and economic well-being is expected to remain an important area of great future concern.[114] All of this will be extremely relevant to the work of the marketing forecaster.

A large body of literature exists relevant to the marketing/technology interface (See Chapter 2). The future of technology is depicted as one of rapid advancement, with the U.S. having less and less of an advantage over foreign competitors. Futurists also tell us that the technological competition will cause many related, sensitive societal issues.[115] Marketing environments are expected to be paradoxical — more keenly competitive, but exhibiting more cooperation among businesses nationally and globally, as well as between business and government. The literature suggests that marketing will be given more importance in the management hierarchy of organizations, and that may change many traditional business approaches.[116] Geo-politically, other nations are expected to increase their presence and power in world markets.[117]

The nine key trends that are expected to affect future strategic marketing environments and operations are:

1. Shifting markets nationally and globally.

2. Increasing competition.

3. Increasing cooperation.

4. Global marketing thrusts.

5. Slow population and economic growth.

6. Rapidly advancing technologies.

[113]Bell 1987; Fly, Harbrecht, Magnusson, McNamee, Dryden, Cahan, Garland, Dwyer, Javetski and Griffiths 1988; Jordan 1987; Magnet 1988; Sethi et al., 1986; Vatter 1986; Whelan 1986.

[114]Cohen and Zysman 1986; Young 1985.

[115]Bocker, Daniels, Prasad and Shane 1986; Brandt 1986; *Broadcasting* 1986-b; Bronson 1986; Bylinski, Moore, Smith, Norton and Slovak 1986; Ebel 1986; Fusfeld and Hanklish 1985; Gantz 1988; Goldhar 1986; Hall, Cahan, Hamilton, Eklund and Therrien 1985; Hamilton, Siwolop, Clark, Therrien and Hoppe, 1986; Hollon and Rogol 1985; Holloway and Hand 1988; Meredith 1987; Schulman, Carson, Norman and Therrien 1985; Smith, DeGeorge, Kelly, Brown and Hamilton 1988.

[116]Cohen and Zysman 1986; *Columbia Journal of World Business* 1987-a; Hannay and Steele 1986; *Harvard Business Review* 1987; Jonas 1986; Jonas, Dreyfack, Port, Wilson, Dobrzynski, Brandt and Pennar 1986; Kirkland 1988; Levine and Byrne 1986; Nasar 1988; Perlmutter and Heenan 1986; Porter 1986-a and -b; Vernon 1986; Young 1985.

[117]Bylinski et al., 1986; Holstein 1986; Keegan 1984; Kotler, Fahey and Jatusripitak 1985.

7. Growth in distributor power.

8. Large social and ecological challenges.

9. Increasing reliance on marketing by business and non-profit organizations in capitalistic and other political environments.

Each is briefly noted below.

Shifting Markets

The literature points to a variety of emerging market opportunities, including:[118]

- The mature market.[119]
- Wealthy baby-boomers and other up-scale markets.[120]
- International markets,[121] especially the Asian[122] and the more unified European Economic Community. (E.E.C.)[123]
- Various geographic and regional markets.[124]
- The gamut of ethnic markets.[125]
- Two-income households.[126]
- Countertrade markets.[127]
- High tech markets.[128]
- Service markets, and service-based markets, such as business services, health care and medical services, security, retailing, restaurants, and leisure services.[129]

---

[118]Nacinovich 1985; Swenson 1988; Walsh 1983.

[119]Bakshian 1986; Lazer 1986-a and 1986-b; Lazer and Shaw 1987.

[120]Colvin 1984; Lazer 1984; Nasar 1988; Rice 1988-b.

[121]Dymsza 1984; Levitt 1983; Walsh 1983.

[122]Terpstra 1985.

[123]Hunsicker 1986; Kirkland 1988; Tully 1988.

[124]Edmondson 1988; Johnson and Friedenberg 1985; *Sales and Sales Management* 1986; *Survey of Current Business* 1985.

[125]Nacinovich 1985; Namakforoosh 1987.

[126]Cherlin and Furstenberg 1983; Exter 1986; *Marketing News* 1983; Waldrop 1988.

[127]Braggs 1988; Cooper 1984.

[128]Bylinski et al., 1986; Chester 1985; Gantz 1988; Goldhar 1986; Hall et al., 1985; Hamilton et al., 1986; Hooper 1986; Meredith 1987; Schulman et al., 1985; *The Economist* 1986; Weindling and Silbet 1987; Wilson 1984.

[129]Brody, Kirkland, Nulty, McComas, Dreyfuss, Breckenfeld, Hector, Saporito, Taylor and Labich 1987; McClenahan and Pascarella 1987; *Occupational Outlook Quarterly* 1987; Personick 1985; Saunders 1987; Su 1985.

The futures literature portrays tomorrow's consumers as being:

1. Slightly more numerous;
2. More demanding and sophisticated;
3. Driven by convenience, service, quality, and value;
4. Better educated;
5. More international and ethnically mixed;
6. Slightly wealthier; and
7. Having more leisure time.

They are also depicted as making use of technological advances, having more job opportunities, demanding a greater number of personal services, and displaying a wider range of acceptable living arrangements.[130] These and related changes are fully expected to affect product and service strategies, channel selection, pricing, communication, and promotion.[131] Human resource strategy in marketing will also be affected, as will workforce composition, which will mirror many larger demographic trends.[132]

Increasing Competition

Increasing competition, especially international competition, is a dominant theme in the literature. Competitive activity is depicted as "boundless,"[133] and is fully expected to impact on domestic and global marketing.[134] Dealing with competition is still viewed by some as "the key factor that marketing strategists face."[135]

Among the visible signs underscoring competitive intensity are:

1. Global over-capacity,[136]
2. Maturing industries,[137]
3. Shakeouts,[138]

---

[130]Bogart 1985; Brody et al., 1987; Keith 1988; *Marketing News* 1984; McClenahan and Pascarella 1987; Michman 1984; *Sales and Sales Management* 1986; Vatter 1987; Zeithaml 1985.

[131]Aaker 1988; Bogart 1985; Crespy 1986; Laczniak and Lusch 1987; Levinson 1986; Marcus and Kaufman 1988; McDonough and Spital 1984; Nasar 1988; Root 1984; Webber 1986.

[132]Zemke 1987; *Management Review* 1984; Taylor 1986-b; Urbanski 1986.

[133]Kirkland 1988.

[134]Bergsten 1985; Bolt 1988; Cohen and Zysman 1986; Dymsza 1984; Hannay and Steele 1986; *Harvard Business Review* 1987; Kirkland 1988; Nasar 1988.

[135]Lynn 1987, p.7.

[136]Levinson 1986.

[137]Frost 1983-1984.

[138]Frost 1983-1984; Shiller, Rossant, Cowan, Miller, Eklund, Power, Terry, King, Zukosky, Norman and Baum 1986.

4. Restructuring processes,[139]

5. Direct foreign investment in the U.S.,[140]

6. Niche closing,[141]

7. Product proliferation and the battle for shelf space,[142]

8. Retail store wars,[143]

9. Success of low-cost producers,[144]

10. Cluttered communication channels,[145] and

11. The intensity of political discussions on competitiveness.[146]

Foreign competition will continue to have a dramatic impact on U.S. firms and this country's economy.[147] Increasing competition among firms, both public and private, will make it more difficult to gain and defend a sustainable competitive advantage in the market.[148] The President's Commission on Industrial Competitiveness reports compelling evidence that the United States' ability to compete has declined over the past twenty years, and indications are that it could continue.[149] Some experts point out that the decline is not particular to manufacturing, arguing that its effects are felt throughout the service sectors, in industries such as distribution and transportation, finance and high-technology.[150]

A continuing theme in the literature depicts increasingly keen future competition from Asian and other lesser developed countries.[151] The total GNP of the Asian Rim countries is expected to surpass that of

---

[139]*Business Week* 1988; Levinson 1986; Nasar 1988.

[140]Dymsza 1984; Holstein 1986.

[141]Levinson 1986; Frost 1983-1984.

[142]Bennett, Donegan and Sullivan 1987.

[143]Bivins 1985; *Chain Store Age Executive* 1987.

[144]Jonas et al., 1986.

[145]Bogart 1985.

[146]Cohen and Zysman 1986; Grossack and Heenan 1986; *Harvard Business Review* 1987; Jonas 1986; Vernon 1986.

[147]Bergsten 1985; Nasar 1988; Young 1985.

[148]Aaker 1988; *Harvard Business Review* 1987; Kirkland 1988; Laczniak and Lusch 1987; Levinson 1986; Porter 1986-a and 1986-b; Webster 1988; Young 1985.

[149]Young 1985.

[150]Berger 1986; Bylinski et al., 1986; *Distribution Research and Education Foundation 1983;* Quinn and Gagnon 1986; Turner 1987.

[151]Dymsza 1984; Kotler, Fahey and Jatusripitak 1985; Root 1984.

Europe and, according to some writers perhaps that of the United States. The future competitive supremacy of the U.S. in world business is in question.[152]

Increasing Cooperation

Although heightened competition was underscored, an opposing phenomenon, that of cooperation, was also highlighted in the literature. As future environments become more competitive and more turbulent, many entities, even arch competitors and rival nations will tend to cooperate with one another. Cooperation will affect a number of key marketing activities, such as piggy-backed distribution networks, R&D, organizing for international activity, warehousing, and waste disposal.[153]

Global Marketing Thrusts

The trends toward international marketing and globalization rank among the most significant forces affecting the strategic landscape of the future.[154] The speed and scope of the growth of global markets is explained in terms of such factors as:

1. Economic and technical imperatives,

2. Advances in transportation and better distribution economies,

3. Flattening domestic markets,

4. A better educated and richer world,

5. Emerging world demand,

6. Movement towards a unified European market,

7. Advanced communications and computing,

8. Flexible production technology and improved control systems,

9. The worldwide youth culture, fostered by music and fashion,

10. The impact of television on consumers all over the globe, and

11. The movement of socialist countries to market economics.[155]

---

[152]Bylinski et al., 1986; Cohen and Zysman 1986; Young 1985.

[153]*Chain Store Age Executive* 1987; *Columbia Journal of World Business* 1987-a; Dymsza 1984; Fusfeld and Hanklish 1985; Grossack and Heenan 1986; *Harvard Business Review* 1987; McCann 1985; Perlmutter and Heenan 1986; Rice 1988-a; Tokarski 1988.

[154]Bolt 1988; Dymsza 1984; Kirkland 1988; Levitt 1983.

[155]Crespy 1986; Kirkland 1988; Root 1984; Tully 1988; Walsh 1983; Porter 1986-b.

Global expansion and targets for global specialization are expected to be central themes underlying the strategies of the world's most powerful, market-savvy corporations. They will continue to foster frenzied jockeying for world-wide strategic position, as evidenced by the recent rash of mergers, joint ventures, spin-offs, and alliances. The success that the Japanese have had in carving out large chunks of global markets will inspire other nations.[156]

Demonstrating adaptability in seeking international opportunities, corporations will develop new organization structures.[157] A key challenge for each firm will be coordinating the elements of its new structure. Coordination has been recognized as the main future challenge, especially as global strategies utilize the resources of, and unite independent firms via joint ventures or alliances.[158]

Slow Population and Economic Growth

The U.S. post-industrial economy is expected to spin out a silver, not golden, age.[159] The most oft encountered economic scenario for most industrialized countries, including the U.S., Japan, and the E.E.C., is slow economic growth through the turn of the century. American economic growth is expected to be strongest in services, but slow across most consumer durable and packaged goods categories.[160]

Growth rates for U.S. GNP are expected to be less than 3% per year to the year 2000. Scores of sober projections are available in the literature for such market dimensions as population,[161] income,[162] and employment.[163]

An increasingly interconnected global economy is expected to produce not only booms in the United States, but economic shock waves.[164] Large, unresolved, future economic problems that are written about include:

- A large federal deficit,

- Dubious loans to third world countries resulting in the continuing vulnerability of the banking system,

---

[156]Kotler, Fahey, and Jatusripitak 1985; Levinson 1986.

[157]Bolt 1988; *Columbia Journal of World Business* 1987-a; Cooper 1984; Dymsza 1984; Levine and Byrne 1986; Morris and Hegert 1987; Perlmutter and Heenan 1986.

[158]*Columbia Journal of World Business* 1987-a.

[159]Brody et al., 1987.

[160]Brody et al., 1987; Carson, Louis and Magnet 1986; *Occupational Outlook Quarterly* 1987; Personick 1985; Saunders 1987; Su 1985.

[161]Saunders 1987.

[162]*Survey of Current Business* 1985.

[163]*Survey of Current Business* 1985.

[164]*Business Week* 1988; Dymsza 1984; Holstein 1986; Karen 1985; Nasar 1988; Root 1984; Terpstra 1985; Wendt 1985.

- Continuing farm belt problems,
- Increasing competition from foreign firms,[165]
- The vulnerability of highly leveraged institutions and individuals,
- The growth of a large underclass, and
- Serious flaws in the tort and liability systems.

Rapidly Advancing Technologies

The increasing speed of technological advances will affect marketing environments and operations. It will spin out a host of new and substitute products of improved quality that will open and close markets. Companies falling behind in technology will find it more difficult to play catch-up.[166] Technology will force more frequent revisions of strategic plans and assessments of capabilities, commanding more attention from marketers than was previously the case.[167]

Technology in the future is depicted as: altering comparative marketing advantages worldwide,[168] shortening product life cycles, increasing product complexity, speeding product introductions[169], and providing new opportunities, capabilities and challenges for marketers.[170] The "factory of the future" will allow marketers to better meet the needs of increasingly fragmented markets and to enjoy returns from cross-selling.[171] Information, computing, and communications technologies will create new competition and change the manner in which marketing has traditionally been executed, as well as create new customer expectations and behavior.[172] Artificial intelligence and expert systems will allow marketing executives to share their expertise, experience, and judgment with subordinates and associates.[173]

---

[165]Bergsten 1985; *Business Week* 1986; Fly et al., 1988; Turner 1987.

[166]Bylinski et al., 1986.

[167]Goldhar 1986; Goldhar and Jelinek 1983; Gordon 1974; Jelinek and Goldhar 1985; Meredith 1987; Papageorgion 1983; Taylor 1986-a; Whaley and Burrows 1987.

[168]Bylinski et al., 1986.

[169]Bylinski et al., 1986; Goldhar 1986.

[170]Clemons and McFarlan 1986; Daniel and Henderson 1984; Foster 1986; Fusfeld and Hanklish 1985; Gilly and Zeithaml 1985; Holloway and Hand 1988; Whaley and Burrows 1987.

[171]Goldhar 1986; Quinn and Gagnon 1986.

[172]Becker 1986; Bush and Schkade 1986; Gantz 1988; Hooper 1986.

[173]Edosomwan 1987-a; Holloway and Hand 1988.

Growth in Distributor Power

The literature on future marketing developments signals a shift in channel power, away from manufacturers and towards distributors and retailers, all of whom will have a vast array of products available and will, of necessity, become more selective.[174] Middlemen will be more demanding of manufacturer marketing support.[175] They will extend the increasing channel responsibility they are now acquiring.[176] More intense competition, rapidly advancing technology, and a greater emphasis on satisfying customer needs will continue to fuel product proliferation. This will increase distributor power in future channel systems.

Manufacturers are expected to respond to such developments by differentiating their products, developing more focused product strategies, and relying on more sophisticated presentations of their offerings to future retailer buying groups. Some retailers see such manufacturer-sponsored activities as providing merchandising suggestions, developing extended advertising campaigns, and providing improved feedback about retail performance as being very important in the future.[177] Manufacturers will also multiply their own options in going direct to the customer, via mail order, manufacturer outlets, and telemarketing.

Large Social and Ecological Challenges

In the future, society, government, and business will likely deal with a number of large social challenges.[178] While the need will be great, resources will not be readily available.[179] Examples of such problems that are projected to have great future impact are:

1. Spiraling medical and health care costs;[180]

2. The declining quality and rising costs of education;[181]

3. The costs of replacing and maintaining the infrastructure;[182]

4. The malaise of the overall economy;[183]

---

[174]Bennett, Donegan and Sullivan 1987; Hiller 1983.

[175]Bennett, Donegan and Sullivan 1987.

[176]*Distribution Research and Education Foundation* 1983.

[177]Bennett, Donegan and Sullivan 1987.

[178]Bell 1987; Fly et al., 1988.

[179]Fly et al., 1988.

[180]Bell 1987; Whelan 1986.

[181]Magnet 1988.

[182]*U.S. News and World Report* 1984-a.

[183]*Business Week* 1988; Fly et al., 1988.

5. National strategy dictates, arising from such international concerns as third world developments, global instability, national security, world peace, and the like;[184]

6. Generational inequality and the "demographic time bomb" arising from the difference in agendas between the young and old;[185]

7. The "polity time bomb," with the nation state becoming too small for the big problems in life, and too big for its small problems;[186]

8. The housing crisis; and

9. The drug crisis.

A widely referenced government study, "The Global 2000 Report to the President," depicted the likely future physical condition of the Earth as being, "more crowded, more polluted, less stable ecologically, and more vulnerable to disruption than the world we live in now."[187] The physical environment is currently depicted as highly fragile[188] and more vulnerable to industrial crises.[189] Among the major future environmental problems discussed are: ozone depletion; species extinction; degradation of forests, croplands, and oceans; expanding deserts and soil erosion; rising temperatures; increasing consumption of oil and coal; water contamination; and garbage, medical, toxic, and nuclear waste disposal.

The impacts of such developments on marketing will be substantial, for marketers may be required to:

- Recycle used products, wrappings, containers, and packages;

- Use materials which when discarded decompose more readily;

- Change packages to bio-degradable packages only;

- Limit packaging, especially non-protective, promotional packaging, and the contents of direct mail letters;

---

[184]Bell 1987; Jordan 1987.

[185]Bell 1987; Vatter 1986.

[186]Bell 1987.

[187]Barney 1980.

[188]Barney 1980; Brown, Flavin and Wolf 1988; Meadows 1985; Rice 1988-a; Rowland 1987; Schwartz 1988; Smart et al., 1987.

[189]*Columbia Journal of World Business* 1987-a; Mitroff 1988; Sethi et al., 1986.

- Use more costly supplies;

- Ban some products;

- Pay for environmental damage.[190]

Industrial crises may become more frequent and more devastating in the future.[191] Executives will likely be prodded to take appropriate steps to develop crises management programs, and deal with products that may be suddenly pulled from retailers' shelves. Socio-political forces will be organized globally to deal with companies that create or contribute to crises anywhere around the world.[192]

Increasing Reliance on Marketing

The theme of the growing role for marketing in both private and public organizations is dominant throughout the literature.[193] Organizations will place more emphasis on the extended marketing concept in response to meeting intensified competition. Executives report that generally, as they place more emphasis on the extended marketing concept, their organizational performance rises.[194] When assessing strategic situations, executives are prodded to focus on marketing factors and strategies, such as R&D, customer requirements, quality, product differentiation, product positioning, and channel development.[195]

Gearing Up For Future Competition

There is an extensive body of literature focusing on marketing imperatives for winning in the future. Some of these are briefly summarized below.

Focus on the Longer Term and Innovation

The literature prods CEOs and marketing executives to focus on longer term results, and relegate short-term impact to considerations of lesser importance.[196] Innovation and adaptability are identified as key

---

[190]*Columbia Journal of World Business* 1987-b; Rice 1988-a.

[191]*Columbia Journal of World Business* 1987-b.

[192]Sethi et al., 1986.

[193]*Business Week* 1983-b; Deshpande and Webster 1989; Gallup 1988; Kiechel 1988; Lusch and Laczniak 1987; Swenson 1988; Taylor 1986-a; Webster 1986 and 1988; Yeskey and Burnett 1986.

[194]Lusch and Laczniak 1987.

[195]Webster 1988.

[196]Booze, Allen and Hamilton, Inc. 1982; Carlisle and Carter 1988; Keane 1987; Varadarajan and Johnson 1987.

prerequisites for future success,[197] with innovation being the toughest challenge for CEOs in the 1990s.[198] The future will require CEOs to make a complete audit of the business to assess its innovativeness and ability to change.

Corporate cultures, organizational structures, operating methods, and other routine procedures and traditions will be changed.[199] Organizational structures will have to display great adaptability to changing environments. In the future, creative organization structures will help companies marshall the power necessary to achieve the previously unthinkable.[200]

Intelligence

Marketing intelligence will be a critical factor, as marketing decisions increase in complexity.[201] A vast array of articles exist about future marketing information systems and their potential, and critical contributions. In an information age, marketing information will become a highly valued asset. Tough decisions will require more insightful, up-to-date, relevant marketing information, which fortunately will become more bountiful.[202] A key future concern will be how to make marketing information even more timely, meaningful, and usable. A large body of literature contains a wide variety of suggestions for doing so.[203]

Global Specialization

Global specialization, whether by niche, region, product/mix differentiation, low-cost producer strategies, or other means, may well become an overriding objective of many powerful multinational corporations.[204] Global specialization is presented as an important future trend. Broad criteria for success in global marketing are beginning to receive attention in the international marketing literature.[205]

---

[197]Booze, Allen and Hamilton, Inc. 1982; Bylinski et al., 1986; *Columbia Journal of World Business* 1987-a; Colvin 1984; Hayes 1985; Keane 1987.

[198]Kiechel 1988.

[199]Guest 1986; Lehmann 1987; Porter 1986-a; Webster 1988; Zemke 1987.

[200]*Columbia Journal of World Business* 1987-a.

[201]Aaker 1988; Lutz 1986; Silverblatt and Korgaonkar 1987.

[202]Becker 1986.

[203]Becker 1986; Bush and Schkade 1986; Chester 1985; Coppet and Sullivan 1986; Edosomwan 1987-a; *EDP Analyzer* 1986; *EDP Analyzer* 1985; Field and Harris 1986; Foegen 1986; Hopper 1986; Lederer and Mendelow 1988; Taylor 1986-a.

[204]Frost 1983-1984; Levitt 1983; Levinson 1986; Shiller et al., 1986; Terpstra 1985.

[205]Bolt 1988; *Columbia Journal of World Business* 1987-a and -b; Cooper 1984; Crespy 1986; Dymsza 1984; Levine and Byrne 1986; Morris and Hergert 1987; Nasar 1988; Perlmutter and Heenan 1986; Porter 1986-a; Tully 1988.

Marketing Management

Niche, company and product/mix differentiation, and distribution and positioning strategies, are all seen as among the keys to successful marketing approaches for the foreseeable future.[206] Product/service uniqueness, customer service, and distribution strategies are all portrayed as growing in future importance.[207] However, some of the literature sees sales management as taking on even greater importance. Future channel strategy is fully expected to challenge the insights and operating decisions of future marketing executives.[208]

Future price competition is depicted as being intense. Some of the pricing literature, however, suggests that some marketers will be able to charge higher than market par prices for items that offer high perceived value, in general, and that will be perceived by buyers as offering determinant attributes, such as: dependability and reliability; timely and convenient delivery; user friendly features; technical or fashion sophistication; convenience; high quality; and product/service uniqueness.[209]

The demographics indicate that marketers will likely face shortages of young workers and may have to make a number of significant operating adjustments.[210] Sales and sales management could be among the marketing areas most directly influenced by demographic shifts, the increasing importance of national accounts and global opportunities, the growing number of small buyers who are better served by direct response marketing, and changing industrial buying requirements.[211]

Corporate affairs and public relations activities are expected to expand, as evidenced by their increasing budgets.[212] Marketing research is expected to change both in technique and orientation, especially where packaged goods are concerned.[213]

And mergers, acquisitions, and divestitures will continue to wreak havoc on marketing management well into the next decade. Marketing executives and professionals will continue to wonder about their job security, corporate longevity, product and distribution strategies, budgets, and resource availability. Morale will be lowered while productivity is

---

[206]*Business Week* 1983-b; Edmondson 1988; *Fortune* 1983; Goldhar and Jelinek 1983; Webster 1988.

[207]Laczniak and Lusch 1987;.

[208]Sutton 1986.

[209]Brody et al., 1987; Lazer 1984; Zeithaml 1988.

[210]*Management Review* 1984; Rosenbloom and Anderson 1984; Zemke 1987.

[211]Cardozo and Shipp 1987.

[212]Crespy 1986; Marcus and Kaufman 1988.

[213]Webber 1986.

expected to be maximized. Marketing 2000 poses great personal and professional challenges for marketing management.[214]

Factory of the Future

Marketing will benefit from advances in the flexible production technologies and product/service quality advancements to be gained through future technologies. The factory of the future will permit the profitable cultivation of thin market niches by providing short production runs without greatly sacrificing scale economies. It is also expected to yield more sophisticated, user friendly, higher quality products, and at the same time, facilitate more cross-selling. Future technology will permit factories of the future to achieve both economies of scope and scale that will be enjoyed by manufacturers and service providers.[215]

Customer Service

The literature suggests increasingly significant improvements in the upcoming customer service era, in the product and service sectors of industrial and consumer markets. Value-added services are expected to account for much of the future market growth.[216] Much of the literature depicts future consumers as being service demanding.[217] However, definitions of customer service will be a lot more innovative and responsive than today's knee-jerk solutions if they are to succeed amidst keen competition.

Upscale Products

Future market opportunities will expand the market potential and availability of upscale products, even those that are not visibly prestigious. While older customers are often characterized as being reluctant to trade up from their current inventory of durable goods, some evidence indicates that is not the case. Mature consumers will buy when compelling advantages are offered.[218]

Many future consumers groups are portrayed as being wealthier and desirous of sophisticated, advanced, easy to use, trouble free new products. They will seek out "the new." They will want variety and change,

---

[214]Urbanski 1987.

[215]Goldhar 1986; Goldhar and Jelinek 1983; Jelinek and Goldhar 1985.

[216]*Distribution Research and Education Foundation* 1983; Feuer 1987; Kiechel 1988; Laczniak and Lusch 1987.

[217]Lazer 1984.

[218]*Fortune* 1983.

and will improve their product inventory,[219] generating attractive markets for improved products. Technology, marketing opportunities, and marketing response will spin out a host of advanced materials and products.[220]

Speed of Response

Future marketers will face more hostile, unstable, and competitive environments. Contingency planning and hedging, two of the approaches to dealing with instability and turbulence, are expected to receive greater emphasis by marketing managers, particularly when competition may quickly close the door on possible opportunities. The notion that marketing managers must speed their actions is expressed widely in the literature. For example, advertising agencies are now striving to permit "instant commercial control" by allowing clients to make immediate judgments of advertising designs through advanced use of satellite and computer technologies.[221] Similarly, distributors who provide just-in-time delivery[222] and product managers who attempt to speed new product development and introduction foreshadow future tendencies to collapse response time.[223]

Technology

Marketers, in the future, will not only expect technical advances but will generate them. Marketers will need technology to more effectively communicate, test and develop, expand services, enter new markets, control expanded activity (especially global marketing), and in other ways remain competitive.[224]

Technology has been depicted as the single most important contributor to enhancing the future well-being of society. However, society has been criticized for the over reliance it places on the "technical fix" for fundamental problems in the physical and social environments.[225]

Marketing Institutions

Manufacturers are now, and will be, more concerned with the costs of promotion and distribution. They will rethink their limited channel strategies. Rising selling costs, proliferation of small accounts, opportu-

---

[219]Brody et al., 1987; Lazer 1984; Lazer and Shaw 1987.

[220]Bylinski et al., 1986; Nasar 1988.

[221]*Association of National Advertisers* 1984.

[222]*Distribution Research and Education Foundation* 1983.

[223]McDonough and Spital 1984.

[224]Edosomwan 1987-b; *EDP Analyzer* 1985; Kiechel 1988.

[225]Bylinski et al., 1986; Meadows 1985; Wendt 1985.

nities for direct marketing, attractiveness of independent distributors, just-in-time delivery, and technological advances underlie the future potential of multiple channel strategy.[226]

Distributors and advertising agencies in the future are seen as using technology to accomplish key objectives, such as:[227]

- Assuming more channel responsibility by performing more functions;

- Entering international markets;

- Servicing unique needs of high-tech manufacturers;

- Better satisfying and locking-in customers by providing value-added services and broader networks.[228]

Retailing will be greatly affected by new marketing and distribution approaches.[229] For example, retailers in the future may employ robots, high-tech safety features, computer-aided design to test both store and shopping center layout design, and artificial intelligence (AI).[230] In fact, up-grading technology is seen as an imperative for all marketing institutions.[231]

Forecasts are that in the future there will be an "overstored America." Some of the retailing literature suggests that, in an overstored America, the keys to future earnings for widely located retailers probably will accrue from improved store operations and merchandising strategies, rather than from expansion into new locations. New forms of retailing, both non-store and store, will continue to prosper, and department stores are expected to continue to face very severe competition. Destination stores are seen among the future winners. Retail stores at either end of the physical size spectrum, both large and small, are expected to prosper more so than medium-sized stores.[232]

---

[226]Sutton 1986.

[227]*Association of National Advertisers* 1984; *Distribution Research and Education Association* 1983.

[228]*Association of National Advertisers* 1984; Berkwitt 1986; Bogart 1985; *Distribution Research and Education Foundation* 1983; Farrell 1986.

[229]Bivins 1985; Bogart 1985; *Chain Store Age Executive* 1987; Loeb 1987; Whittemore 1986.

[230]*Chain Store Age Executive* 1987; Jones and Ledger 1986.

[231]*Chain Store Age Executive* 1987; Clemons and McFarlan 1986; *Distribution Research and Education Association* 1983.

[232]Bivins 1985; *Chain Store Age Executive* 1987; Loeb 1987.

Developing Future Executives

Tomorrow's marketing challenge includes a greater emphasis on education and training programs necessary to prepare for Marketing 2000. Future marketing managers, according to the literature, will have to possess an expanded set of managerial, technical, and social skills.[233] Needs are generally described in terms of education about business functions and the total business system. Specific references are made to training focused on integrating marketing research and R&D, the development of strategic marketing plans under turbulent conditions, enhancing people skills, and gleaning useful information from large data bases.[234] In addition, future marketing managers may well need international exposure and skills in managing marketing activities under international alliances and joint ventures.[235]

Information specialists who understand not only marketing and business, but information technology, will be valued.[236] Marketing executives will also need education and skills that relate to increasing product/service quality, enhancing customer satisfaction, improving productivity, and dealing effectively with the media.[237]

Some authors perceive a return to basic marketing principles as another part of the prescription for future success. Such marketing basics as consumer behavior, segmentation, product/mix differentiation, improved quality, relationship management, positioning, channel development and distribution strategy, customer service, negotiation, and motivation will be infused into executive development programs.[238]

Conclusions

Six likely developments impacting on marketing in the future which are referred to over and over again, either directly or by implication, are: growing turbulence in marketing environments; the growing importance of marketing and having a marketing orientation; more sophisticated executives; the development of global perspectives and operations; greater attention to assessing and planning for the future; and the mandate to market change effectively.

Marketing strategies will be implemented in environments that are characterized as: more dynamic, rapidly evolving, and more turbulent,

---

[233]Olson and Cooper 1987.

[234]Bush and Schkade 1986;

[235]*Columbia Journal of World Business* 1987-a; *Research Management* 1986.

[236]Lutz 1986; Stubbart 1985.

[237]Edosomwan 1987-b; Pinsdorf 1987.

[238]*Business Week* 1983; Webster 1986 and 1988.

more complex and more highly interactive, more international and competitive, more hostile and less forgiving, and more ecologically fragile. Marketing executives will be challenged to both adjust to sudden shifts and to purposely set out to create desirable change. Greater flexibility and more rapid adjustment to change will become a way of life for marketing managers.

Future marketing planning, strategy, and management are described as being: more critical to business success, conducted under much tighter time constraints, more flexible, efficient, and effective, more responsive to emerging opportunity and to solving customer problems, more closely coordinated, evaluated, and controlled, effective for shorter durations due to increasing turbulence, more frequently revised, and longer term in overall perspective.

Marketing strategies, in the future, will likely be the domain of executives who have, to a considerable extent, broken free from the "short-term planning only" tradition, in order to develop longer range and more imaginative visions. They will address uncertainties and be open to alternative possibilities while carrying responsibilities across broader business areas.

Future marketing success will require greater international commitment than ever before, in both outlook and operation. Keener competition for global markets via low-cost producer strategies, and carefully selected, specialized, international niche strategies, are anticipated. New organization structures, including joint ventures, global partnerships, and a wide variety of linkages, will develop and grow in both market and socialist economies. These new structures will complement organizational weaknesses and overcome barriers to international opportunities. A multinational and global philosophy will be deeply embedded in corporate and government cultures. Increasingly, American investments will cross national boundaries, with more international firms continuing to invest in the U.S. A truly global business community will emerge with global marketing operations developed to match.

Executives, in dealing with tomorrow's highly turbulent marketing environments, are prodded to pay great attention to: trends and shifts, imaginative philosophies and varied perspectives on marketing strategy, perceptions of normative value held by key publics, developing innovative and responsive organizations and distribution channels, and putting creative marketing management in place.

A new emphasis on marketing and managing change is advocated by many authors. Emphasis is given to anticipating, reacting to and creating change. The literature underscores the need for systems thinking, cross-functional perspectives, enhanced flexibility, and competitive orientations on the part of executives. A major theme, expressed over and over again, is that of the great resistance to change. The tendency to resist change, and the devastating impact that it has on creative and innovative marketing approaches, is well documented. The marriage of futures studies and strategies planning will be a critical underpinning to successful marketing management in Marketing 2000.

REFERENCES

Aaker, David A. (1988) *Strategic Market Management*, 2nd Edition. New York: John Wiley & Sons.

Achrol, Ravi S. and Louis W. Stern (1988), "Environmental Determinants of Decision-Making Uncertainty in Marketing Channels," *Journal of Marketing Research*, 25 No. 1 (February), 36-50.

Aldred, Carolyn (1987), "Pollution Risks a Growing Concern: Experts," *Business Insurance*, 21 No. 42 (October 19), 27-28.

Amara, Roy (1978), "Probing the Future," in *Handbook of Futures Research*, J. Fowles (ed.) Westport, Connecticut: Greenwood Press, 41-51.

Armstrong, J. Scott (1985), *Long-Range Forecasting: From Crystal Ball to Computer*, New York: John Wiley & Sons.

Association of National Advertisers (1984), "Advertising in the Year 2000: A Series of Presentations to the Federal Trade Commission," Transcript of Speeches, Barbara Pressin (Moderator), 155 East 44th Street, New York, NY 10017, (October 24).

Ayres, Robert U. (1984), "Limits and Possibilities of Large-Scale Long-Range Societal Models," *Technology Forecasting and Social Change*, 25 No. 4 (July), 297-308.

Ayres, Robert U. (1979), *Uncertain Futures: Challenges for Decision makers*, New York: John Wiley & Sons.

Bakshian, Araur Jr. (1986), "America's Gray Wave of the Future," *Nation's Business*, 74 No. 4. (April), 4.

Barney, Gerald O. (1980), "The Global 2000 Report to the President," Washington: U.S. Government Printing Office.

Beasley, J. E. and R. Johnson (1984), "Forecasting Environmental Protection Legislation Using Cross-Impact Analysis," *Long Range Planning*, 17 No. 6 (December), 132-138.

Becker, Hal (1986), "Can Users Really Absorb Data at Today's Rates? Tomorrow's?" *Data Communications*, 15 (July), 177-191.

Behrman, J. N. (1986) "The Future of International Business and the Distribution of Benefits," *Columbia Journal of World Business*, (20th Anniversary Issue: 1966-1986), 15-22.

Bell, Daniel (1987), "The World and the United States in 2013," *Daedalus*, 116 No. 3 (Summer), 1-32.

Bennett, Stephen, Priscilla Donegan, and Erin Sullivan (1987), "The Pot is Bigger But It's the Same Game," *Progressive Grocer*, 66 No. 11 (November), 53-71.

Berger, Joan (1986), "The False Paradise of a Service Economy: If Basic Industry is Allowed to Wither, the Service Sector Can't Thrive," *Business Week*, (March 3), 78-81.

Bergsten, C. Fred (1985), "The Second Debt Crisis is Coming," *Challenge*, 28 (May-June), 14-21.

Berkwitt, George (1986), "The Future Years: 1986-2000," *Industrial Distribution*, 75 (October), 38-120.

Bivins, Jacquelyn (1985), "Store Wars: Is America Big Enough for All?" *Chain Store Age Executive*, 61 (August), 15-17.

Bocker, Hans J., John P. Daniels, Jyoti N. Prasad and Hugh M. Shane (1986), "The Factory of Tomorrow: Challenges of the Future," *Management International Review*, 26 No. 3, 36-49.

Boddewyn, J. J. (1982), "Advertising Regulation in the 1980s: The Underlying Global Forces," *Journal of Marketing*, 46 (Winter), 27-35.

Bogart, Leo (1973), "The Future in Retailing," *Harvard Business Review*, (November-December), 16-176.

Bogart, Leo (1985), "War of Words: Advertising in the Year 2010," *Across the Board*, (January), 21-28.

Bolt, James F. (1988), "Global Competitors: Some Criteria for Success," *Business Horizons*, 31 No. 1 (January February), 34-46.

Booze, Allen & Hamilton, Inc. (1982), "New Product Management for the 1980s," Found in: *Marketing Management and Strategy: A Reader*, Philip Kotler and Keith K. Cox, (eds.) Englewood Cliffs: New Jersey: Prentice Hall, 265-277.

Braggs, Arthur (1988), "Bartering Comes of Age," *Sales and Marketing Management*, 140 No. 1 (January), 61-82.

Brandt, Richard (1986), "Biotechnology Down on the Farm," *Business Week*, (September 15), 180-184.

Broadcasting (1986-A), "ARF Gathering Ponders the Media Climate of 2010," 110 (March 24), 94.

Broadcasting (1985), "Media Evolution to the Year 2000," 108 (April 22), 78-79.

Broadcasting (1986-B), "Satellites: Flying Higher Than Ever," 111 (July 14), 41-57.

Brody, Michael, Richard I. Kirkland, Jr., Peter Nulty, Maggie McComas, Joel Dreyfuss, Gurney Breckenfeld, Gary Hector, Bill Saporito, Alex Taylor III and Kenneth Labich (1987), "The Economy of the 1990s: Special Report," *Fortune*, 115 (February 2), 22-63.

Bronson, Gail (1986), "Science & Technology: Where's the Demand," *Forbes*, 138 (October 20), 138-142.

Brown, Arnold and Edith Weiner (1984), *Supermanaging: How to Harness Change for Personal and Organizational Success*, New York: McGraw-Hill Book Company.

Brown, Barbara (1984), "Baby Boom Generation Now Mirrors the Values and Attitudes of its Elders," *Marketing News*, 18 No. 8 (April 13), 9.

Brown, Lester, Christopher Flavin, and Edward Wolf (1988), "Earth's Vital Signs," *The Futurist*, 22 No. 4 (July/August), 13-20.

Brown, O. and E. Davis (1983), "The Implications of the Supreme Court's California Nuclear Moratorium Decision," *Public Utility Fortnightly*, 111 (May 26), 35-38.

Bush, Chandler M. and Lawrence L. Schkade (1986), "Fifth Generation Challenges for System Managers," *Journal of Systems Management*, 37 (January), 24-27.

Business Week (1983-A), "Deregulating America," (November 28), 80-86.

Business Week (1983-B), "Marketing: The New Priority," (November 21), 96-106.

Business Week (1986), "The Biggest Villain Is Still the Trade Gap," (October 13), 39-40.

Business Week (1988), "Made in the U.S.A.," (February 29), 60-71.

Bylinski, Gene, Alicia Hills Moore, Lee Smith, Robert E. Norton and Julianne Slovak (1986), "Special Report: The High Tech Race, Who's Ahead," *Fortune*, (October 13), 26-44.

Carbone, Robert and Spyros Makridakis (1986), "Forecasting when Pattern Changes Occur Beyond the Historical Data," *Management Science*, 32 No. 3 (March), 257-271.

Cardozo, Richard and Shannon Shipp (1987), "New Selling Methods Are Changing Industrial Sales Management," *Business Horizons*, 30 (September-October), 23-28.

Carlisle, A. Elliot and Kent Carter (1988), "*Fortune* Service and Industrial 500 Presidents: Priorities and Perceptions," *Business Horizons*, 31 No. 2 (March-April), 77-83.

Carson, David (1978), "Gotterdammering for Marketing," *Journal of Marketing*, 42 No. 3 (July), 11-19.

Carson, Lorraine, Arthur M. Louis and Myron Magnet (1986), "America's New Economy," *Fortune*, 113 (June 23), 18-31.

Carson, Rachel (1962), *Silent Spring*, Boston: Houghton Mifflin.

Chain Store Age Executive (1987), "Retailing In the Year 2000," 63 No. 5 (May), 19-244.

Challenge (1977), "Forging America's Future: Strategies for National Growth and Development," Reprint of the Report of the Advisory Committee on National Growth Policy Processes, (February), 7-61.

Cherlin, Andrew and Frank F. Furstenberg, Jr. (1983), "The American Family in the Year 2000," *The Futurist*, 17 No. 3 (June), 7-14.

Chester, Jeffrey A. (1985), " Artificial Intelligence: Is MIS Ready for the Explosion," *Infosystems*, (April), 74-78.

Clemons, Eric K. and E. Warren McFarlan (1986), "Telecom: Hook Up or Lose Out, "*Harvard Business Review*, (July-August), 91-97.

Cohen, Stephen S. and John Zysman (1986), "Can America Compete?" *Challenge*, 29 (May-June), 56-64.

Cohen, Stephen S. and John Zysman (1987), "Why Manufacturing Matters: The Myth of the Post Industrial Economy," *California Management Review*, 24 No. 3 (Spring), 9-26.

Cole, Sam (1987) "Global Models: A Review of Recent Developments," *Futures*, 19 No. 4 (August), 403-430.

Columbia Journal of World Business (1987-A), "Special Focus Issue: International Corporate Linkages," 22 No. 2 (Summer), 3-104.

Columbia Journal of World Business (1987-B), "Special Focus Issue: International Industrial Crisis Management," 22 No. 1 (Spring), 3-112.

Colvin, Geoffrey (1984), "What the Baby-Boomers Will Buy Next," *Fortune*, (October 15), 28-34.

Cooper, Richard N. (1984), "Why Countertrade," *Across the Board*, 21 No. 3 (March), 36-41.

Coppet, John I. and Cornelius H. Sullivan (1986), "Marketing in the Information Age," *Business*, 36 (July-September), 13-18.

Cravens, David W. (1986), "Strategic Forces Affecting Marketing Strategy," *Business Horizons*, 29 (September-October), 77-86.

Crespy, Charles T. (1986), "Global Marketing Is the New Public Relations Challenge," *Public Relations Quarterly*, 31 (Summer), 5-8.

Daniel, Kenneth J. and Thomas R. Henderson (1984), "Labs Will Be Fully Automated in 2020," *Research & Development*, 26 (November), 230-234.

Deshpande, Rohit and Frederick E. Webster, Jr. (1989), "Organizational Culture and Marketing: Defining the Research Agenda," *Journal of Marketing*, 53 No. 1 (January), 3-15.

Distribution Research and Education Foundation (1983), "Future Trends in Wholesale Distribution: Time of Opportunity," 1725 K Street, N.W., Washington, DC, 1-48.

Dowling, Grahame R. and Paul K. Walsh (1985), "Estimating and Reporting Confidence Intervals for Market and Opinion Research," *European Research*, 13 (July), 130-133.

Drucker, Peter (1980), *Managing in Turbulent Times*, New York: Harper & Row Publishers.

Dymsza, William A. (1984), "Trends in Multinational Business and Global Environments: A Perspective," *Journal of International Business* Strategy, 15 (Winter), 25-46.

Ebel, Karl H. (1986), "The Impact of Industrial Robots on the World of Work," *International Labor Review*, 125 No. 1 (January-February), 39-51.

The Economist (1986), "Beyond Factory Robots," 300 (July 5), 61.

Edmondson, Brad (1988), "Targeting America's Hot Spots," *American Demographics*, 10 No. 1 (January), 24-30.

Edosomwan, Johnson A. (1987-A), "Artificial Intelligence/Expert Systems — Computer Role in Decision Making in the Year 2000," *Computers & Industrial Engineering*, 13 No. 1-4, 1-6.

Edosomwan, Johnson Aimie (1987-B), "The Challenge For Industrial Managers: Productivity and Quality in the Workplace," *Industrial Management*, 29 No. 5 (September-October), 25-27.

EDP Analyzer (1985), "Six Top Information System Issues," 23 No. 1 (January), 1-12.

EDP Analyzer (1986), "Organizing for the 1990s," 24 No. 12 (December), 1-16.

Enzer, Selwyn (1984), "Anticipating the Unpredictable," *Technical Forecasting and Social Change*, 26 No. 2 (September), 201-205.

Exter, Thomas (1986), "The Census Bureau's Household Projections," *American Demographics*, 8 No. 10 (October), 44-47.

Fahey, Liam, W. King, and Vadake K. Narayanan (1981), "Environmental Scanning and Forecasting in Strategic Planning. The State of the Art," *Long Range Planning*, 14 (February), 32-39.

Farrell, Jack W. (1986), "An Inside Look at Current Logistics Trends," *Traffic Management*, 25 (June), 77-87.

Feuer, Dale (1987), "Poof! You're in Sales," *Training*, 24 No. 8 August), 44-48.

Field, Anne R. and Catherine Harris (1986), "The Information Business," *Business Week*, (August 25), 82-90.

Fly, Richard, Douglas A. Harbrecht, Paul Magnusson, Mike McNamee, Steven J. Dryden, Vicky Cahan, Susan B. Garland, Paula Dwyer, Bill Javetski, and Dave Griffiths (1988), "After Reagan: America's Agenda for the 1990s," *Business Week*, (February 1), 56-68.

Foegen, J. H. (1986), "Is Computer Backlash Growing," *Business*, 36 (July-September), 51-53.

Fortune (1983), "The Mass Market is Splitting Apart," (November 28), 76-82.

Foster, Richard N. (1986), "Working the S-Curve: Assessing Technological Threats," *Resource Management*, 29 (July-August), 17-20.

Fowles, Jib (1978), *Handbook of Futures Research*, Westport, Connecticut: Greenwood Press.

Fox, Robert W. (1988), "Population Images," *The Futurist*, 22 No. 2 (March-April), 29-32.

Frost, W. H. (1983-1984), "Interpreting the Mature Industry Situation," *International Studies of Management and Organization*, 13 No. 4 (Winter), 63-76.

Fuerst, Judith A. (1985), "Piloting Toward the Year 2,000," *Handling and Shipping Management*, 26 (September), 36-46.

Fullerton, Howard N., Jr. (1987), "Labor Force Projections: 1986 to 2000," *Monthly Labor Review*, 110 No. 9 (September), 19-29.

Fusfeld, Herbert I. and Carmela S. Hanklish (1985), "Cooperative R&D for Competitors," *Harvard Business Review*, 63 (November-December), 60-76.

Galbraith, John K. (1968), "The Theory of Social Balance," in *Social Issues in Marketing*, Lee E. Preston (ed.) Glenview, Illinois: Scott, Foresman and Company, 247-252.

Gallup, George, Jr. (1988), "Survey Research: Current Problems and Future Opportunities," *The Journal of Consumer Marketing*, 5 No. 1 (Winter), 27-30.

Gantz, John (1988), "A Look into the Future: The Personal Computing Industry at the Millennium," *Infoworld*, 10 No. 9 (February 29), 38.

Garde, V. D. and R. R. Patel (1985), "Technological Forecasting for Power Generation - A Study Using the Delphi Technique," *Long Range Planning*, 18 (August), 73-79.

Garrett, Dennis E. (1987), "The Effectiveness of Marketing Policy Boycotts: Environmental Opposition to Marketing," *Journal of Marketing*, 51 No. 2 (April), 46-57.

Gilbreath, Robert D. (1987), "Planning for the Unexpected," *Journal of Business Strategy*, 8 No. 2 (Fall), 44-49.

Gilly, Mary C. and Valerie A. Zeithaml (1985), "The Elderly Consumer and the Adoption of Technologies," *Journal of Consumer Research*, 12 No. 3 (December), 353-357.

Goldhar, Joel D. (1986), "In the Factory of the Future, Innovation Is Productivity," *Resource Management*, 29 No. 2 (March-April), 26-33.

Goldhar, Joel D. and Mariann Jelinek (1983), "Plan for Economies of Scope," *Harvard Business Review*, 61, No.6 (November/December), 141-148.

Gordon, Theodore J. (1974), "Changing Technology and the Future of Marketing," *The Conference Board Record*, 11 No. 12 (December), 22-26.

Grossack, Irvin and David A. Heenan (1986), "Cooperation, Competition and Antitrust: Two Views," *Business Horizons*, 29 (September-October), 24-28.

Guest, Robert H. (1986), "Management Imperatives for the Year 2000," *California Management Review*, 28 No. 4 (Summer), 62-70.

Hall, Alan, Vicky Cahan, Joan O'C. Hamilton, Christopher S. Eklund and Lois Therrien (1985) "The Race for Miracle Drugs," *Business Week*, (July 22), 92-96.

Hamilton, Joan O'C., Sana Siwolop, Evert Clark, Lois Therrien and Richard Hoppe (1986), "The New War on Cancer," *Business Week*, (September 22), 60-62.

Hankinson, G.A. (1986), "Energy Scenarios - the Sizewell Experience," *Long Range Planning*, 19 (October), 94-101.

Hannay, N. Bruce and Lowell W. Steele (1986), "Technology and Trade: A Study of U.S. Competitiveness in Seven Industries," *Research Management*, 29 No. 1 (January-February), 14-22.

Harvard Business Review (1987), "Competitiveness Survey: HBR Readers Respond," 5 (September-October), 8-12.

Hayes, Tom (1985), "15 Future Trends in U.S. Food Consumption," *Progressive Grocer*, 64 (May), 29-30.

Hill, Kim Quaile (1978), "Trend Extrapolation," in *Handbook of Futures Research*, J. Fowles (ed.) Westport, Connecticut: Greenwood Press, 249-272.

Hiller, Terry R. (1983), "Going Shopping in the 1990s: Retailing Eaters the Future," *The Futurist*, 17 No. 6 (December), 13-19.

Hollon, Charles J. and George N. Rogol (1985), "How Robotization Affects People," *Business Horizons*, 28 (May-June), 74-80.

Holloway, Clark and Herbert H. Hand (1988), "Who's Running the Store, Anyway? Artificial Intelligence!!!" *Business Horizons*, 31 No. 2 (March-April), 70-76.

Holstein, William J. (1986), "Japan, U.S.A.," *Business Week*, (July 14), 44-46.

Hopper, Grace (1986), "Exciting Changes, New Possibilities Are Described For the Future of the Communications Industry," *Communications News*, 23 (July), 75-77.

Hunsicker, J. Quincy (1986), "Vision, Leadership and Europe's Business Future," *The McKinsey Quarterly*, (Spring), 22-39.

Jelinek, Mariann and Joel D. Goldhar (1985), "Strategic Implications of the Factory of the Future," *The McKinsey Quarterly*, (Autumn), 20-33. See also: *Sloan Management Review* (1984), 25 No. 4 (Summer), 29-37.

Johnson, Kenneth P. and Howard L. Friedenberg (1985), "Regional and State Projections of Income, Employment and Population to the Year 2000," *Survey of Current Business*, 65 No. 5 (May), 39-63.

Jonas, Norman (1986), "A Strategy for Revitalizing Industry: America Should Start by Correcting Its Self-imposed Disadvantages in World Competition," *Business Week*, (March 3), 84-85.

Jonas, Norman, Kenneth Dreyfack, Otis Port, John W. Wilson, Judith H. Dobrzynski, Richard Brandt, and Karen Pennar (1986), "The Hollow Corporation: The Decline of Manufacturing Threatens the Entire U.S. Economy," *Business Week*, (March 3), 57-85.

Jones, Gil and John Ledger (1986), "Expert Systems in Decision Support: Opportunities for the Retailer," *Retailer and Distribution management*, 14 No. 5 (September-October), 18-19.

Jordan, Amos A. (1987), "A National Strategy for the 1990s," *The Washington Quarterly*, 10 No. 3 (Summer), 15-24.

Journal of Marketing (1970), "Marketing in the 1970s: A Symposium," Eugene J. Kelley (ed.), 34 No. 1 (January), 1-30.

Kahle, Lynn R., Sharon E. Beaty, and Pamela Homer (1986), "Alternative Measurement Approaches to Consumer Values: The List of Values (LOV) and Values and Life Style (VALS)," *Journal of Consumer Research*, 13 No. 3 (December), 405-409.

Kahn, Herman and Anthony J. Wiener (1967), *The Year 2000: A Framework for Speculation on the Next Thirty-Three Years*, New York: The MacMillan Company.

Karen, Ruth (1985), "A Mosaic of Opinion: 12 International Business Leaders Speak Out," *FE* 1 (December), 22-29.

Keane, John G. (1987), "Focusing on the Corporate Future: Not a Trivial Pursuit," *Business Horizons*, 30 No. 1 (January-February), 25-33.

Keegan, Warren J. (1984), "International Competition: The Japanese Challenge," *Journal of International Business Studies*, 15 (Winter), 189-193.

Keith, Bill (1988), "Consumer Changes Tied to New Definition of Time," *Drug Topics*, 132 No. 3 (February 1), 44-47.

Kiechel, Walter III (1988), "Corporate Strategy for the 1990s," *Fortune*, 117 No. 5 (February 29), 34-42.

Kirkland, Richard I. Jr. (1988), "Entering A New Age of Boundless Competition," *Fortune*, 117 No. 6 (March 14), 40-48.

Knee, Richard (1986), "Five Views on the Future of Ports," *American Shipper*, (July), 70-72.

Kotler, Philip (1988), *Marketing Management: Analysis, Planning, Implementation and Control*, 6th Edition, Englewood Cliffs, New Jersey: Prentice Hall.

Kotler, Philip, Liam Fahey, and S. Jatusripitak (1985), *The New Competition*, Englewood Cliffs, New Jersey: Prentice Hall, Inc.

Laczniak, Gene R. and Robert F. Lusch (1987), "Environment and Strategy in 1995: A Survey of High-Level Executives," *Journal of Business and Indus-*

trial Marketing, 2 No. 1 (Winter), 5-23. Same article also appears in *The Journal of Consumer Marketing* (1986), 3 No. 2 (Spring), 27-45.

Laczniak, Gene R., Robert F. Lusch, and Von G. Udell (1977), "Marketing in 1985: A View From the Ivory Tower,"*Journal of Marketing*, 41 No. 4 (October), 47-56.

Larreche, Jean-Claude and Reza Moinpour (1983), "Managerial Judgments in Marketing," *Journal of Marketing Research*, 20 No. 2 (May), 110-121.

Lazer, William (1969), "Marketing's Changing Social Relationships," *Journal of Marketing*, 33 No. 1 (January), 3-9.

Lazer, William (1986-A), "Dimensions of the Mature Market," *Journal of Consumer Marketing*, 3 No. 3 (Summer), 23-34.

Lazer, William (1984), "How Rising Affluence Will Reshape Markets," *American Demographics*, 6 No. 2 (February), 16-21.

Lazer, William (1970), "Marketing Education: Commitments for the 1970s," *Journal of Marketing*, 34 No. 3 (July), 7-19.

Lazer, William (1986-B), "Soviet Marketing Issues, A Content Analysis of Pravda," *Journal of Business Research*, 14 No. 2 (April), 117-131.

Lazer, William and James D. Culley (1983), *Marketing Management: Foundations and Practice*, Boston: Houghton Mifflin Company.

Lazer, William and Eric H. Shaw (1987), "How Older Americans Spend Their Money," *American Demographics*, 9 No. 9 (September), 36-41.

Lederer, Albert L. and Aubrey L. Mendelow (1988), "Information Systems Planning: Top Management Takes Control," *Business Horizons*, 31 No. 3 (May-June), 73-78.

Leemhuis, J. P. (1985), "Using Scenarios to Develop Strategies," *Long Range Planning*, 18 (April), 30-37.

Lehmann, Jean Pierre (1987), "Ten Corporate Commandments for the Year 2000," *Personnel Management*, 19 No. 6 (June), 26-29.

Levine, Jonathan B. and John A. Byrne (1986), "Corporate Odd Couples: Joint Ventures Are All the Rage, But the Matches Often Don't Work Out," *Business Week*, (July 21), 100-105.

Levinson, Marc (1986), "The Pitfalls in Global Restructuring," *Dun's Business Month*, 128 (October), 40-42.

Levitt, Theodore (1983), "The Globalization of Markets," *Harvard Business Review*, (May-June), 92-102.

Linstone, Harold A. (1978), "The Delphi Technique," in *Handbook of Futures Research*, J. Fowles (ed.), Westport, Connecticut: Greenwood Press, 273-300.

Loeb, Walter (1987), "Retailers with Destination Store Image Will Prosper in '90s," *Discount Store News*, 26 (May 11), 171-172.

Lusch, Robert F. and Gene R. Laczniak (1987), "The Evolving Marketing Concept, Competitive Intensity and Organizational Performance," *Journal of the Academy of Marketing Science*, 15 No. 3 (Fall), 1-11.

Lutz, Tom (1986), "Information the Catalyst for Corporate Change," *Data Management*, 24 (June), 25-29.

Lynn, Robert A. (1987), "Anticipating Competitive Reaction: Marketing Strategy in the 1980s," *Journal of Consumer Marketing*, 4 No. 1 (Winter), 5-12.

Maddox, Nick, William P. Anthony, and Walt Wheatly, Jr. (1987), "Creative Strategic Planning Using Imagery," *Long Range Planning*, 20 No. 5 (October), 118-124.

Magnet, Myron (1985), "Who Needs a Trend Spotter?" *Fortune* 112 No. 13 (December 9), 51-56.

Magnet, Myron (1988), "How to Smarten Up the Schools," *Fortune*, 117 No. 3 (February 1), 86-94.

Management Review (1984), "The New Salesperson," (May), 54.

Marcus, Alfred A. and Allen M. Kaufman (1988), "The Continued Expansion of the Corporate Public Affairs Function," *Business Horizons*, 31 No. 2 (March-April), 58-62.

Marketing and the Future (1981), D. F. Mulvihill (ed.), Chicago: American Marketing Association Proceedings Series. Order No. 326.

Marketing News (1983), "Changes Found In Attitudes, Shopping Behavior of U.S.'s Two-Income Couples," 17 No. 22 (October), 12.

Marketing News (1984), "The Year 2000: A Demographic Profile of Consumer Market," 18 No. 11 (May 25), 8-10.

Martino, Joseph P. (1972), "Technology Forecasting: Tools for Looking Ahead," *IEEE Spectrum*, (October), 32-40.

Masini, Eleonora B. (1978), "The Global Diffusion of Futures Research," in *Handbook of Futures Research*, J. Fowles (ed.), Westport, Connecticut: Greenwood Press, 17-29.

McCann, John and David J. Reibstein (1985), "Forecasting the Impact of Socioeconomic and Demographic Change on Product Demand," *Journal of Marketing Research*, 22 (November), 415-423.

McCann, John E. (1985), "Analyzing Industrial Trends - A Collaborative Approach," *Long Range Planning*, 18 No. 5 (October), 116-123.

McCarthy, E. Jerome (1978), *Basic Marketing: A Managerial Approach*, 6th ed. Homewood, Illinois: Richard D. Irwin, Inc.

McClenahan, John S. and Perry Pascarella (1987), "America's New Economy," *Industry Week*, 232 (January 26), 26-32.

McDonough, Edward F. III and Francis C. Spital (1984), "Quick-Response New Product Development," *Harvard Business Review*, (September- October), 52-61.

McHale, John (1978), "The Emergence of Futures Research," in *Handbook of Futures Research*, J. Fowles (ed.), Westport, Connecticut: Greenwood Press, 5-l5.

McLean, J. Michael (1978), "Simulation Modeling," in *Handbook of Futures Research*, J. Fowles (ed.), Westport, Connecticut: Greenwood Press, 329-367.

Meadows, Donella H., Dennis L. Meadows, Jorgen Randers and William W. Behrens III (1972), *The Limits to Growth: Report for the Club of Rome's Project on the Predicament of Mankind*, New York: Universe Books.

Meadows, Donella H. (1985), Charting the Way the World Works, "*Technology Review*, 88 No. 2 (February-March), 54-63.

Meredith, Jack R. (1987), "The Strategic Advantage of the Factory of the Future," *California Management Review*, 24 No. 3 (Spring, 27-41.

Mesarovic, Mihajlo and Eduard Pestel (1974), *Mankind at the Turning Point*, New York: E. P. Dutton & Co., Inc. Readers Digest Press.

Metz, Edmund J. (1984), "The Missing "H" in Strategic Planning," *Managerial Planning*, 32 No. 6 (May-June), 19-23.

Michman, Ronald D. (1984), "Linking Futuristics with Marketing Planning, Forecasting, and Strategy," *Journal of Consumer Marketing*, 1 No. 3, 17-23.

Michman, Ronald D. (1984), "New Directions for Lifestyle Behavior Patterns," *Business Horizons*, 27 No. 4 (July-August), 59-64.

Miles, Ian (1978), "The Ideologies of Futurists," in *Handbook of Futures Research*, J. Fowles (ed.), Westport, Connecticut: Greenwood Press, 67-97.

Mitroff, Ian I. (1988), "Crisis Management: Cutting Through the Confusion," *Sloan Management Review*, 29 No. 2 (Winter), 15-20.

Mockler, Robert J. and D. C. Dologite (1988), "Developing Knowledge -based Systems for Strategic Corporate Planning," *Long Range Planning*, 21 No. 1 (February), 97-102.

Morris, Deigan and Michael Hergert (1987), "Trends in International Collaborative Agreements," *The Columbia Journal of World Business*, 22 No. 2 (Summer), 15-2l.

Morris, Elinor (1987), "Vision and Strategy: A Focus for the Future," *Journal of Business Strategy*, 8 No. 2 (Fall), 51-58.

Moy, Joyanna (1985), "Recent Trends in Unemployment and the Labor Force," *Monday Labor Review*, 108 (August), 9-22.

Nacinovich, Tony (1985), "The Kaleidoscope of New Audiences," *Marketing and Media Decisions*, 20 No. 2 (February), 102-108.

Naisbitt, John (1982), *Megatrends: Ten New Directions Transforming Our Lives*, New York: Warner Books.

Namakforoosh, Naghi (1987), "Targeting the Elusive, Yet Lucrative Hispanic Market," *Bank Marketing*, 19 No. 11 (November), 36-38.

Nasar, Sylvia (1988), "America's Competitive Revival," *Fortune*, 117 No. 1 (January 4), 44-52.

North, Harper Q. and Donald L. Pyke (1969), "Probes of the Technological Future," *Harvard Business Review*, (May-June), 68-80.

Occupational Outlook Quarterly (1987), "Projections 2000," U.S. Department of Labor, Bureau of Labor Statistics, (Fall), 2-35.

Olson, James E. and Thomas A. Cooper (1987), "CEOs on Strategy: Two Companies, Two Strategies," *Journal of Business Strategy*, 8 No. 1 (Summer), 51-57.

Papageorgion, John C. (1983), "Decision Making in the Year 2000," *Interfaces*, 13 No. 2 (April), 77-86.

Patterson, James M. (1966), "What Are the Social and Ethical Responsibilities of Marketing Executives?" *Journal of Marketing*, 30 (July 1966), 12-15.

Perlmutter, Howard V. and David A. Heenan (1986), "Cooperate to Compete Globally," *Harvard Business Review*, 64 No. 2 (March-April), 136-152.

Personick, Valerie A. (1985), "A Second Look at Industry Output and Employment Trends Through 1995," *Monthly Labor Review*, 108 (November), 26-41.

Peters, Thomas J. and Robert H. Waterman, Jr. (1984), *In Search of Excellence*, New York: Warner Books.

Petroleum Economist (1986), "Looking to the Year 2000," 53 (November), 400.

Pinsdorf, Marion K. (1987), "Ten Business Trends and What They Mean to a Communicator," *Communications World*, Vol. 4, No. 1, (January), 20-22.

Porter, Michael E. (1979), "How Competitive Forces Shape Strategy," *Harvard Business Review*, 47 (March-April), 137-145.

Porter, Michael E. (1986-A), "Changing Patterns of International Competition," *California Management Review*, 28 (Winter), 9-40.

Porter, Michael E. (1986-B), "Why U.S. Business is Falling Behind," *Fortune*, 113 No. 9 (April 28), 255-262.

Post, James E. (1985), "Assessing the Nestle Boycott: Corporate Accountability and Human Rights," *California Management Review*, 27 (Winter), 113-131.

Progressive Grocer (1987), "1987 Nielsen Review of Retail Grocery Store Trends: Part II," (September), 3-31.

Quinn, James Brian and Christopher E. Gagnon (1986), "Will Services Follow Manufacturing Into Decline?" *Harvard Business Review*, 64 (November-December), 95-103.

Renfro, William L. (1987), "Future Histories: A New Approach to Scenarios," *The Futurist*, 21 (March-April), 38-41.

Research Management (1986), "CEOs' Perspectives," 29 (September-October), 4-5.

Rice, Faye (1988-A), "Where Will We Put All That Garbage?" *Fortune*, 117 No. 8 (April 11), 96-100.

Rice, Faye (1988-B), "Wooing Aging Baby-Boomers," *Fortune*, ll7 No. 3 (February 1), 68-77.

Richardson, John M. (1984), "The State of Futures Research Personal Reflections," *Futures*, 16 (August), 382-395.

Root, Franklin R. (1984), "Some Trends in the World Economy and Their Implications for International Business Strategy," *Journal of International Business Studies*, (Winter), 19-23.

Rosenbloom, Bert and Ralph E. Anderson (1984), "The Sales Manager: Tomorrow's Super Marketer," *Business Horizons*, 27 (March-April), 50-56.

Ross, Joel E. and Ronnie Silverblatt (1987). "Developing the Strategic Plan," *Industrial Marketing Management*, 16 No. 2 (May), l03-l08.

Rowland, Sherwood (1987), "Can We Close the Ozone Hole?" *Technology Review*, 90 No. 6 (August-September), 50-58.

Sales and Sales Management (1986), "USA 2000: America's Statistical Future, Part II: 1986 Survey of Buying Power," 137 No. 6 (October 27), 1-175.

Saunders, Norman C. (1986), "Sensitivity of BLS Economic Projections to Exogenous Variables," *Monthly Labor Review*, 109 No. 12 (December), 23-29.

Saunders, Norman C. (1987), "Economic Projections to the Year 2000," *Monthly Labor Review*, 110 No. 9 (September), 10-18.

Schulman, Roger, Teresa Carson, James R. Norman, and Lois Therrien, (1985), "The Gene Doctors: Scientists Are on the Verge of Curing Life's Cruelest Disease," *Business Week*, (November), 76-80.

Schwartz, Joe (1988), "The Real Price of Water," *American Demographics*, 10 No. 9 (September), 28-32.

Sethi, S. Prakash, Hamid Etemad, and K.A.N. Luther (1986), "New Socio-political Forces: The Globilization of Conflict," *Journal of Business Strategy*, 6 (Spring), 25-31.

Shama, Avraham (1978), "Management and Consumers In An Era of Stagflation," *Journal of Marketing*, 42 No. 3 (July), 43-52.

Shiller, Zachary, John Rossant, Alison L. Cowan, Frederic A. Miller, Christopher S. Eklund, Christopher Power, Edith Terry, Resa W. King, Jerome Zukosky, James R. Norman, and Laurie Baum (1986), "Deals, Deals, Deals: Mergers, Buyouts, Takeovers, the Pace is Faster Than Ever," *Business Week*, (November 17), 64-68.

Silverblatt, Ronnie and Pradeep Korgaonkar (1987), "Strategic Market Planning in a Turbulent Business Environment," *Journal of Business Research*, 15 (August), 339-358.

Silvestri, George T. and John M. Lukasiewicz (1987), "A Look at Occupational Employment Trends to the Year 2000," *Monthly Labor Review*, 110 No. 9 (September), 46-63.

Smart, Tim, Emily T. Smith, Todd Vogel, Corie Brown, Karen Wolman, Richard Brandt, Russell Mitchell, Gail DeGeorge, and Antonio N. Fins (1987), "Troubled Waters: The World's Oceans Can't Take Much More Abuse," *Business Week*, 3020 (October 12), 88-104.

Smith, Allen, James MacLachlan, William Lazer, and Priscilla LaBarbera (1989), *Marketing 2000: Future Perspectives on Marketing, An Annotated Bibliography of Articles.* Chicago, IL: American Marketing Association.

Smith, Emily T., Gail DeGeorge, Kevin Kelly, Corie Brown, and Joan O'C. Hamilton (1988), "Aging: Can It Be Slowed?" *Business Week*, (February 8), 58-64.

Stambler, Irwin (1986), "Uncertainties Pervade Forecasts of U.S. Energy Consumption," *Research & Development*, 28 (July), 41-42.

Stevens, Benjamin H. and George I. Treyz (1986), "A Multi-regional Model Forecast for the United States Through 1995," *American Economic Review*, 76 (May), 304-307.

Stover, John G. and Theodore J. Gordon (1978), "Cross-Impact Analysis," in *Handbook of Futures Research*, J. Fowles (ed.), Westport, Connecticut: Greenwood Press, 301-328.

Stubbart, Charles (1985), "Why We Need A Revolution In Strategic Planning," *Long Range Planning*, 18 (December), 68-76.

Su, Betty W. (1985), "The Economic Outlook to 1995: New Assumptions and Projections," *Monthly Labor Review*, 108 (November), 3-16.

Survey of Current Business (1985), "Metropolitan Area Projections of Income, Employment and Population to the Year 2000," 65 (October), 32-36.

Sutton, Howard (1986), "Marketing: Changing Channels," *Across the Board*, 22 (January), 12-13.

Swenson, Chester A. (1988), "How to Sell to a Segmented Market," *Journal of Business Strategy*, 9 No. 1 (January-February), 18-22.

Taylor, Bernard (1984), " Strategic Planning - Which Style Do You Need?" *Long Range Planning*, 17 No. 3 (June), 51-62.

Taylor, Bernard (1986-A), "Corporate Planning for the 1990s: The New Frontiers," *Long Range Planning*, 19 No. 6 (December), 13-18.

Taylor, Thayer C. (1986-B), "Meet the Sales Force of the Future: Older Female and More Productive," *Sales and Marketing Management*, 136 (March 10), 59-60.

Terpstra, Vern (1985), "The Changing Environment of International Marketing," *International Marketing Review*, 2 No. 3 (Autumn), 7-16.

Toffler, Alvin (1970), *Future Shock*, New York: Random House.

Toffler, Alvin (1981), *The Third Wave*, New York: Bantam Books.

Toffler, Alvin (1985), *The Adaptive Corporation*, New York: McGraw-Hill.

Tokarski, Kathy (1988), "Public Outcry Forces Hospitals to Confront Medical Waste Issue," *Modern Healthcare*, 18 No. 37 (September 9), 26-32.

Tonn, Bruce E. (1986), "500-Year Planning: A Speculative Provocation," *Journal of the American Planning Association*, 52 No. 2 (Spring), 185-193.

Tully, Shawn (1988), "Europe Gets Ready For 1992," *Fortune*, 117 No. 3 (February 1), 81-84.

Turner, Graham (1987), "The Future Ambitions of Japan's Financial Giants," *Long Range Planning*, 20/5 No. 105 (October), 11-20.

Urbanski, Al (1986), "Incentives: The Spouse Factor," *Sales & Marketing Management*, 137 No. 4 (September), 104-110.

Urbanski, Al (1987), "Merger Mania: What Marketers Need to Know," *Sales and Marketing Management*, 130 No. 2 (February), 30-35.

U.S. News and World Report (1984-a), "Ten Forces Reshaping America," (March 19), 40-52.

Van-Dam, Andre (1977), "Future of Global Business Forecasting," *Business Horizons*, 20 No. 4 (August), 46-50.

Varadarajan, P. Rajan and Mark W. Johnson (1987), "The Corporate Priorities of New CEOs: Implications for Marketers," *Akron Business and Economic Review*, 18 No. 4 (Winter), 57-68.

Vatter, Robert H. (1987), "Demographics: An Aid to Long-Term Forecasting and Planning," *Journal of Business Forecasting*, 6 No. 2 (Summer), 5-8.

Vatter, Robert H. (1986), "Generational Equality: The Issue of the 1990s," *Review of Business*, 7 No. 4 (Spring), 24-25.

Vernon, Raymond (1986), "Can U.S. Manufacturing Come Back?" *Harvard Business Review*, 64 (July-August), 98-106.

Verwayen, Henri (1984), "Social Indicators: Actual and Potential Uses," *Social Indicators Research*, 14, 1-28.

Wack, Pierre (1985), "Scenarios: Unchartered Waters Ahead," *Harvard Business Review*, 5 (September-October), 72-89.

Waldrop, Judith (1988), "The Fashionable Family," *American Demographics*, 10 No. 3 (March), 22-26.

Walsh, Doris (1983), "World Futures," *American Demographics*, 5 No. 8 (August), 38-39.

Webber, John C. (1986), "Packaged Goods Marketing Research - Where's It All Going?" *Journal of Advertising Research*, 26 (October-November), RC 3-RC 5.

Webster, Frederick E., Jr. (1986), "Marketing Strategy in a Slow Growth Economy," *California Management Review*, 28 No. 3 (Spring), 93-105.

Webster, Frederick E., Jr. (1988), "The Rediscovery of the Marketing Concept," *Business Horizons*, 31 No. 3 (May-June), 29-39.

Webster, Frederick E., Jr. (1981), "Top Management's Concern About Marketing: Issues for the 1980s," *Journal of Marketing*, 43 No. 3 (Summer), 9-16.

Weindling, Ralph and Sigmund Silbet (1987), "Landscape of the Industry to Come," *Computerworld*, 21 No. 46 (November 16), 83-92.

Weiner, Edith (1976), "Future Scanning for Trade Groups and Companies," *Harvard Business Review*, 54 No. 5 (September-October), 14, 174, 176.

Wendt, Henry (1985), "The Multinational of Tomorrow," *Across the Board*, 22 (September), 49-54.

Whaley, Richard and Brian Burrows (1987), "How Will Technology Impact Your Business?" *Long Range Planning* 20/5 No. 105 (October), 109-117.

Whelan, Elizabeth M. (1986), "Wishful Thinking About An Epidemic," *Across the Board*, 23 (October), 30-36.

Whittemore, Meg (1986), "Franchising's Future," *Nation's Business*, 74 No. 2 (February), 47-53.

Wildawsky, Aaron (1973), "If Planning Is Everything, Maybe It's Nothing," *Policy Sciences*, 4 No. 2, 127-153.

Wilson, David Gordon (1984), "Moving People and Goods Before the Year 2000," *Technology Review*, 87 No. 4 (May-June), 60-87.

Wilson, Ian H. (1978), "Scenarios," in *Handbook of Futures Research*, J. Fowles (ed.), Westport, Connecticut: Greenwood Press, 225-248.

Wilson, John W. and Scott Ticer (1985), "Superchips: The New Frontier," *Business Week*, (June 10), 82-85.

Yeskey, Dennis P. and C. Don Burnett (1986), "A Marketing Outlook for U.S. Businesses," *Journal of Business Strategy*, 7 (Fall), 5-6.

Yip, George S. (1985), "Who Needs Strategic Planning," *Journal of Business Strategy*, 6 (Fall), 30-41.

Young, John A. (1985), "Global Competition: The New Reality," *California Management Review*, 27 No. 3 (Spring), 11-25. See also: *Vital Speeches* (1985), 51 No. 15 (May), 466-470.

Zeithaml, Valerie A. (1988), "Consumer Perceptions of Price, Quality, and Value: A Means - End Model and Synthesis of Evidence," *Journal of Marketing*, 52 No. 3 (July), 2-22.

Zeithaml, Valerie A. (1985), "The New Demographics and Market Fragmentation," *Journal of Marketing*, 49 No. 3 (Summer), 64-75.

Zeithaml, Carl P. and Valerie A. Zeithaml (1984), "Environmental Management: Revising the Marketing Perspective," *Journal of Marketing*, 40 No. 2 (Spring), 46-53.

Zemke, Ron (1987), "Training in the 90's," *Training: The Magazine of Human Resource Development*, 24 (January), 40-53.

CHAPTER 6

A VIEW FROM THE TOP: VISIONARY EXECUTIVES

"The present has only a being in nature; things past have a being in memory only; but things to come have no being at all, the future being but a fiction of the mind..." Thomas Hobbes

Introduction

The problem-solving styles of experts have attracted a great deal of recent attention with much of it focusing on the use of computers to "expert systems." These systems help "non experts" function in a manner similar to experts.

While computers can facilitate performance, the purpose of this chapter is to help accomplish just that, to help understand and appreciate actual mind-sets of experienced, insightful CEOs as they consider Marketing 2000.[1]

As compared with novices, experts exhibit two important abilities:

1. They seem to sense, or know somewhat intuitively, what information to acquire and how to acquire it.

2. They are able to integrate large amounts of information into meaningful patterns.

Consider, for example, the formidable task facing soldiers who must be able to identify battlefield tanks as those of friends or foes. Since NATO and the Warsaw Pact countries have many different sizes and styles of tanks, and since their appearances are quite similar, this would appear to be a most difficult task. Experts, however, can quickly train novices to distinguish among them by focusing on one or two important discriminating features (Biederman and Shiffrar, 1987).

---

[1]A list of the executives interviewed is given in the Appendix on Methodology.

Thus, when it comes to discriminating between friendly and enemy tanks a little advice about where to look and what to look for suffices. When tasks are more complex, however, such as playing chess at the Master's level, experts bring into play the second capability — that of being able to integrate large amounts of information into meaningful patterns. For example, "Master chess players reconstructed with greater than 90% accuracy mid-game boards that they had seen for only five seconds" (Adelson 1984). Also in studies of the recall clusters of Master Go players, Reitman (1976) found abstract representations that were based on the attack and defense relationships in the game board.

The implication of the above for marketing is that individuals desiring to function in a more expert manner can usually profit by observing experts, to determine what information they use and how they structure it. Marketers desiring to become more adept in evaluating future developments may be able to hone their skills by considering the information in this chapter. It uses insights and verbatim quotations from CEO interviews.

The Style of the Experts

When asked to predict the future, the CEOs nearly always began by looking into the past, searching for trends and considering those that might be projectable. They also looked for propositions, generalizations, and relationships that have proven consistently true in the past. An example is the executive who stated "I kind of vote the way history does on textiles, cameras, televisions, and so forth. The low cost producer eventually, no matter where he is located, wins." Thus, he feels able to offer more accurate predictions about various other producers and industries, internationally.

The CEOs were quick to find concrete examples which illustrated abstract concepts they articulated, such as the practical examples stemming from Japanese experiences. These data points were then put in a larger context to form patterns, delineate trends, and permit generalizations about the future.

The CEOs were cautious about making too many extrapolations. They did not always proceed in a linear fashion. They were well aware that trends can reverse themselves, and often in their considerations of the future pointed out that "we may now come about full circle." They cautioned that for every trend there may be a countertrend, and their experiences rendered them sensitive to such possibilities. This was illustrated in the discussion of designer labels in department stores.

The CEOs also exhibited a pervasive readiness to acknowledge that changes which will affect the very foundations of their businesses will take place, and that they, as CEOs, needed to accommodate. Being attuned was seen as a requisite for success in tomorrow's marketplace. As one CEO put it, "...if you're not, somebody else will take your place. The question is how best to do it."

Objective

The interviews summarized in this chapter are designed to furnish insights from practitioners on the forefront of marketing and business decisions about how the future might impact on marketing. We hope to:

1. Show what relevant information experts seem to reference.

2. Show their integration of the information as they project out into the future.

3. Use the views of these executives to help identify future changes and their implications for Marketing 2000.

We have structured the information under rubrics usually included in typical marketing plans. The framework of our discussion is as follows:

    I.   Marketing Mix Considerations
        a. Product Strategy
        b. Price Strategy
        c. Distribution Strategy
        d. Promotion and Advertising
        e. Marketing Research
        f. Coordination with Other Business Activities
   II.   Marketing Targets
  III.   Strategic Considerations

Product Strategy

The U.S. is no longer the global standard of superior products. "The standards of excellence (are) higher in many countries than they are here," and that may well continue to be the case. That was the general opinion of CEOs. Japan was singled out, and the typical comment was that Japanese consumers "are asking for much higher quality than we tend to think is adequate, and they are getting it."

The fact that Japanese consumers are so demanding helped make Japanese companies globally superior and will continue to do so. A CEO in the food processing industry said:

I think a good illustration of that is that in Japan, we sell X Juice. We sell X Juice all over the world. Japan is the only market where the only way to get into the market is to have a lithographed can, and it cannot be a can that has any sign of a dent, any sign of any kind of rust or imperfection; it is just taken off the shelf. They do not allow that. Now, if you went into an American supermarket, you would find a ripped can, you would find a wrap-around label, you would find some scuffed. You are liable to find some dented on the shelf as I do every Saturday when I go to shop, and I keep trying to get them off there. In Japan you just do not see that because the supermarket operator, or the store operator, would never think of antagonizing his customers by putting anything on the shelf that was not absolutely perfect.

"You have got to come up with worldwide standards of excellence and options....You have got to have the innovations." "We have a thing or two to learn because we have to compete in their own yards (at) their levels of excellence." Thus, the combination of demanding consumers from other parts of the world and alternative product offerings from non U.S. corporations will raise future American marketing and product standards. They will force the U.S. to pay more attention to consumer desires and demands, to motivate American companies to provide better value, and to deliver the quality consumers deserve.

Things that might have been tolerated and not thought of in the past are, of course, very important to customers today — the sound of a door closing, a loose thread in a seat, the trim between the seat and the cushion. Those types of things are very much in the customers' minds today to a much greater degree than in the past; and certainly they are very strongly influenced by some of the kinds of things that have been important in the foreign markets in the past and now are available to our customers. Quality is definitely viewed differently today than it was a few years ago.

This focus on quality is altering the emphasis of the CEOs in their day-to-day managing:

We spent yesterday afternoon talking quality. Before, we looked at inventory and receivables. Now, we look at what our quality ratings are with each one of our customers; what are rejects; what's our cost of quality; what was our defect performance before.

Achieving actual quality, and developing and maintaining an image of quality will be high among marketing management priorities of the future. The era and aura of quality will be a dominant future marketing theme.

Targeting Products

With increasing emphasis on segmenting, niching and targeting markets, our CEOs said, "we shall see a great deal more of focused products...(products) for specific groups of people...very targeted products." This will mean vastly improved products in terms of performance and design and increased customer value and satisfaction. "If you design (a product) for a specific situation it is going to be better than if you slap (adjustments) on after." The result will be a change in philosophy from adjusting standardized products to designing and tailoring products for specific purposes — doing it right the first time so that products will look and function as though they were designed as part of the system rather than as individual units or parts. The approach will be one of designing products to meet customer requirements, rather than shoe-horning customer needs into available production capabilities.

The CEOs also noted the recognition of varying regional tastes. Regional products will be developed so that there may be a California, Florida, New York or mid-western version of the same nationally branded item. In this way, products will mesh better with market needs. Sample quotes from CEOs are:

> Regionalization is growing: we've been very aggressive in certain areas...carrying specific products for them.

> I would like to point out that we have made specific models, for example, a California (version) that we specifically tailored with different type of appointments, different type of exterior accouterments, specifically for the California market. We were quite successful in that.

Regional products, like all targeted products which are more precisely tailored to consumer wants and needs, are often based on the availability of flexible manufacturing capabilities, which in turn hinge on technological developments.

Developing Products More Quickly

Several respondents noted that in the past, the product development process was highly centralized, and there was a staff orientation that created various difficulties and slowed the product introduction process.

One CEO stated "We attacked this (product development) as marketers...and the central marketing crew did everything out of the textbook...we bombed." With such a high degree of centralization, by the time everything was done according to the procedures specified, and "all was coordinated and directed from headquarters, market conduct had changed." Cutting product development time will have high management priority in future years. The situation with regard to automobiles was summarized by a CEO who noted:

> Our current new car development is approximately a five-year process; a venture too long. We are trying to get down to three or three and one-half years...Time is cost.

Another executive agreed that the product development process just took too much time, there were too many staff people involved and too many branches and executives. We "had to find another way to get the product back into the market...we got the line managers to invent the product and get in the market...I think successfully this time." Another CEO stated:

> Getting the line people involved and compressing the time needed to develop and alter products will be important in the future.

Two future avenues to success were thus underscored: reducing the product development time-cycle and greater involvement of line executives. This means that products will not only be altered during annual model changes, but there will likely be continuous product change. There will be a lot of small product improvements, over time, that will add up to better quality and heightened consumer satisfaction.

According to one senior executive, "Everybody is doing his work from a timing standpoint. We have to be able to respond to changes and we are getting as fast as anybody. The re-organization of (our company) provided the ability to move much more rapidly than in the past." He talked about reducing future design time, finding ways to make money at much lower production levels, and keeping track of and adjusting to consumer preferences as constantly moving targets. Technology was seen as being an invaluable aid in many aspects of cutting response time. So was decentralization.

Several CEOs noted that the trend is away from centralization because of the need to address diverse markets quickly. Two observations shared were:

Centralization...does not work as well when companies expand across states and nations. Internationally we find as much as we try, it is difficult to provide the same product for Germany and England, and have it be totally satisfactory in each market. They are becoming more alike, but it's a relatively small trend. The German market is technically the more educated market that we deal with on a global basis. They will accept a higher purchase price for a technical feature. Not only will they be willing to pay for it, but they consider the products that don't have it as not in the running. We introduced (items) which you might sell as an option, or might even put up as standard in Germany because it's a requirement.

In a future attempt to both speed and improve product development, suppliers, and retailers, as well as consumers, will be very actively and directly involved in what was previously seen as the manufacturer's domain. In addition, they will be involved much earlier in the product development process. The CEO of a supplier noted:

One of the things you see today is that you get much earlier involvement in things than you did before. Soon they are expecting you to do a lot more design work all the way through. The major suppliers have their CAD/CAMs talking to customer CAD/CAMs.

The future will see a closer linking of manufacturers, suppliers, dealers and customers providing opportunities for developing a more coordinated and integrated marketing system, thereby improving marketing efficiency and productivity.

The respondents generally agreed that products and technologies will change much faster, which in turn will speed up the rates of product obsolescence. This has significant future implications, managerial and social, for marketing management. In one CEO's words:

The most recent example is the city of Norwood; we closed a plant there and they are suing us for leaving their community. Yet in today's world obsolescence of products is coming at a faster rate; plants will be closing and opening at a much faster rate as products and technologies...become obsolete. It is going to be very difficult to try and manage that in a way that minimizes the impact on communities and people; yet it is a fact of life. We're in a faster and faster rate of change which really says that obsolescence of any product will probably happen at a much faster rate than it has previously, and those facilities, in many cases, are not going to be adaptable to the next generation or the replacement-type products.

> Herein lies a future marketing challenge: to alleviate the undesirable effects of product changes while capitalizing on the benefits.

In the factories and service firms of the future, the emphasis will shift away from just achieving economies of scale to achieving economies of scope. The latter refers to the ability of manufacturers and distributors to provide great product variety while still significantly containing costs of manufacturing and distribution. In the case of the service firm, it refers to providing additional revenue-producing services, through existing systems, at little or no increase in fixed cost.

Price Strategy

CEOs fully expect future markets to be much more competitive, for both differentiated products and commodities. The result will be continuing pressure on both prices and costs. The very nature of competition is expected to change, somewhat limiting future price discretion, because competition is taking place amongst "a wave of giants...big, big companies that are smart...not making a lot of mistakes, very capable of being innovative and strong."

In Marketing 2000, "competitors are going to be well funded, and skillful." International suppliers will exert much more pressure on domestic prices. This will generate some difficult marketing situations for domestic producers and distributors. International companies "are dramatically trying to improve their cost structure and pricing. We can't price as they do." The statements of many CEOs indicate that foreign companies may be better poised to meet future pricing situations than U.S. companies will be. Several respondents explained, for example, that in order to maintain competitive prices, foreign producers would take actions that U.S. companies cannot or will not — the Japanese are now absorbing adverse currency fluctuations "as a reduction in profits." It was noted that this will eventually be offset by future cost reductions as a result of increasing productivity. The implications were that continuing pressures will be placed on future prices that U.S. firms can charge and that profit margins could suffer.

On the other hand, in considering future consumer purchase reactions, many CEOs also saw price as becoming less of an overriding consideration. "People are interested in much more today than where can I get the lowest priced (product)...In fact, the lowest priced (ones) are not the (ones) that are selling." Several CEOs noted that large segments of the population will place more emphasis on quality, value, service, and durability in their future purchases.

As product changes, innovations, and adjustments become more frequent, the time period to recapture costs will be shortened. This is expected to impact on future pricing strategies, suggesting higher initial margins, and prices. Unanticipated contingencies as well as anticipated profit squeezes will have to be taken into consideration. The pricing/time compression, was further emphasized by one respondent who, in discussing prices, stated "you have to reduce your planning horizon...your planning time." Others commented on the need for price flexibility with the capability of making rapid price adjustments to meet changing competitive conditions.

Commenting on the changing perspective of price in market segmentation, one CEO underscored the need to target prices in a more focused manner. He stressed that segmentation based simply on price sensitivity will not be sufficient. He said,

> In the past, our strategy was to have something in the product line that was low priced, medium priced, and high priced to satisfy the whole market. That just doesn't work. The future approach is seen as one of great precision in setting prices that are pinpointed to better meet both market and company needs.

Distribution Strategy

The CEOs, almost unanimously, saw significant change in future distribution strategies. They affirmed distribution's increasingly important role in future marketing management decisions. In particular, those respondents representing consumer goods companies seemed to agree that not only will distribution be a more important component of the marketing mix, but that there will be widespread changes in future distribution channels which will reverberate throughout marketing. "Companies are now adapting products, and indeed the whole marketing mix, to move into new distribution channels that match up with market segments more precisely and effectively."

Future executives will pay more attention to their selection of distribution channels. In the past, distribution channels seemed to spring up rather haphazardly, on a patched-up and piece-meal basis, and to expand illogically with the company becoming locked in. Distribution channel decisions predicated on past situations tended to become "encased in cement" a situation that respondents felt could not be tolerated in the future.

One CEO, commenting on the less than logical development of his company's distribution system, succinctly stated, "We haven't intentionally gone out to build branches, but...We've acquired a very broad distribution system...We'd better know how we're doing." Another commented, "We've been trying for two years to figure out what to do with at least our hub branches. ...We've had several major projects underway...to retrofit our branch system...we now try and get an efficient fit...go back in and rebuild the distribution system." The point underscored was that past distribution patterns will not serve future marketing requirements effectively, and that the haphazard approaches to distribution strategies will not suffice in the future. Effective and efficient distribution will become an important competitive requisite of Marketing 2000. It will be a most essential component of the delivery of customer value.

Among the marketing management implications are that in the future, companies here and abroad will be forced to reassess their distribution systems and bring them more into line with market changes. Distribution systems will be rehabilitated, redeveloped, retrofitted, and changed significantly to meet future market requirements. They will become key determinants of marketing success. The appearance of absolutely new product lines, products of the type that were never before available, that require different support and delivery systems, will spur many changes in distribution.

In the future, real estate will become an even more important ingredient in channel considerations than it has been in the past. One CEO, expressing a common theme, noted that current distribution channels of most U.S. companies are rooted in properties that were "good ten to fifteen years ago." This favors the more recent and future international competitors entering U.S. markets. They will be able to select properties more in tune with current and future market requirements. They can develop a more efficient and effective distribution structure, which can be a distinct marketing advantage. Compounding this, in many international markets, where distributors are linked to single sources of supply, and where neither established distributors nor desirable locations are available, there is a substantial barrier to U.S. companies.

Cultural factors can become barriers that prevent distributors from accepting foreign franchises and products. This can force "foreigners to get brand new distributors...to set up their own system...with dealers with no experience...and in less desirable locations," which will be a major handicap. This often happens in countries like Japan and may be widespread.

Retailing

Changing patterns of retailing are seen as better able to accommodate the expanding variety of future consumer needs and desires. Mid-sized stores will be challenged competitively, consolidation will occur and the development of larger retailing units is expected. At the same time, efficient smaller stores will exist side-by-side with their larger counterparts, featuring "a homestyle approach, with personalized attention, and becoming touchy feely."

To obtain goods with some universal fashion acceptability, designer labels have been embraced in the department store. But, in the future, it was noted, the basis for this "marriage of convenience" may erode.

> When I was growing up in this business, we did not have designer labels. The Bonwit Teller label was the label, and you went to Bonwit Teller because they had it for you if you were that kind of customer. If you wanted more jazz, maybe you went to Saks; that was their look. You went to Lord & Taylor for the American, country look, which was predominant at Lord & Taylor. Each store had something special to offer. All at once, these stores took on the designer labels and retailing became a real estate deal. It was whether Calvin Klein had more space than Bill Blass. Every store had the same merchandise because they had to have solid representation of each designer and each store was trying to out-do one another, without taking the consumer to mind.

> What has happened now is that those very same designers that insisted on being very well-placed in the stores are not pleased with how the stores are representing them. Ralph Lauren has opened up his own boutique, and that's not new news, but others are starting to do it and that is new news. The department stores are no longer only competing with other department stores, they are competing with the designer for the same customer. This means the pie is getting smaller. I feel this will lead the stores to search for new and different areas of merchandising. For example, they are going into their own labels and are doing private labels. What we see taking place is a defense mechanism; and what other routes they may take is still to be seen.

This insightful comprehensive statement, supported by the opinions of many CEOs, highlighted the overlapping of future retailing images and segments, the desire for control of labels and merchandising support, the lack of attention to consumers, the movement to direct channels, and the diffusion of the range of competitors. The future retailing challenge of being new, innovative, and differentiated, as a result, may become more difficult to achieve.

In the past, large retailers have used computers to centralize buying and consolidate operations, thereby generating distribution efficiencies and lower operating costs. This centralization of control, however, makes it more difficult for chains to be attentive to the market shifts and to consider the changing preferences, and local and regional desires of customers.

A current major retailing development related to computers and control was singled out and described as a "retailing revolution...computerization at the back door." It will affect future retailing management, ordering, stocking, inventory control, and physical handling operations.

Computers will give retail chains the ability to individualize their stores while still maintaining efficiency. The ability of individual stores to maintain a computerized perpetual inventory, and have computer assisted ordering, will be facilitated by the widening use of technology such as scanning devices and standardized bar codes:

> I see a time where virtually every product will have some universal bar code. UBC's will be far more subtle in their presentation rather than looking like something that you buy in the supermarket, and therefore those will be applied to all goods that we could buy. Readers will become more sophisticated and much less visible.

In addition, new technologies can refine conventional methods of distribution making them more efficient and effective. For example:

> In upstate New York there has been a trial of UPC coded coupons, which have the bars on them so that when the coupon is cashed in, it goes over the scanner, and is checked against the proper evaluation of proper couponing and all the rest of it. There is a big move on to see if that is a workable approach to the whole industry because they are just saturating these coupons out there with a lot of rip-off applications, and a lot of inefficiencies.

Powerful, low-cost computer systems may make it impossible for individual stores, within chain organizations, to get back to more of the entrepreneurial approach. In the future, intrapreneurship in retailing will be encouraged. Some retailers are already moving in that direction:

> I do see a possibility of a regional breakup so that we do get back to the possibility of the entrepreneurial system. There are some large chains in the world of retail today that have specific buyers for each of their stores and that is an expensive way of doing business. However, it works well for them because they know what the customer's needs are and what they will purchase. This leads to fewer markdowns and increased sales because the buyers are meeting the cus-

tomer's needs, because they know the pulse of that specific market. This might be a format which more stores may use in the future.

Because producers throughout the world have been increasing capacity, they will be fighting for access to customers. One implication is that there will be more manufacturer involvement in direct distribution. "You need to go right to the store with your own controlled distribution system to get the kind of quality assurance...that you really need." Some manufacturers may follow the example of Ralph Lauren and attempt to deal directly with "their customers" if they have a strong brand name — but retailers may try to hold shoppers, as "their customers," by emphasizing private store brands and offering special services, such as personal shoppers, alterations, and home decorating consultants.

As manufacturers and retailers in Marketing 2000 compete for customers, and distribution outlets scramble and multiply, consumers will succeed in imposing their preferences to a much greater degree. It was also pointed out that preferences may conflict with those of channel members; wholesalers, retailers, and manufacturers. In foods, for example, retailer preferences, ranging from the most to the least desirable, are for: canned, frozen, refrigerated, then fresh foods. Consumer preferences, however, are usually just the reverse: fresh, refrigerated, frozen, and then canned. The trend among consumers is an increasing emphasis on freshness, which complicates distribution. It was suggested that in the future there may be more future channel conflicts between intermediaries and customers, as in the above example, as opposed to the more traditional channel conflict situation between intermediaries.

As future technology makes available new methods for reaching consumers, manufacturers will be receptive to them. Commenting on an evolving new method of distribution, a CEO stated:

> Homeshopping is one of the biggest things to come along and I believe its going to be with us in one form or another — and the capability of interacting. ...You have the job still to be done of the marriage of the entertainment, and the motivating side of television, and the random access capability of the computer. Those things have not yet been put together, but I believe in 15 years they will. Rather than watching Home Network and just whatever comes along, and every merchandise offer that comes along, you would be able to say "I'm interested in automobiles" and have a whole segment on automobiles that somebody will prepare; and "I'm interested in magazines," and a whole segment on magazines would come up. That's what we're trying to figure out now — if we want to be involved in

this business, and, of course, if you're not, somebody else will take your place. The question is how to do it.

Non-store retailing was identified as a trend that may see future reinforcement. Among the change factors which may well speed the trend are:

1. An increased emphasis on consumer self-identity which will necessitate more product variety due to the fragmentation of markets, which in turn will foster increased inventories and display space, straining the physical capacity of the store;

2. Growth in the number of working women;

3. A desire for more leisure time;

4. Increasing costs of going shopping;

5. Improved information about products and retailers; and

6. Technology.

Consumers are becoming more time-conscious as they confront a poverty of time to carry out and enjoy their preferred lifestyles. This will be increasingly reflected in how merchandise is marketed, how it is displayed, where it is offered, and how it is packaged. Any distribution system, particularly retailing, will have to focus on expanding discretionary and enjoyable consumer time, and reducing the undesirable time spent on chores. "User friendly" will be a key quality of future distribution systems:

> Everybody is busy today, whether you have a career or not, everyone is time conscious. Consequently, it isn't the same casual shopping spree that women used to undertake. In order to capture your audience, you have to service them quickly. The merchandise must be pulled together so they can target it quickly; also a lot of it is self-service. From that aspect, mail-order is going to continue to grow and become very strong. I still feel tele-shopping is going to take a while, especially for soft goods, because people still like to touch and feel to a great degree, but eventually this will also become stronger.

> Distribution and packaging are inextricably intertwined, and there is an enormous revolution of packaging going on. In foods, "the microwave thing" is driving everybody. We are dual ovenable...we are into aseptic packaging...plastic squeezables...we keep looking for the ultimate packages that are, what I call, user friendly.

Service and Repair

Revised approaches to product development, particularly among durable products, will change the product/service nexus. Formerly, products were built with a great emphasis on cost, embodying the philosophy that there would be some defective products made, that defective products would be repaired and serviced later, and that it was up to the buyer, in making purchases, to beware. Under this approach, distribution channel members made significant profits from servicing products, often defective products. In the future, there will be a philosophy of achieving zero defects, with an emphasis on quality, on doing it right the first time, on standing behind products, and on a modular approach encouraging self-service and less servicing. Thus, there could be a decline in the product maintenance and repair sector of the business. As a result "we shall see a restructuring of distribution...maybe a new policy of extending geographical areas for exclusive dealers, or combining (product) lines. Distributors in the future will have to downsize service facilities and turn more of that space into other operations." Service, sometimes seen as a most profitable part of past business opportunities, may now become an unprofitable segment.

Manufacturer/dealer cooperation regarding servicing will be increased. Manufacturers will play more of a lead role. Computers will permit manufacturer/dealer/consumer linkages that provide accurate and instantaneous information to diagnose and solve consumer problems.

The future will see a trend to more hi-tech and smart products. Currently, "products are technically much more sophisticated and (authorized dealers) are about the only ones that can service them and even they have trouble." Product sophistication is projected to increase by leaps and bounds in the future, providing a challenge to educate and train technicians to service them. Continuous product development and improvements, moreover, will create continuing needs for servicing and education support. Manufacturers, therefore, will likely assume greater responsibility for servicing their products, for updating and training dealers, and for monitoring consumers about product/service satisfaction.

Sales Force Management

Regarding future changes in the sales force, CEOs stressed two expectations: one concerning perspectives, and the other concerning market knowledge. As to perspectives, more members of the sales force will see themselves not as selling a product or a commodity, such as plastic or telephones, but as total problem-solvers. They will be a part of a marketing team assisting customers in solving their problems efficiently and in generating satisfaction. They will be expected to bring additional services and capabilities to customers. They will help customers capitalize on their business or personal opportunities and to readily overcome hurdles and difficulties.

"We have a reservoir of materials technology that we can bring to our customers," said a CEO who went on to explain that it will not matter what materials are required. The sales rep, as the total problem-solver, will be able to oblige customers and meet their total needs, rather than just specializing in one material such as stainless steel. This will provide some future insurance for companies, for it was explained that such an approach limits specialization, "and we can also hedge our bets." The result may indeed be company diversification, but diversification to extend customer service, rather than to spread company risks by serving new markets and customers. It was emphasized that, under this approach, the core business "becomes our customers, with a focus on adjusting to serve them better."

As to market knowledge, sales reps in the future will take a longer run perspective to market opportunities and will be much more knowledgeable and informed. "You could talk to any of our salespeople and they will tell you what's out there in five years — what the opportunities are; what we can get and not get." In the emerging information age, the sales organization will become front-end problem-solvers and critical providers of market information.

Promotion and Advertising

Along with distribution, advertising is the component of the marketing mix that many of the senior executives saw changing the most in Marketing 2000. The thought was often expressed that more resources will be put into advertising — both new funds and money redirected from some of the other business and marketing activities.

The theme of moving from mass to segmented markets, was again reflected in the discussion of future advertising developments. Several respondents noted that the rapid increase in advertising costs of the past will likely continue, and that companies will not be able to afford advertising to the general market "when only 10% of them are going to buy." The expectation for the future is an increase in effectiveness by the use of more focused and specialized advertising (as with cable-directed marketing), and the allocation of more money to pinpoint potential customers and markets.

The future will see increasing personalization of advertising and the tailoring of messages. The movement will be "from mass media to more directive media," from more general advertising and media, to decisions that "get media closer to the action," from avoiding frequency and continuity decisions to the timing of typical advertising to reach people when they are ready to make purchase decisions. The comments reinforcing such ideas were: "In the future, I shall transfer some of the mass media dollars I used to spend on TV and radio (advertising) into the stores. Local television advertising will replace network advertising."

Several executives expressed the belief that not only will local media and advertising become relatively more important in the future, but that these will be coupled with specialized communications and market segmentation. This can lead to more precise targeting of advertising, as was described by the CEO who elaborated with the following example:

> If you are a person who has bought a boat, lives in California, lives in certain areas, we know that you are highly likely to buy a truck, not a car. So, we want to talk to you about four-wheel drive, trailer towing, about a matched boat and a vehicle called a truck.

It is expected that more local and regional ad agencies will be used:

> In order to focus our advertising, we actually hired a different advertising agency just for California to be sure that we were focusing on the specific demographics of California. I guess you can say California psychographics count more than demographics.

The resulting regional and even international advertising specialization was emphasized by several respondents. Typical was the CEO who explained: "In Europe, we may have 20 major countries, and marketing and advertising (will be) done by country." That, of course, can be costly. It was explained that some economies can be gained by using common elements such as the same film background for every country and interposing a different voice and language.

Another more general advertising trend was forecast, related to company positioning and image. One CEO summarized this by stating that management will desire to position the company as "caring." And this will have many organizational and personnel ramifications. It will also prescribe a new role for advertising. For the "caring company is the kind of organization that we want to be and have our employees feel a part of. And we want the marketplace to perceive us that way. That positioning theme has set in motion not only part of our advertising effort, but a lot of our internal training. ...It's becoming a core strategy for management." This highlights the integration of future advertising strategy with the overall marketing approach that will be adopted by companies in the future.

Marketing Research

With the availability of improved information technology, marketing is going to become more investigative than it already is, furnishing unprecedented amounts of insightful, timely information about markets, consumers, and purchase behavior. Marketers will learn to follow people's electronic "paper" trails. For example, they will use credit card records, add in a credit reporting service's data base, utilize a file of warranty card registration forms, and so on, to obtain a pretty clear picture of an individual customer — complete with name, address, and phone number. This undreamed of aggregation of data can provide companies with opportunities for pinpointing and understanding actual and potential consumers, and satisfying their needs. This will result in improved design, increased product functionality, higher quality, better value, and the specific tailoring of products and services. CEOs noted that, in the future, they will have to pay greater heed to consumers. They cautioned companies "to get rid of all inhibitions," "to get outside and deal with customers," and "don't say that you don't have a budget...if the consumers want it, do it anyway."

Referring to the heightened use of marketing research in future product development, one CEO used present actions to reflect on the future, noting:

> We spend probably more market research money by a factor of two or three than we have in the past to try to identify what the consumer wants.

To get a feel for marketing themes and consumer trends, it was suggested that special consideration be given to those geographic areas that are "leading indicators" of consumer preferences.

> California is the hottest thing and out of California will come California cuisine, California clothes, and the California pallet in paint and home furnishings. Right now it's California, tomorrow it could be Maine.

Cautions were raised about marketers becoming "locked into an image (of) certain perceptions that are not shared on the outside." Still marketing research will be helpful in spreading and lowering per unit costs by finding common denominators that will make a product successful across markets. In discussing research seeking common tastes across countries, an executive emphasized that:

> The only common element we find is lifestyle. Lifestyle is the only one that transcends markets. ...If you take a certain lifestyle, the people in Britain will like it as much as the people in Germany and rate it the same. However, the people of that particular lifestyle might be only 10% in Britain and 40% in Germany.

While it could be important to research geographic indicators and existing demands, companies still have an obligation to be on the cutting edge of innovation. One CEO cautioned: "It's not always the customer who knows what he wants," and another looking to the future stated, "There will always be a time when you've got to develop (products) even if the customer does not know what he wants." That philosophy will likely lead to greater future reliance on test marketing, not only by manufacturers, but also by retailers. This will create difficulties for many. A CEO explained:

> Everybody is tired of hearing about The Limited, but they test market and it has been successful. They will find something, test market it and, if it works really well, go after it in a big way. But most of the stores really don't have the time to test market; they are buying so close to the time of need. Consequently, they don't give themselves the opportunity to test. Testing is viable where there is a controlled atmosphere like The Limited which is autonomous, vs. Macys or Saks, where there are so many layers of management that by the time you get an order placed, the time is gone.

Future product development will be more costly. Thus, it will be more important than ever to develop prototypes and to test features, which in turn will add to marketing research activities and costs. But, it was pointed out that the stakes of not testing are very high. "It costs a lot of money, money well worth it... (to) find out what actual and potential customers like and dislike."

Although the use of marketing research is expected to increase, managerial judgment will not be reduced significantly. Decisions will not be made automatically by the numbers. Rather, as one executive explained insightfully, "when you get done with the marketing research, it really involves 30 to 40% of your decisions. ...Some of it is still gut feel." Regardless of the data available, "you still have to take a chance." And it was explained that in the future more, not less, executive "gut feel," may be required.

In Marketing 2000, it will be more important "to be aware of the direction of the market, of the trends...what you know is going on and take cues." Marketing research will be able to furnish executives with more pertinent, relevant, and timely information with which to assess market opportunities, increase efficiency and effectiveness, and improve customer satisfaction. It will remain an important contributing force for overall company profitability. But its insights will increasingly permeate the total operating system. Combined with better futures information, marketing research will help marketing managers carry out their responsibilities more effectively.

Coordination With Other Business Activities

Among the factors deemed most important in future economic growth and competitive advantage, the CEOs cited the future "cost of money." One noted that in the past our "competitive advantage grew out of the fact that we were a generator of relatively low cost cash," which gave the U.S. a big advantage. We will not enjoy that advantage in the future. Now the Japanese have the advantage and "will pay less for their money in the market. Therefore, they will be able to compete for a piece of the business more effectively somewhere else." "From a competitive standpoint, what you pay for money is very important."

The changing value of money has become critical. CEOs emphasized that actual profits may have little or "nothing to do with the operation...you are doing well down there, but the minute there is a devaluation — that goes through your balance sheet and you have nothing to do with it." This requires greater focus on predicting future market risks and vulnerabilities. It also points to the need for new standards to evaluate future international marketing operations. As global markets increase in general importance the problems are compounded. Future marketing managers may feel great frustration because of their lessened direct influence over profitability. The dominance of exogenous factors over internal marketing decisions and operations will lead to the need for increased knowledge and competence in the use of tools associated with international finance, and for the coordination of marketing activities with finance. The marketing manager's job requirements will thus be extended — greater reliance on international financial skills — but the risk will be increased, nonetheless.

Market Targets

Previously, marketing organizations were geared for mass, mass production, and mass distribution, which is consonant with centralization, organizational control, homogeneity, standardization, and uniformity. But CEOs see future divisions as seeking uniqueness, individuality, distinction, heterogeneity, and the advantages that flow from relating operations closely to specific markets. This is more in tune with decentralization, organizational diversity, flexibility, variations, and individualization, which can in turn generate "continentality between divisions."

Almost all CEOs addressed the topic of segmentation, pointing out that the mass markets of yesteryear would be replaced by mini-mass, thinner, more focused, and fragmented market segments of the future. The future importance of adopting niche strategies was underscored. Some of the comments made were: "You cannot address the mass market anymore; instead of going mass, you are going segmented, small market;" "Market fragmentation will abound. ...There will be fewer, very large markets of the past;" "We are developing products for specific niches." A transformation away from the mass to more focused, narrower market targets is consonant with CEO thinking about the future.

The future emphasis on the segmentation process now in place was underscored by CEOs who noted: "The market segmentation process is used to determine the image and constraints — the boundaries within which a division works." "The breakup of mass markets into finer segments and narrower fragments means that products will be fine-tuned to specific markets; this requires different design, flexible manufacturing facilities." "We have a segmentation plan as to each division's marketing identity, market focus, brand equity, and so forth."

Future requirements for putting effective segmentation programs in place were cited as being: good information about segments, insights into how to adjust and tailor products and services, the capacity to make the required adjustments, the selection of appropriate distribution channels, and the tailoring of communications. And it was cautioned that "you have to keep looking at those segments every year because the next group moving up does not behave the same." Future market segments were perceived as becoming even more dynamic moving targets than is presently the case.

One executive, commenting on future segmentation, emphasized that, "there are two pieces to segmentation — distribution segmentation and product/strategy segmentation." He explained that both will receive increasing future attention. Another CEO summarized future segmentation bases as including: "demographics, the tastes and preferences of older consumers, regional rather than national markets, individual con-

sumers, individual households, and individual stores." A third commented that "Markets will be segmented on an individual store level with
products available for the demographic and cultural profile of that store."
Moreover, he noted that "stores can be patterned after...demographics
surrounding the store."

Respondents expressed general agreement that information technology
will lead to an increased ability to identify specific market segments. In
addition, it was explained that in the future, computer-assisted design and
manufacturing (CAD/CAM), coupled with flexible manufacturing systems, will permit companies to deliver products tailored to specific segments.

Supermarket scanners, consumer credit data bases, and computerized
magazine circulation lists will be among the billions of bits of information that computers have stored about who buys what, when, and where,
which is going to change the face of marketing. They will help transform the concept of a mass marketed good by providing marketers with
ready access to more precise information about consumer buying habits.
Stated one CEO:

> I think we'll see a great deal more focused products. Probably a good
> example is what Pontiac did with Fiero. There is a two passenger car
> with almost no trunk space. It's obviously not a car for everybody.
> But it's a car for a single female, working woman whose traveling is
> done in the city. This is an example of a very targeted vehicle.

When the likelihood of increased segmentation is combined with
expected overcapacity, new industry entrants, and keener competition,
the manufacturing premiums that will be placed on flexibility and short
runs in the future becomes clearer.   Regarding shorter manufacturing
runs, one manufacturer reported, "That's our niche. That's what we do
well. We were the people who got the shorter run...that is a bonanza to
us." Similarly, they can provide future market opportunities for many
companies now geared to the mass.

Several CEOs noted that future strategic marketing thinking will be
more in line with the "small can be profitable" perspective, which will
replace the "bigger is better" mass marketing theories of the past. One
CEO's insightful comment, summarizing those of several others, is the
statement that in the past "we have adopted a mass philosophy along
with a modus operandi of sloppy marketing." He explained that a lot of
slack was permitted in the marketing system. Products and programs
were thrown at the mass market with varying results. The future strategy

however, will be "to pick worthwhile segments and build up a mass by appealing to each segment. Companies must adjust to the wants and needs of each segment."

Key future segmentation activity, it should be noted, will include not just the decomposition of markets. It will also include their reconstitution to create an adequate, critical, profitable mass. The strategy of adding together small niches across demographic and national boundaries, that comprise profitable market segments, will represent another thrust in Marketing 2000.

Strategic Situation

The CEOs, without exception, referred to fundamental changes occurring in international markets, including the future emergence of a global economy with keener international competition and manufacturing overcapacity. Overcapacity was seen as resulting in heightened emphasis on marketing considerations: increased quality, improved customer value, and improved marketing productivity. Some CEOs saw this leading to a restructuring of specific industries and the modification of management philosophies, including those of marketing management.

Typical is the statement by the CEO who emphasized that "the whole world is in a state of overcapacity...all of these products at one time had growth rates that were unbelievable ...now industry is operating at 60%, 70% or 75% of capacity worldwide." This oversupply will be heightened by continuous streams of imports of offshore products. In the past, "most of the prosperity of lesser developed countries has resulted from access to the United States market." The U.S. will remain a relatively open market. The U.S. will also pressure its trading partners to open their markets. But with markets saturated, the lesser developed countries will suffer in many ways — e.g., in exports of raw materials — even as they become attractive locations for low-cost manufacturing.

As a result of oversupplies, several CEOs expect to see "a big shake-out in most industries," with only the most efficient producers surviving. Markets are not able to support current productive capabilities, let alone the future capacities that will be coming on-line from newly industrialized countries. It was suggested by several CEOs that international accommodations will be made, and that future international marketing efforts "are going to get more compatible...somebody is going to say we can't all sell." The implications are that orderly market agreements, voluntary restraints, and cooperative arrangements will be reached, implicitly or explicitly, among competitors in global markets. Such marketing accommodations will tend to harmonize future production capacities and reduce some of the destructive competitive practices.

Several CEOs also pointed to developments that may create a kaleidoscope of new markets — in Asia, in a less regulated and more open European market, and among upscale shoppers in the U.S. And it was pointed out that market opportunities exist for U.S. firms in many countries because they have not yet been targeted.

Still, the perception of the U.S. as a market may change. If nationalism and protectionism become endemic on a global basis, the American market will not be quite as open. With keener international competition, U.S. companies losing money, markets becoming more fragmented, and foreign governments involved in protecting their own companies and markets, the U.S. would adopt a posture of being more protective of its own long-run global market interests, with government working more closely with business and encouraging international business cooperation.

Consumerism and Environmental Concerns

The CEOs in our study saw the consumer movement, at present and in the near future, as being less active than it was during the 1960s and 1970s. However, various important future issues of the environmental movement were noted, and it is believed by some that the two would combine to affect marketing. For example, the possibility of shortages was not cast aside. One CEO commented, "everybody has forgotten about waiting in line (for gas). I suppose there will be another crisis and it will come full circle."

Several years ago, when we conducted our interviews, the respondents were not overly concerned with future consumerist or environmental issues. But even then, the futures literature indicated that the crisis cycle could peak by the year 2000. The CEOs, however, did not expect fuel shortages to be the root cause of future concerns. Then, as now, it seemed more likely that any impact on marketing may be more likely attributed to the fruition of several of the following speculations: (Brown, Flavin, and Wolf, 1988; Dworkin and Sheffet 1985; Manley 1987; *Petroleum Economist*, 1986; Stambler, 1986.)

> 1. International industrial crises become pervasive global problems. As industrial accidents occur and scandals mount, managers will be operating in a fishbowl where product problems and ethical considerations will have to be confronted and cannot be swept under the rug. Examples are the Valdez accident,

Chernobyl, and the current investigation of false test result reports of some generic pharmaceutical products.

2. The consumer movement, temporarily dormant, awakens, and is organized to span national boundaries, as is evidenced by some international boycotts, and human and animal concerns. Products made of fur and ivory may be precursors of future actions.

3. The rush to enter markets overrides new product safety testing, resulting in a renewed liability crisis and/or increased demand for product recalls.

4. Insurance companies show mounting concern over how to spread the risk of environmental and industrial hazards, catastrophes, and wastes.

5. More severe penalties become associated with damage, as is evidenced in recent product liability legislation. The expansion of strict liability increases awards of punitive damages. This leads to new theories regarding product liability, such as "delayed manifestation." Organization leaders are forewarned about the likelihood of more severe penalties for damaging the environment or individuals, even from actions whose long-term consequences are yet to be determined.

The future impacts of these events are likely to be far worse for some firms and for society than was the case in yesteryear. Executives will be wise to closely monitor the pulse of domestic and international situations, by gathering and analyzing data from local, national, and worldwide surveys.

Keeping Customers

One executive explained: "We have been such an earnings-driven organization, as opposed to market-share driven, that we have skilled ourselves in exploiting the next product. ...We exploit the product/market rather than the customer base that the company already has in house." CEOs agreed that attention is now directed to company capacities and productive capabilities rather than customers, and customers are not being served as effectively as possible. When companies are solely committed to earnings, profit and growth goals, it was felt they "search out the next profitable product as opposed to trying to (satisfy) the existing customer." "That will change over the next ten years" and the emphasis will be on the "satisfaction of existing customers; serving present customers well to build market share."

Diversification

The preponderance of opinion seemed to be that specialization, concentration, and doing that which a company can do well will be dominant future tendencies. "Companies have to build a niche for themselves," and that "requires a focus."

Regardless of the diversification spurt of the 1970s, CEOs expressed concern about future diversification and see a general return to core markets, core products, and activities. "We'd rather stay at something that we know something about." "It (diversification) has been a very difficult experience for us because we just don't understand that kind of business." A CEO observed:

> Corporations will divest big hunks of what they built up because they are not getting the kind of return expected. They are going back to basics and will become more powerful and competitive.

Uncoupling of past diversification thrusts rids companies of inefficient units. Expectations are that greater productivity and market satisfaction will accrue, value will be enhanced and profits may be improved. Staying with core businesses that have growth opportunities can enhance company competitiveness, as was pointed out:

> It is difficult to maintain organizations that are highly proficient in vastly different types of businesses. ...It is difficult to mesh corporate cultures.

> Diversify slowly in the future, and make sure that you know the business you are going into,

A continuing trend to more careful diversification was seen at two levels:

1. Existing companies will continue to diversify into new markets and products, with diversification closely related to current operations.

2. Companies outside an industry will still enter via diversification, but will enter into new industries more carefully. This can mean increasingly competitive future markets and more market fragmentation.

So, companies will build on the efficiency and effectiveness of specialization, capitalizing on the knowledge, and insights of a core business. Then, by developing global strategic partnerships, and further extending the base of the core business, companies can penetrate markets worldwide.

Competition and Competitive Strategy

The CEOs expressed widespread agreement that the impact of competition, especially international competition, will be substantially intensified in Marketing 2000. "International competitors will move into more of our fundamental industries — industries where we have always been the leaders, such as food and food-processing." One CEO cautioned, "Just don't stand there looking...and saying, oh well, they will not come into (this) business...(think) rather, someone will do it and we must expect that."

> Everybody who has a design is trying to sell into this market. It's probably the only profitable market in the world. Toyota is the only (automobile) company making money in Japan. Hardly anybody is making a significant amount of money in Europe. The profitable automobile market is here. In Japan, there is far greater capacity than there is the ability to absorb more products, so the market is saturated there. Europe is in a situation where it has been for many years — a more limited market than the U.S. by far. It's a very fragmented market.

> There has been a watershed change. We are now something different than post World War II America. We are no longer kingpin in anything.

Global competition will set the tone for the U.S. and for U.S. companies marketing abroad. A new twist: arch-rival competitors appear to be using cooperation as a competitive weapon. The high cost of R&D, lack of resources (financial and human), the rush toward emerging global markets, the need to build distribution, and having to overcome trade restrictions are among the factors that will alter competitive philosophies. Such philosophies were previously built on distrust, secrecy, centralized authority, and the like. International cooperation, resulting in various forms of co-venturing and market sharing, was espoused as a future trend.

Government and Legal Influences

Most of the CEOs interviewed felt that there will be more governmental regulation and legal red-tape facing marketing in the future in both domestic and international markets. This was seen by some as boding ill.

> The price of entering any business now is getting more and more expensive. I despair because this nation was made great because people could enter a business easily and watch it grow with a minimum of regulatory agencies hovering around them. As we raise the thresh-

old of what it costs to enter a business, we lower our chances of being competitive in the future.

There will likely be more regulation concerning citizens' privacy (giving out or selling telephone numbers, customer information, purchase histories, and other personal data), environmental issues, (e.g. pollution control), and consumer protection and safety (e.g. air bags in cars).

The ability of marketing executives to access detailed information about consumers is already conflicting with consumers' felt need for privacy. Legislation will address how far marketing can go. For example, a CEO in the direct marketing field observed:

> There isn't a week that goes by that a state legislator doesn't come up with some kind of bill that would limit the rights of mailers and telephoners to access either information or people. That is a very important issue. As we move out toward the year 2000, databases are going to be very complete and very refined. And so, on the legal and regulatory side, I see potentially a great deal of activity to regulate the use of this data.

Product liability concerns will continue to have great impact and can cause executives to rethink whether they should market particular products. In discussing product liability, a CEO commented:

> The biggest thing that we're concerned about (is that)...all of a sudden there are a lot of lawyers coming in.

Another stated:

> We are constantly in court over wheels. It's not that we are building bad wheels. It's just that we will sell a 16 1/2 inch wheel and some guy will put a 16 inch tire around it and it will blow up in his face. We will get a law suit that contends it's our duty to warn.

Tort reform is seen as critical to the continued competitive ability of the U.S. Most other nations are not hampered by the liability costs and judgments that have plagued American companies for a decade. But the situation has not improved. A very concerned CEO noted:

> ...We haven't seen the kind of legislation we anticipated on the limitation of product liability. Most of the people who make the laws are lawyers.

However, some companies are moving toward reducing their involvements with courts and lawyers by going to specified arbitration systems which could provide a future model, particularly for product/customer concerns.

> We've addressed this through arbitration processes with the Better Business Bureau as the arbitrators. That's been probably our key thrust in that area. It certainly has forced us to try and look at ways to come to an accommodation with our customers. It's an on-going problem. We will have to continue to focus on finding more and more ways of settling our differences outside the courtroom.

Regarding international legislation and protectionist trade legislation, the thinking is that marketplace economics will eventually come into play.

> I kind of vote the way history does on textiles, cameras, televisions, and so forth. The low cost producer eventually, no matter where he is located, wins. You get some aberrations and protection for a year, two years, three years or five years. But not if you're talking the year 2000.

Consumer Behavior

Somewhat surprisingly, the CEOs gave little attention to the important demographic trends and future income trends that will shape and structure markets. Perhaps these areas are perceived of as a major concern of others, such as planning and marketing departments. Relatively little information was shared in the interviews about likely future consumer behavior, lifestyles or demographics. However, a few executives mentioned the obvious aging and greying of America.

The leader of a major food manufacturing company was one of the few CEOs to focus specifically on future consumer trends. He indicated that "a revolution is occurring on the consumer front" and referred to such developments in food as the microwave revolution, eating out, grazing, health concerns, the importance of ethnic factors, and convenience. Other executives agreed that increasing concern with health and fitness will be a lifestyle theme of the future.

It was noted that consumers will continue to try to rid themselves of burdensome, time consuming, repetitive, and undesirable "nitty gritty" chores associated with everyday living. "People are moving their life styles over to convenience." Consumers will become much more time conscious and companies must be able to react to their needs for fast service and self-service, including mail-order, tele-shopping, personal shopping, and overnight delivery. Helping consumers overcome the time scarcity that limits enjoyment and discretionary activities was seen as a major future opportunity.

While some of the literature indicates that income polarization may cause a decline in the number of middle class people, and that future demand will be found near either end of the price-quality spectrum, this tendency was not discussed. References were made to some related factors. On the one hand, trends were mentioned which are expected to catapult some consumers toward the higher end of the income spectrum, such as the: 1) maturing of the baby-boomers, who are expected to enjoy sizeable incomes, 2) rising affluence of senior citizens, and 3) increasing numbers of households headed by two wage earners. On the other hand, there were references to trends which may drop some consumers toward the lower range, such as the: 1) loss of manufacturing and clerical jobs to technology, and to overseas producers, 2) increase in the number of single parents, 3) national education dilemma resulting in a large pool of unskilled workers, and 4) emergence of service-based jobs, which typically pay much less than jobs in manufacturing. An implication is that companies positioned to market products toward either end of the price/quality spectrum may do better than those targeting consumers in the middle. However, this has become a marketing platitude and it may be too simple a statement for the complex demographic and economic environment of Marketing 2000.

Marketing Management Implications

The results of these CEO interviews, combined with the contributions of Marketing 2000 Presidential Advisory Committee members, the literature, and the deliberations of the Commission, strongly indicate that marketing managers, in Marketing 2000, will face a marketing environment that is different in kind and magnitude from that of the 1970s and 1980s. The following ideas present some of the anticipated and implied differences, and are intended to be illustrative and not exhaustive.

The Changing Marketing Focus

Marketing will be recognized and accepted as a top-level organizational concern. Its critical role in overall strategic decisions will be more widely recognized. Fostering this change will be the heightened needs to improve productivity, meet competition, gain market share, and improve customer satisfaction. External forces driving these will include industry overcapacity, global competition, new technology, and rapid innovations. The overall management shift will be more market-driven rather than manufacturing and product driven business systems.

The strategic aspects of marketing will come to dominate the current functional focus. That is to say, there will be more of a corporate focus, moving from mainly or exclusively functional concerns to CEO concerns. The end result will be a repositioning of marketing activities at higher levels of authority and concern.

Targeted Marketing Effort

Increased understanding of consumer behavior at both group and individual levels will accrue from paper trails and vastly improved information systems. Customers will be targeted and pinpointed more precisely along many dimensions. And products and services will be more specifically tailored to customer demand.

A host of suggested Twenty First Century developments will aid in this process, including more flexible manufacturing and faster product introduction. Companies will be able to narrow and bridge the gap between themselves and their customers, and bring their marketing mixes more into line with customer wants, needs, and desires. Volume will not be the overriding goal; rather, profitability will be the driver of strategy. Niches and segments will be agglomerated, when possible, to create the critical mass needed to mirror volume goals of yesteryear.

Consumers and Consumption

Consumers will have a much broader array of product/service choices, and a vast amount of market information that will generate greater chances for confusion as well as increased satisfaction. Consumer choices are more likely to center on value and quality as opposed to price. Still, design, color, and style will be as important as functionalism; taste and graciousness will exist as aspects that rival utility and durability; and time saving and extension will be stressed.

Pricing

Price increases will be constrained by severe competitive pressures, both domestic and international, that will work to encourage cost containment and result in increasing pressures for greater marketing productivity and efficiency. Longer time periods and different bases may be utilized to establish cost/price relationships for many products. International competition will play an increasing role in setting domestic prices. Other variables in the marketing mix will take on increasing importance relative to prices.

Market Information

Market information will be recognized as one of the most valued company resources. More timely and complete information will be available to marketing personnel in user-friendly modes. More money will be put into the development of marketing information, both relatively and absolutely, as it becomes an integral component of the total corporate intelligence system. Social and demographic information will be gathered at disaggregated levels, then grouped and correlated with other consumption data. Marketing research will interface with data from other company sources including finance, manufacturing, R&D, purchasing, and so on, to provide up-to-date comprehensive decision information of use to all facets of the business, making the entire information process more productive.

Distribution Channels

Distribution channels will be a major factor in the effective development of market share, particularly internationally. They will undergo dynamic change. Retrofitting and adjustment of distribution channels will occur, allowing for much greater flexibility in what has been one of the more fixed and rigid aspects of the marketing mix. Real estate concerns and values will become a more important factor in the selection and maintenance of distribution outlets. To maintain quality and insure service, more direct distribution may be undertaken by many manufacturers. Also, the use of multiple methods of distribution will expand and include such approaches as tele-marketing, television sales, mail-order, and computer-assisted buying.

Organization

Accompanying the focus on the marketplace, the development of market-driven organizations, and the need for greater flexibility, will be the trend to decentralization. Companies will strive to get closer to consumers, move decision authority to markets and to speed marketing decisions. The tendency will also be to integrate both backward and forward to gain efficiency. Hence, manufacturers will move more directly into marketing, while retailers and wholesalers will move into some manufacturing. They will give greater attention to their core businesses rather than to widespread, unrelated diversification. Companies will tend to pursue specialization in markets and products to enhance productivity and effectiveness.

Advertising

Advertising will be used to help differentiate companies and their products, create more favorable images, achieve closer matches with markets, communicate more efficiently and effectively, and target various niches and segments. This means that the dollars spent on advertising, both proportionately and absolutely, will be more focused dollars, thus increasing the productivity of advertising.

Marketing Flexibility

The rapidity of market changes, the speedy reactions of competitors, the emergence of new products resulting from technological developments, and the universally available monitoring and information capabilities will place a premium on the ability of marketing management to sense changes immediately and to move rapidly. Marketing programs will be comprised of much more flexible elements, including more flexible advertising programs, reduced product development time, the ability to change products and packages readily, alternative pricing strategies, contingency planning, and decentralized marketing authority. Marketing will become a major means of adjusting to dynamic business environments. Marketing 2000 will mark an era of flexible marketing, increasing marketing productivity multifold.

Products and Product Development

The product development process will be streamlined and compressed to get products into the marketplace faster, to foster profitable innovations and to generate new marketing approaches and themes. Product development will be seen more as a continuous stream of steady improvements rather than as periodic model changes. The time between the identification of market opportunities and product introductions will be greatly compressed. Emphasis will be placed on: developing quality products; enhancing customer satisfaction; increasing value; developing smart products that require less service, are self-monitoring and can be cared for by consumers; utilizing modularization; and creating products that can be changed readily in color, design, and style to reflect individualization and customization. The internationalization of tastes and standards will occur as consumers are exposed to products of the world marketplace. But people will still maintain many of their national preferences and identities. Blended tastes will result, reflecting not only an Americanization of foreign products, but also the globalization of American products.

Marketing Education and Training

All the considerations above suggest that marketers will require continuing education and training over and beyond that which comprises mainstream marketing education and training today. While today's traditional base of marketing skills will be highly valued, tomorrow's marketing managers may need further education in such areas as:

- Containing marketing costs effectively

- Increasing productivity

- Accepting and generating marketing changes

- Negotiating domestically and abroad

- Monitoring consumers and environments to develop insights into future opportunities

- Developing licensing agreements and other joint ventures on a global basis, particularly among socialist and lesser developed countries

- Marketing in many other cultures

- Fostering beneficial cooperative agreements with actual and potential competitors worldwide

- Accessing international markets effectively

- Managing markets in more consultative organizational structures

- Encouraging entrepreneurship in small and large companies

- Coordinating large scale risky and complex marketing projects

- Collecting, correlating, and using large quantities of marketing information from new sources

- Managing marketing under conditions of global currency fluctuation.

Marketing 2000 portends greater opportunities to better satisfy consumer wants and needs and to meet company growth objectives by remaining attuned to the marketplace. It bodes well for marketing as having a critical role in shaping and guiding future organizational destinies, because it places a higher order of importance on marketing in the business world of tomorrow. It highlights the guiding influence of market trends in shaping future business organizations. And, it underscores the fundamental requirement of having a future focus in order to meet the leadership challenges of tomorrow.

REFERENCES

Adelson, Beth (1984), "When Novices Surpass Experts: The Difficulty of a Task May Increase With Expertise," *Journal of Experimental Psychology: Learning, Memory and Cognition*, 10 No. 3, 483-495.

Biederman, Irving and Margaret M. Shiffrar (1987), "Sexing Day-Old Chicks: A Case Study and Expert Systems Analysis of a Difficult Perceptual-Learning Task," *Journal of Experimental Psychology: Learning, Memory and Cognition*, 13 No. 4, 640-645.

Brody, Michael, Richard I. Kirkland, Jr., Peter Nulty, Maggie McComas, Joel Dreyfuss, Gurney Breckenfeld, Gary Hector, Bill Saporito, Alex Taylor III, and Kenneth Labich (1987), "The Economy of the 1990s: Special Report," *Fortune*, 115 (February 2), 22-63.

Brown, Lester, Christopher Flavin, and Edward Wolf (1988), "Earth's Vital Signs," *Futurist*, 22 No. 4 (July/August), 13-20.

Dworkin, T.M. and M. J. Sheffet (1985), "Productibility in the 80s," *Journal of Public Policy and Marketing*, 4, 69-79.

Hannay, N. Bruce and Lowell W. Steele (1986), "Technology and Trade: A Study of Competitiveness in Seven Industries," *Research Management*, 29 No. 1 (January-February), 14-22.

Harvard Business Review (1987), "Competitiveness Survey: HBR Readers Respond," 5 (September/October), 8-12.

Manley, Marisa (1987), "Product Liability: You're More Exposed Than You Think," *Harvard Business Review*, 5 (September-October), 28-40.

Petroleum Economist (1986), "Looking to the Year 2000," 53 (November), 400.

Porter, Michael E. (1986), "Why U.S. Business is Falling Behind," *Fortune*, 113 No. 9, (April 28), 255-262.

Reitman, J.S. (1976), "Skilled Perception in Go: Deducing Memory Structures from Inter-Response Times." *Cognitive Psychology*, 8, 336-356.

Stambler, Irwin (1986), "Uncertainties Pervade Forecasts of U.S. Energy Consumption," *Research & Development*, 28 (July), 41-42.

Vernon, Raymond (1986), "Can U.S. Manufacturing Come Back?" *Harvard Business Review*, 64 (July/August), 98-106.

Walsh, Doris (1983), "World Futures," *American Demographics*, 10 No. 8 (August) 38-39.

Young, John A. (1985), "Global Competition: The New Reality," Calfornia Management Review, 27 No. 3 (Spring), 11-25.

Zeithaml, Valerie A. (1985), "The New Demographics and Market Fragmentation," *Journal of Marketing*, 49 No. 3 (Summer), 64-75.

CHAPTER 7

THE INSIDERS' VIEW

"You have to catch the future. It is not moving toward you, it is moving away." African Proverb

Introduction

The purpose of this book, as was emphasized in an earlier chapter, is not to attempt to make accurate predictions about the future, but to enhance marketing management preparedness for the future. To this end, a variety of experts, from academe, consulting, journalism and business, shared their opinions and insights, providing interesting vistas into future marketing developments. Since many of them are influential, they are also likely to have significant impact on the shape of marketing as a discipline and an operational function.

This chapter presents ideas about Marketing 2000 offered by seventeen contributors who shared their thoughts with us. We believe that readers will find their comments insightful, stimulating and provocative. The speculations offered are more than just commentaries about hypothetical developments in the future. They have practical implications of direct relevance for the future management of profit and non-profit organizations.

The contributors selected were not directed to cover any particular marketing areas or topics. No questionnaire or interview guide was used. Instead, they were given free reign to express their ideas on any future aspect of marketing. The major restriction imposed was that of space. The contributions are presented as given, with the exception of shortening the remarks in a couple of cases. Where this was necessary, the final document was approved by the authors to assure that the integrity of their statement was maintained.

Organizing the papers proved to be challenging. The contributors touched on many different issues and developments. The material, therefore, has been loosely organized around several major themes. (Within each theme the contributions are presented in the alphabetical order of the authors.)

> Marketing Management
> Macro/Micro Trends in Marketing
> The Environment in Which Marketers Will Operate

Several of the contributors focused their thinking on marketing management:

- Leonard Berry, Foley's Federated Professor of Retailing and Marketing Studies, Texas A & M University.

- Fred Danzig, Editor, *Advertising Age*.

- John Howard, George E. Warren Professor Emeritus of Business, Graduate School of Business, Columbia University.

- Theodore Levitt, Edward W. Carter Professor of Business Administration, Harvard University and former Editor, *Harvard Business Review*

- Burt Nanus, Director, Center for Futures Research, University of Southern California.

Berry describes a key shift from the marketing department era to the marketing performance era. He also discusses the change in the criteria by which marketing executives will be judged. Danzig talks about critical aspects of marketing management that will not change as well as aspects that will change. Howard highlights six reasons why the marketing operation will be much better and more effective than it is today. Levitt zeros in on the essence of business success and how marketing managers can be prepared. Nanus points out why marketers will need to learn to do more with less and how top marketing executives will need to take on the role of long-term strategists.

Macro/micro trends were discussed by:

- Leo Bogart, Executive Vice President/General Manager, Newspaper Advertising Bureau.

- Jane Fitzgibbon, Senior Vice President, Ogilvy & Mather Trendsights and Fred Elkind, Vice President, Ogilvy & Mather Trendsights.

- Phil Kotler, S.C. Johnson & Son Distinguished Professor of International Marketing, Kellogg Graduate School of Business, Northwestern University.

- Sidney Levy, Charles H. Kellstadt Distinguished Professor of Marketing, Chairman, Department of Marketing, School of Business, Northwestern University.

- Edith Weiner, President, Weiner-Edrich-Brown, Inc.

Bogart presents predictions of marketing trends within and outside the corporation. Fitzgibbon and Elkind analyze why the relationship between marketer and consumer will shift from mass provider to personal customizer. Kotler offers insightful predictions regarding aspects of the salesforce, advertising, direct marketing, sales promotion, trade channels, price, and product. Levy discusses the advent of two distinct marketing tiers or challenges, "obligatory marketing," which involves the provision of essentials, and "permissive marketing," which involves the provision of novelty or distinctive products. Weiner discusses both upside and downside factors that will impact on future marketing developments and details several constants in good marketing management. She includes predictions about important differences in marketing over the next decade and marketing trends within and outside the corporation.

Six contributors emphasized various aspects of the environment in which marketers will operate:

- Hal Becker, President, New Perspectives, Inc.

- Richard N. Cardozo, Curtis L. Carlson Chair in Entrepreneurial Studies, University of Minnesota

- Howard V. Perlmutter, Professor of Social Architecture and Management, The Wharton School, University of Pennsylvania.

- Frederick E. Webster, Jr., Osborn Professor of Marketing, Amos Tuck School of Business Administration, Dartmouth College.

- William D. Wells, Executive Vice President, Director of Marketing Services, DDB Needham Worldwide, Inc.

- Jerry Wind, Director, SEI Center for Advanced Studies in Management and The Lauder Professor of Marketing, The Wharton School of the University of Pennsylvania.

Becker expresses his perspectives on changes in technology, foreign firms and markets, demographics and truth in marketing and advertising. Cardozo focuses on concentration, globalization, technology, politics and labor, while Perlmutter emphasizes globalization and develops some of the marketing implications as well. Webster provides an overview of five forces that will re-shape marketing: globalization, information technology, disintegration of large corporations, defunctionalization of marketing, and the public consequences of private consumption. Wells offers his insightful views on technology, global marketing, and demographics as they will affect and influence marketing in the future. Finally, Wind contributes viewpoints on the changing environment and how it is likely to drastically affect the nature of marketing in the 21st century.

The original versions of our contributors' comments, which follow, should serve as a significant stimulus in extending the readers' own ideas and insights about Marketing 2000.

MARKETING MANAGEMENT

Leonard L. Berry
Foley's/Federated Professor of Retailing and Marketing Studies
Texas A&M University

I believe one of the key changes for the year 2000 will be the shift from the marketing department era to the marketing performance era. In the marketing department era, the marketing department "does marketing" for the company. In the marketing performance era, the marketing department helps the company to be more effective in marketing. This may sound like a play on words but it is much more.

Although the shift from one era to the other will be most pronounced for so-called service organizations, this won't matter so much in ten years because executives in many more manufacturing firms will consider their firms to be "service organizations." There will be less and less distinction between goods and service businesses as manufacturers compete more and more on service. It will be increasingly difficult to create sustainable, technology-based competitive advantages, making service an even bigger competitive weapon than it is today. Marketers of goods will see service quality as a key competitive weapon and will be just as interested in services marketing as executives in banking, health-care and transportation are today.

As the shift to the marketing performance era evolves, the criteria by which marketing executives are judged will change. Increasingly, marketing directors will be required to have comprehensive knowledge of the business, strong interpersonal and "teaching" skills, a capacity for true service-oriented leadership, and a solid grounding in finance. Technical skills in advertising, sales or research will not be enough to become or remain a marketing director.

Fred Danzig
Editor
Advertising Age

Two things will not change: the need for talented people and the need for marketers to pursue growth through the delivery of coherent, relevant and consistent sales messages.

Business will need, more than ever, talented people to come into the creative and administrative ranks of the advertising and marketing fields. This ranges from the writers, artists, directors, and producers, to the account-service people, the media planners and buyers, researchers, promotional marketing experts, and creative persons selling media. In one word: People. That need will not only continue; it will increase because the background noise will be elevated. Clutter-crackers will be needed.

Those in the advertising business will be both blessed and cursed by having at their fingertips more information. To deal with the extra time needed to contend with the swelling volume of data, they will have backup teams of data organizers who will gather, organize, and update data; teams to interpret and disseminate data. They will have the equipment that will help them keep up with this mountain of data, sort it out, deliver it when needed, discard it and channel it into the right offices. Media options will continue to change for advertisers as interactive applications in TV, fax equipment, etc., offer opportunities now unavailable.

The irony is, as all this occurs and as worldwide marketing efforts become more numerous, micro-management of advertising agency work will be required. We will have "fighting brands" — smaller-volume brands that must serve as price-monitors in various competitive product categories — forcing rival products to maintain an unprofitable position. And we will have the introduction of "fighting squads" in marketing. Instead of planning campaigns on a grand scale, agencies will have to learn to apply their local/regional expertise to foreign markets, where the equivalent local/regional programs will be needed. Instead of more echelons to go through before decisions can be made, there will be fewer. As with an infantry, agencies will be set up in squads, platoons and companies. Squads will do the tactical work while platoon leaders and company commanders handle the strategies. Input will flow in both directions — up and down the line.

John A. Howard
George E. Warren Professor Emeritus of Business,
Graduate School of Business
Columbia University

In the next 10 to 20 years, in the typical company, the marketing operation will be much better integrated and effective than today for at least six reasons.

First, the typical company then is more likely than now to be guided by corporate strategic planning. By corporate strategic planning is meant a company that plans at the corporate level for at least 5 years ahead with the major objective of market growth. This type of planning will encourage better integration of marketing than is displayed by non-planning or financial planning where the objective is financial, and may be either short-term or long-term.

Second, the strategic planning firms have three characteristics which facilitate integrating the marketing operation of the company. The strategy of emphasizing market growth focuses company effort upon new products and so encourages integration. The strategic planning company is oriented toward environmental analysis, and a key aspect of its environment is the product market. Finally, the organization structure and climate of the strategic planning company encourages emphasis in the market such as placing the product development activities in the division.

Third, the much better understanding of the nature of the customer that has been attained through years of research will aid the integration of marketing into the company. Because of this research there has been a break-through in theory-based application to marketing practice, which has two elements. First, the theory, such as the Customer Decision Model (CDM) which informs the managers of what they must do to favorably influence the customer. The CDM is made up of a set of concepts which describe how the customers consider, buy, and use the product. Hence, these are aspects of the customers' thinking that the manager must cater to if the company is to be successful.

Then, the CDM and its extensions tell the managers how successful they have been in marketing to the customer and what changes they should make in their marketing planning to be more effective. This happens because the CDM specifies data that should be collected from customers and analyzed to determine the strength of the relations among the elements of the CDM. The resulting structural model indicates what the pay-off will be from changing the various aspects of the marketing strategy or plans. In this way the managers can decide which changes, if any, will better serve their objectives.

Fourth, knowing the consumer theory will enable the managers to explain their marketing recommendations to others in the organization such as members of finance, operations, R&D, and human resources. This is possible because the labels of the theory's concepts will provide a vocabulary that the entire management team can learn, thereby greatly improve the communication about marketing issues in the company. The lack of a marketing vocabulary has been a serious handicap for effective marketing within a company. The marketer's inability to communicate often causes others in the management team to doubt his/her effectiveness and this is especially true in dealing with advertising issues.

Fifth, there appears to be a need for a major development in American business schools of comparable effort to the Ford Foundation and Carnegie programs in 1950s and 60s. This effort has led to better intellectual foundations for teaching each of the individual business functions. However, now there is a great need to integrate these individual functions together, in the context of the total enterprise, in our teaching. Because marketing is just now going through this task of integrating itself into the firm, it should be in a good position to exert leadership in the integration of all functions. This could help yield a truly effective total enterprise in meeting the growing foreign competitive onslaught that many American firms are now, and will continue, experiencing.

Sixth, the importance of the company's marketing operation to the long-term success of the U.S in world competition has become recognized by non-marketing experts. A recent MIT report states, "In such areas as product quality, service to customers and speed of product development, American companies are no longer perceived as world leaders, even by American consumers." A study of the social benefits of innovation states, "Marketing strategy often had an important affected social benefit." Such views will encourage all company managers to accept and support improvements in marketing effectiveness.

I believe these six factors will contribute in the future to corporate performance as measured by long-term financial performance.

Theodore Levitt
Edward W. Carter Professor of Business Administration
Harvard University
former Editor, *Harvard Business Review*

Three years ago, the sixty-year-old newly-appointed CEO of one of the world's largest chemical companies stopped by to talk. "We've been fantastically successful, but the new thing is to get marketing oriented and customer driven. We've got to learn how to do that."

Recently, at a university Board of Trustees meeting, the forty-year-old CEO of a thriving publishing company advised the president to think in terms of "the newest concept that's now so hot in business" — "being marketing oriented" and "getting close to the customer."

What's suddenly so fashionably new is the discovery of what's been actively around since 1959. Sir Isaac Newton told us authoritatively that a body at rest tends to remain at rest unless subjected to an equal opposing force. No matter how powerful the accelerating forces that drive the world, it seems unlikely that in just over ten years — by "The Year 2000" — they will change marketing or how managers think three times faster or differently than in the last tumultuous thirty years.

There is now a huge effulgence of direct marketing, but it is hardly new. It is just more abundant and sophisticated. Data inundate digitally at the speed of light, but nobody feels or performs discernibly better than anybody else, and rarely has any company suffered irreparably for only having hooked late into the information pipeline. Professors profess, students attend, demographics convulse, life styles transform, factories flexibilize, fiber optic networks link and thrive, telephones cellurize and fax, and business functionaries congregate in great indoor halls, as they have since the invention of post and beam construction, to listen solemnly to hustling futurists and evangelical fixers uttering the same dire warnings and making the same liberating promises that they always have.

Things change, of course. But the unending task remains the same — to become constantly better, which does not necessarily mean being different, doing different things, or doing things radically differently. Betterness will always be defined by evolving conditions, and by those who must make decisions and do the work. Nobody else can. If they don't make the necessary decisions and do the needed work that these three conditions require, what they have not done can only be known retrospectively. There is no reliable guide to knowing what to do in advance of events that are unknowable until they happen.

Like the weather, the best prediction of what will happen in this world is "More of the same;" that is, what is and has been. The powerful thing that "is" and "has been" for over a generation is micro-electronics — how, with unabated acceleration, it has shaped everything. Nothing has been exempt from its transforming power and influence, whether we speak of other sciences such as micro-biology, of family life, of ideologies, of management practices, globalization, or, to mention the obvious, of all manner of goods and services. The transformational pervasiveness of micro-electronics will surely continue and intensify, if for no deeper reasons than this has been its trajectory from its very beginning, while the field keeps attracting eager, bright, venturesome talents and massive amounts of capital.

Some of the specific directions all this will take can be imagined, some can be confidently foretold, but the most important are unpredictable. What is not predictable is, definitionally, the most importantly influential, owing precisely to its unpredictability. When things unexpectedly happen, they require responses, adjustments, and positive actions that will often be hurried, not easily or carefully considered, and therefore likely to cause trouble. That is what makes them so important, and why agility is so critical to survival and success.

In another realm, speaking sociologically, the most significant thing that "is" and "has been" for quite awhile is the simultaneous thriving of opposites in almost all things: markets divide into ever smaller segments, and simultaneously they scramble; discrete segments emerge, but they are both porous and migratory; the more the technological and competitive pace accelerates, the greater the inertia and nostalgia for what was; the more secular and materialistic society gets, the more religion, mysticism, and fundamentalism thrive; the more diets we go on, the more we need to go on diets; the bigger and more powerful the established old large corporations become, the more numerous and vigorous become the small new ones; the more technologically intensive and rational the way we do our work, the more sybaritic and hallucinogenic we make our lives; the more tethered to our work and associates, the more escape and release we seek and get. These are not predictions or forecasts. They are demonstrably extant.

We are headed in directions that cannot be precisely foretold, except for the further unravelling of what already exists, such as the increasing use of specialized knowledge in doing the world's work, including especially scientific and technological knowledge. And there are the rising numbers of older people in the developed world and of younger ones everywhere else. With respect to these and everything else, we are destined to function in ways that humankind has always functioned — reactively, and, if possible, imaginatively and responsibly. But what is imaginative is a function of how things are, not of what we define it abstractly to be. Reality, as always, will determine what is done and thrives.

We can define some of the continuing forces, sentiments, and unravelling events that will help shape the future, but can have little confidence in specific or detailed social predictions. Instead of trying to predict or describe the future, it is best to make oneself strongly aware of the forces that shape it. And, above all, it is important to enlist historical perspective so as to help to know what is told to us by the past. The past suggests that success in business will be a matter of constantly doing better those realistically right things that the marketing concept has prescribed since its formation long ago. That is the one abiding truth. In business, unless you get and keep customers, nothing else much matters. Indeed, all else is only engineering.

Burt Nanus
Director, Center for Futures Research
University of Southern California

The next decade will be likely marked by high economic stress as America works itself out of budget and trade deficits, and fights off aggressive competitors from Europe and Asia. Under such circumstances, customers will seek value and durability in products, demanding more in the way of real substance and less of image. Under such circumstances, companies will be strongly motivated to invest in productivity, quality and cost improvements, possibly leading to proportionately less generous marketing budgets. Thus, marketers will need to learn to do more with less. With more niche markets and rapid new product introduction and obsolescence, large marketing research budgets may give way to less expensive and more effective methods of tracking and responding to customer feedback after new product introduction.

Major changes in marketing will follow from the rapid spread of the information economy. With the cost of micro-electronics and micro-miniaturization continuing to plummet, computer intelligence will be everywhere and there will be more information content in all products and services. It will be more common for customers to order custom-designed products and to participate in the design process, since computers will make such orders inexpensive to produce and to process. Computer networks will also stimulate catalog sales and will make it possible for advertising and promotion to be delivered at the customer's convenience and keyed to specific inquiries.

Ethics in marketing may take on much greater importance, with keen international competition to gain the consumer's trust. Simple compliance with the law in such matters as labelling and advertising may not be enough. Many companies will find it in their interests to conform to ever higher ethical standards to avoid not only lawsuits, but even the possibility of being seen as anything less than totally committed to full product value and complete customer safety.

Finally, the top marketing executive will have to become much more of a leader than a manager, providing the vision that can bridge current marketing decisions to long range strategies. Indeed, he or she will have to become an ombudsman for the future in the organization, helping others to see what must be done to build long term market positions.

MACRO/MICRO TRENDS IN MARKETING

Leo Bogart
Executive Vice President/General Manager
Newspaper Advertising Bureau

The future of marketing has been the subject of five separate Delphi studies I have conducted since 1971 at the Newspaper Advertising Bureau. In these studies, small groups of knowledgeable decision makers have first identified possible emerging trends, developments, or events that might affect their businesses, and large samples of their peers have evaluated both the probability and impact of these events through mail questionnaires.

Looking back on the earlier of these studies, it is apparent that people in positions of industry leadership have a pretty good track record of forecasting. However, they tend to think in terms of the continuation or extrapolation of existing trends. Not surprisingly, they can rarely envision sharp discontinuities from what is present and familiar. In thinking about the future, we find it hard to envision wars or catastrophes that might destroy our well-ordered scheme of things. When we talked about the "Greenhouse Effect" in the early 1970s, it was almost something of a joke.

The marketing world of the year 2000 is really very close. It will not be all that different from the one we see around us today. What are the trends that the experts think will continue and that will alter the practice of marketing as we know it? To summarize the most significant themes makes them appear commonplace.

1. An economy growing in real terms, fed by an expanding base of technology, producing an ever greater variety of new and improved products and services.

2. A society that is more affluent and better educated, with the elderly and minorities playing more important parts and an impoverished self-perpetuating underclass continuing to sap morale and economic strength.

3. An increasingly global marketing system.

4. Greater concentration of corporate ownership and control.

5. Continued expansion of corporate interests across the traditional dividing lines among different types of enterprise.

6. Further expansion of services in relation to goods.

7. An accelerated effort to differentiate consumers by appeals to segmented motivations or interests and through product positioning and niching.

8. More exploitation of geographic cultural variability through regionalized marketing programs.

9. A vast proliferation of data (partly through widened applications of product scanners, partly through access to government information bases) and greater dependence on data.

10. A shift in the balance of power from manufacturers to retailers and a growing sophistication in the use of research by retailers.

11. More emphasis on trade promotion and immediate sales results from consumer promotion at the expense of image-building advertising.

12. An exponential growth of disseminated advertising messages and heightened competition for the public's diminished time resources.

All of the above dozen points represent the conventional wisdom, and I don't disagree with any of them. I would add just a few other thoughts:

I think in the next dozen years we will see new applications for social marketing. Marketing skills must and will be used to urge people to consume less individually so that they can consume more public goods that reflect their collective interests. The essential social expense of maintaining a livable environment must be reflected in higher pricing of consumer merchandise. As waste disposal becomes a growing public issue in the 1990s, marketers will face a growing conflict between the financial interests of their employers and their own private beliefs and professional judgments. Within the corporate enterprise, they will, if they do their job well, play the part of public advocates with their eye on the long-term picture rather than on the next balance sheet.

They may face another role conflict as they confront two of the significant trends I mentioned earlier — toward bigness in industry (and in the retail, advertising agency, and research businesses as well) and toward the surging volume of research data. Both of these trends carry the danger of bureaucratized formula thinking that discourages innovation and shies away from fresh ways of solving problems. A major task for marketers in the year 2000 may be to market to management the principle that reflection can be creative but systems cannot.

Jane R. Fitzgibbon
Senior Vice President
Ogilvy & Mather TrendSights

Fred Elkind
Vice President
Ogilvy & Mather TrendSights

The character of the relationship between marketer and consumer will shift from mass provider to personal customizer.

- Advertising will sell the broad concept and imagery of a product; but the actual sale of the merchandise will involve tailoring the product to the specific tastes and requirements of each consumer.

- The growing power of the new telecommunications technologies will facilitate this custom tailoring. This is already occurring at a group or segment level with many cable TV channels targeting product and service offerings to more select and homogeneous micro-audiences.

- But there is a big difference between micro-segment targeting and individual customization. Segmentation means "getting something that is closer to what I want because it more closely fits the needs or tastes of the group to which I belong." Customization means "getting a product made, fit, styled, or configured precisely in the way I want it."

- The customization trend is being driven by the substantial move, in the U.S. and around the world, towards greater personal control and individualism.

- The move towards individualism and personal choice is being driven by the proliferation of globalized mass communications and the myriad of opportunities and options it presents to people.

- Growing affluence and discretionary spending is combined with the new technologies to make customization not only a highly desirable possibility, but a feasible one.

Marketers and marketing managers will utilize sophisticated models and systems to master the strategic and logistical challenges of the increasingly complex markets of 2000. These markets will be more complex because:

- Markets will continue to fragment, due to growth in the population of diverse ethnic groups and the need to develop efficient and coherent marketing and advertising programs to reach these groups with brands that mesh with their needs. Managers will have to become more like cultural anthropologists and sociologists, to develop an empathetic understanding of and sensitivity to these cultures.

- The cross-influences of these ethnic groups on the customs, tastes and preferences of the mainstream populations — e.g., in the U.S., the growing impact of the various Hispanic groups from Mexico, Cuba, Puerto Rico, Central and South America, and the influx from the Orient, will affect prevailing orientations. The challenge will be to develop products that bring appealing aspects of these cultures to the rest of the population, without losing the authenticity of the original — i.e., not creating a blurred and meaningless polyglot.

- The complexity for marketers will be expanded due to the ever increasing tidal wave of market research information that will be flooding their desks — as U.S. national surveys are joined by regional, local, ethnic and micro-segmentation data, e.g., Prizm, AIM, ACORN, NDS, etc.

PC networks and expert support systems/artificial intelligence programs will be required to help these managers cope with and navigate through the complexities and challenges of these markets of the future.

New computerized design and manufacturing machines will make it possible for manufacturers to efficiently respond to the demands created by growing segmentation and customization, as will some recent legal changes.

- Machines will create custom and semi-custom clothing and home decor items; or computers will identify and direct orders to the appropriate outside artisans, who will complete the order by hand or machine.

- Recent changes in the law will be favorable for customization and home-grown ethnic and native industries, by encouraging at-home manufacturing.

Other technological changes, such as those in credit card information storage, will enhance the ability of manufacturers to efficiently deliver custom tailored goods.

- Credit cards and card codes will contain details on personal preferences, clothing sizes, food seasoning choices, service preferences, etc., making it easier for businesses to instantly cater to the customers' wants.

More and more manufacturers will operate on the full spectrum of marketing channels.

- They will continue to communicate through the mass media and sell through conventional stores.

- But they will find it necessary to join the ranks of direct marketers, selling through printed and electronic catalogues.

- Catalog sales will be revolutionized by self-scanning holographic computers, which will allow a consumer to send a clothing manufacturer or distributor a precise three dimensional measurement of his or her body. As a result, it will be possible to obtain a custom tailored suit, dress, shirt, etc. without leaving the comfort of one's living room.

Services will also be impacted by the new customizing technologies.

- Physicians will be able to diagnose many problems from a distance, using the new scanning computers. The patient can be treated without leaving the safety and security of the home, and most importantly, with incredible speed. Such technology is already being used by physicians to monitor coronary patients.

- Other outside service providers, ranging from home maintenance and security businesses to dentists and psychologists/

stress therapists, can get in tune with the consumer with such technologies.

Product packaging also will be revolutionized by the new technologies, resulting in greater competition on the one hand, and greater customer satisfaction, on the other.

- Printed usage instructions on packages will become obsolete. They will be replaced by computer encoded mini-compact discs or magnetic cards that will explain exactly how to use or operate the product — and will also be able to program the appliance used in preparation.

- These cards also will visually show how a product is to be used; and will also be capable of answering a limited number of questions — through an interactive video.

- This new technology/concept will, in effect, represent more than just a new way of delivering instructions — it will become part of the product benefit package. Those marketers who do it better — will do better in the marketplace.

Children and teenagers will become more important target segments — as shoppers, as *tabula rasa* consumers for brand loyalty development, as sophisticated mini-adults with financial management needs, media needs, medical needs, etc.

More marketing and distribution activities will come to the home — electronically or via fully equipped "shopping vans," *Viz*: gym-in-a-van, decorator-in-a-van, office commuting van.

Credit cards will become increasingly smarter in terms of information needed by retailers at point-of-purchase and in terms of financial feedback to card owner.

- Possible adoption of a Japanese card, that is purchased for a set monetary fee, with decreasing balance, available as purchases are made.

All media will become more visual and sensory. Argument-style advertising will be less common.

- HDTV will encourage more visual experimentation, as well as print techniques using audio chips, holography, etc.

Philip Kotler
S.C. Johnson & Son Distinguished Professor of International
Marketing, J.L. Kellogg Graduate School of Management
Northwestern University

To quote Yogi Bera, "the future ain't what it used to be." We thought that the bedrock of America would always be "the married family with a working husband, a homemaking wife, and two children." We designed and aimed our products largely at this market. Today, this family is only seven percent of the American public.

We also thought that the typical American consumer would be Caucasian. Today Caucasians are a minority in several American cities. Because the "future ain't what it used to be," we must constantly revise our picture of the marketplace. Change is the only constant.

We can anticipate certain things about the marketplace in the year 2000. First, American consumers will be older; we have an aging society. The Gross National Product (GNP), therefore, will shift in favor of health products and retirement homes. Second, a growing proportion of our products will be sourced abroad, where wages are lower or skills are higher. Hopefully, we will also be able to sell more abroad in order to pay for the growing import bill.

Third, the buying market will be bimodal in its income and tastes. Low-income consumers will look for basic products, low prices, and no frill service. High-income consumers will search for well-crafted products and personalized service. If the size of the middle class continues to shrink, marketers will have to choose which bimodal market they want to serve.

Even these forecasts are tentative. Forecasters do not have impressive records. A few years ago, we were told to prepare for an Ice Age and people were ready to move to the Equator. Today we are warned of a "Greenhouse effect" heating up the earth; people are ready to move north to high altitude places.

What about marketing mix elements? Here are some speculative predictions.

1. *Salesforce.* There will be a reduction in the relative size and importance of salesforces in the marketing mix. The CEO of a major pharmaceutical company told me that he hopes to "drastically reduce the size of the salesforce within ten years; it's too expensive a way to sell." Drucker observed some years ago that "people are too expensive to use in selling."

2. *Advertising.* Advertising channels will increase in number but not in mass reach. Supermarkets are creating new in-store

advertising channels, including audio messages in the aisles, carts that advertise, and store floor tiles bearing national brand names. Media and messages will increasingly be focused on target markets, thereby reducing wasted exposure. Advertising agencies will be increasingly accountable for advertising effectiveness; they will be put on performance pay schedules.

3. *Direct marketing.* Direct mail and telemarketing will continue their strong growth in complementing or replacing other media. Direct mail pieces will include audio and video tapes. Faxed and computer messages will show explosive growth. More households will make their purchases through televised home shopping programs and electronic catalogs. More businesses will do their buying through electronic shopping systems.

4. *Sales promotion.* Sales promotion expenditures will continue to grow as a percentage of the promotion budget. Sales promotion tools will undergo further invention and refinement. Companies will collect better measures of their sales promotion effectiveness.

5. *Trade channels.* Power in the marketing channel will continue to shift from manufacturers to retailers. Giant retailers, armed with optical scanning devices at checkout counters, will know item-by-item profitability. They will demand better terms from weaker national brands or drop them. In many product categories, retailers will carry one or two leading national brands, one or two store brands, and a generic ("no name") brand. Manufacturers of weak national brands will be reduced to supplying the store brands.

6. *Price.* Buyers will grow more sophisticated in assessing value. Companies will be under increased pressure to supply price justifications. They will have to price-justify each product/service feature and allow customers to buy on a more "unbundled" basis.

7. *Product.* Products will continue to improve in quality, partly because consumers demand it and partly because sellers will discover that high quality costs less. As products achieve quality parity, buyers will look for other factors in choosing vendors, such as superiority in service, design, features, and so on. Today, General Motors is spending its time catching up to Japanese quality when a growing number of consumers are seeking design superiority. "Better late than never" is no longer a safe assumption in an intensively competitive marketplace.

Given these probable changes in the role and relative importance of marketing mix elements, what new practices and strategies will appear in marketing management? Here is my list of some major changes.

1. *Niche marketing.* Niche marketing will continue to attract more practitioners. Market demassification will provide endless niching opportunities. Instead of targeting one of six social classes, consumer marketers will scan forty or more lifestyle groups in search of high potential users. Today the Rolex company can buy mailing lists of "bluebloods" to promote their $11,000 oyster shell watches. The Toro company can buy lists of "fur and station wagon" households to promote their snowblowers. Miller Beer can aim their ads at the "pickup truck" crowd. Industrial marketers are also finding niches, often global niches, to penetrate and dominate. Segments are too big and crowded for these nichers. The nichers are unlayering these segments in search of micro-segments.

2. *Customized marketing.* Advances in computer technology, telecommunications, and factory automation will permit more industries and companies to give each customer what he or she wants. Instead of a male who measures size 41 trying to fit into a size 40 or 42 ready-made suit, he can be measured electronically and the information sent to a factory which cuts out a unique fitting suit for him. "A tailor-made suit without a tailor." Banks will customize their banking relationship with each customer separately. Advances in industrial housing will let each family design its own home.

3. *Turbo marketing.* Companies will substantially speed up their innovation and distribution time. U.S. auto manufacturers will be able to design and build new cars in three years instead of five years. Customers won't have to wait eight weeks for home furniture delivery. Clothing manufacturers will receive daily information on their sales at retail so that they can manufacture replacement stock continuously. Retailers who offer one-hour film development service or one-half hour pizza delivery service will lose out to faster competitors.

4. *Megamarketing.* Good marketing skills alone will not help companies sell in global markets. Many attractive markets will be "blocked" by political barriers. Tomorrow's marketers will need "megamarketing skills." They will need to analyze and influence political elites and publics of host countries.

5. *Geo-marketing.* All markets are local. No matter how tempting it is to produce one product and advertise it and sell it

everywhere in the world in the same way, some adaptation is always necessary, if only in language, packaging, etc. Even the same motorcycle needs to be sold as a "transportation vehicle" in Bangkok and as a "recreation vehicle" in Los Angeles.

6. *Cybernetic marketing.* Marketers will increasingly plan and implement on a continuous real-time basis. They will know the impact of their marketing expenditures on customer sales and satisfaction. They will continuously correct weaknesses in their products. Marketing managers will be aided in their decision making by expert system software.

7. *Stand-alone marketing.* Some organizations will operate as pure marketing companies. They will spot unfulfilled needs and contract out all the functions required to fill it. Pure marketing companies require only a desk, telephone, and computer. These pure marketing companies are made possible by the rapidly developing network of global telecommunications and fast transportation.

CONCLUSION

All forecasting can take two directions, either extrapolating the "seed" trends now being observed, or claiming that every current trend will reverse itself. Speculation about the future is valuable primarily for its thought-provoking effect on today's marketers, and not for any claim to predictive accuracy.

Marketing will continue as a major force affecting global lifestyles and institutional organization. Hopefully, it will succeed better in its intended mission of delivering a higher standard of living to the world's population.

Sidney J. Levy
Charles H. Kellstadt Distinguished Professor of Marketing,
Chairman, Department of Marketing, School of Business
Northwestern University

Many authors have stressed the significance of the role of marketing in the coming decade. There seems little doubt that the growth of the global marketplace will continue to enhance the necessity for increasing awareness and sophistication on the part of all participants in the world economy.

Nevertheless, it seems worth pointing out that as ever, there will be stability as well as change. The passage of a decade will produce little alteration in the circumstances of vast numbers of people. They will continue to strive to sustain their standard of living, in many cases at subsistence levels, or at quite modest degrees of comfort. The growth of population in many places continues to outpace the productivity of the local society; and even assuming that the globe is capable of providing for its total population in some adequate manner, there is little indication that the world society is going to develop a universally satisfying distribution of goods and services in the near future.

In an ideal world, governments would be benign, the religious would save us, doctors heal us, teachers educate us, and the marketers provision us all. In doing so, product development and distribution would succeed without destroying the rain forest or polluting the atmosphere. I believe there will be progress made toward these optimistic goals, that some marketing managers will recognize the need to have larger perspectives, that new products will take advantage of technological innovations to enhance consumption patterns.

At a more mundane level, there will continue to be the proliferation of goods and services, limited only by the ingenuity of marketers to find means of differentiating their offerings and segmenting their customers. The impact of women in the work force will continue to pervade the marketplace with changing perceptions of social roles, shifting arrangements, and opportunities for new businesses.

There might be more awareness of two levels or types of marketing challenges, as implied above. The two marketing tiers may be termed *obligatory marketing* and *permissive marketing.* Obligatory marketing refers to the marketing systems that require the involvement of governments, non-profit organizations, and multi-national corporations in their provision of life's fundamentals.[1]

This is the kind of marketing that keeps the great millions of people fed, clothed, and housed in basic, ongoing ways. It is commodity-oriented and economics-oriented, geared to seeing to it that neighborhoods keep going with a viable housing stock, that the stores always have potatoes, hamburgers, milk and bread — or whatever the local cultural versions are; and that there is fabric for dresses, shirts and trousers. Keeping this great tonnage moving to enable a basic contentment in all societies is a core task for marketing. Obligatory marketing sees people as large social groups, not only as welfare recipients, but also with essential needs for education, health, and participation in the arts.

---

[1]Salamon, Lester M. (1987).

Beyond that is the permissive marketing that is more directed by individual choices. It is geared to innovation, variation, and style. It is excited by novelty, changes of a few percentage points in consumption patterns, interesting consumer subgroups, and the latest fad. It is important because it enables the expression of individuality, it relates more to the development of the human personality and its psychological aspirations for distinction. Also, out of its inventiveness and elite discoveries come products and services that in time become part of the obligatory system.

The vitality of the marketplace is due to the interplay between the essential and permissive, the core and the periphery. The specific content of change in the next decades will move toward enhancing the great engine of marketing as people of good will struggle to take care of the obligatory process, absorbing from the margin the imaginative, quirky elements that make for variety and surprise.

Edith Weiner
President
Weiner-Edrich-Brown, Inc.

We have come so far in each decade of the Twentieth Century, and the last decade will be no exception. On the upside, space exploration will resume; telecommunications will become all pervasive; adult education will be commonplace; the old major superpowers will be at peace with each other and the new ones will be facing stepped-up pressures to democratize and commercialize. Globally, the world will be re-mapped, corporations will be multi-cultural, and there will, as always, be a lot of wealth migrating around the earth.

On the downside, the underclass in every nation, especially the western industrialized countries, will place increasing burdens on the quality of life; medical advances will be balanced by resurgence of disease in poor, drug-infested and crowded environments, as well as the need to ration health care in the face of an aging society. Illiteracy and productivity lags will drag down nations that under-invested in children and education (including our own); the gap between rich and poor nations will continue, and the fear of technology (genetic, biological and nuclear warfare and accidents) will remain potent. Environmental issues will go on posing a major challenge to those who care about the Twenty First century, and the costs of a college education will go on posing a serious threat to our system of classless democracy.

Through it all, marketing will be, as it always has been, the cornerstone of commercial enterprise. Even though the biggest business in the world today is the transfer of funds electronically around the globe, exchanging currencies and manipulating eighths of a point 24 hours a day, money is only as good as what it will buy in the hands of its ultimate recipients. Whether it will buy financial security, designer clothes, opera tickets or a United Way donation is all up to the marketing establishments. There will never be a substitute for effective marketing in attracting spendable income.

Going forward, the constants in good marketing will be as true at the turn of the century as they always have been. These include:

- *Listening to the marketplace*

- *Listening to the customer*

- *Taking advantage of* trends when they are still *countertrends.*

  (Every trend gives birth to a countertrend, and early detection of these provides competitive advantage. Examples currently include upscale chic moving to downscale chic, high tech moving to neo-traditional.)

- *Moving away from ethnocentrism*, which sees the new multi-national, multi-cultural markets through a narrow, white middle-class perspective.

- *Following the course of disintermediation* (the bypassing of traditional channels of delivery of goods and services in the marketplace) to see how best to bring products and ideas to market. (Currently popular are use of mail, consumer warehouses, and telemarketing. In the next ten years, we may see a return to value-added personal service, as well as more sophisticated forms of simulation purchase, such as using holographic imagery to buy a car or video-surround immersion to choose a vacation package. Employment-related group sales will also likely increase, as will the office as a site for personal purchases. The latter is part of the melding home/office marketplace, and itself is worthy of a whole paper.) The compatibility of disparate products, like washing machines with telephones, will become important as products are co-marketed into environments like the "smart home."

What will be some of the more important differences over the next decade? Perhaps a starting list might include the following:

- *Marketing professionals will not occupy their positions* in the Twenty First century as long as did their counterparts in the latter part of the Twentieth century. Tenure in any career suffers as a result of life extension (to age 85 or older), economic turmoil and uncertainty (which is a major new factor heading into the year 2000), and personal life style revolution, which will take place one or more times in the course of today's and tomorrow's working population. No one will want to be in marketing for 45 years, so rather than being uniformly trained and permanently oriented, marketing professionals will be coming from and going on to multiple fields of background and endeavor. This should help enrich the profession immensely.

- *Consumer activism* will come to the fore again and we will see new targets of attention and action. These will include lease/purchase contracts (because more institutions are pulling back from granting credit to the increased number of poor and near-poor), invasion of privacy (via use of such things as tele-marketing, bloc modelling techniques and sales of mailing lists), and provision of selective shopping/boycotting guides to aid customers who wish to patronize socially/environmen-tally/morally responsible stores or products.

- *Corporate entities will have merged and consolidated world-wide*, making the advent of the *nationless product a fait accompli.* This will not only relate to cars and computers, but to financial services, research services and retailing as well.

- *The Northern hemisphere will be increasingly inhabited by the Southern* as immigration patterns and birth rate patterns lead to Asian, Hispanic, and African pushes northward. Eco-nomic, environmental and political conditions will continue to keep illegal as well as legal migration rates very high, and as a result, markets, work forces and cultural orientation of the North will reflect the newcomers and their offspring genera-tion.

- *Globally, formerly insignificant markets* will increasingly become significant ones as growing numbers and incomes attach to such segments as the aged, the handicapped and the non-marrieds.

- *Transitioning* will characterize the most important life style change at the dawn of the Twenty First century. The past 20 years marked a time of increasing incidence of change for individuals: multiple marriages and divorces, multiple retire-ment phases, multiple jobs and careers, and multiple experi-ences with education into adulthood. But the emerging, more fundamental shift is that these changes no longer merely increase in number...their eventuality permeates the entire life process, such that almost everyone, almost always, seems to be transitioning. If you ask someone today, "What do you do for a living?," or "Are you married?," the answer frequently begins with the disclaimer, "Well currently I'm..." This will lead to a need to completely reorient marketing strategy, segmentation, psychographics, traditional uses of demographics, and even the new applications of these, such as geographic cluster analysis and bloc modeling.

• *Products and services that address personal health, safety, and security* will consume larger percentages of disposable income as we face higher crime rates, more environmental mega-threats, greater concern for children and breakdowns of public health and safety delivery and oversight mechanisms.

There you have a very abbreviated list of some of the things we can expect as we face the challenge and thrill of the beginning of a new century. As with any list of things to come, there is a healthy measure of more of the same as well as the bold and the new.

Perhaps the most important ingredient through all of this is the ethical one. So long as marketers can face themselves in the mirror in the morning with pride at having done a good job, and having served well both the customers and one's employer, the marketer of 2050 will be just as able to cope as his or her counterpart of 1950.

THE ENVIRONMENT IN WHICH MARKETERS WILL OPERATE

Hal Becker
President
New Perspectives, Inc.

Formulating, choosing and directing marketing activities in the year 2000 will include approaches and actions both the same as and different than our actions in the late 1980s. This may not seem very startling or insightful. However, the year 2000 is closer than many of us would like to believe. And, we typically overestimate changes that will occur in the near term (the next 5 to 10 years) while underestimating what will take place in the long term (beyond 10 years). As to change, I believe four areas, in particular, will create, or continue to create, changes in our marketing activities. These areas are: 1) communications and data processing technology, 2) foreign firms and foreign market places, 3) demographic shifts in the U.S., and 4) truth in marketing and advertising.

Technology

There is little disagreement about the many ways advancements in communications and related technologies have impacted marketing activities over the last two decades. Changes will continue in our abilities to analyze and communicate with the consumer. Changes will come from new applications of existing technologies and the emergence of new technologies. New ways of reaching consumers in a host of settings (the home, work place, while travelling to and from work and even during leisure) will be found and exploited. It will become easier and easier to present messages to a broader range of consumers in more focused ways.

Our technologies will allow us to track consumer segments to collect information about the consumer and his/her household (demographics, economics, lifestyles) and their buying decisions (items purchased, where purchased, why purchased, how utilized, prices, etc.). This information will comprise comprehensive data bases and it will be possible to analyze movements and changes in essentially real time. We will be more able to spotlight the real decision maker and the reasons underlying purchases. Clearly, technologies of data collection and analysis, coupled with high speed communications techniques, will allow us to be more adept at segmenting our markets.

Possibly, most important will be the ability of the analyst to effectively communicate with the decision maker(s) in his/her own organization. Ways must be continually sought to improve our abilities for converting enormous masses of statistical data to meaningful messages that can be easily communicated to those deciding on the marketing approaches for our company. The compulsion that many of us have to generate data frequently results in a feast of numbers and a famine of visibility. Preventing or minimizing this tendency should be a challenge we always keep in mind.

Foreign Firms and Foreign Markets

Foreign firms will be an increasing participant in the U.S. market. Domestic firms will find themselves under greater competition from such firms. It will be incumbent on our domestic companies to continually improve their ability to understand, design appropriate products for and successfully communicate with the changing U.S. consumer to compete with foreign firms from around the world. To do that, it will be more and more important for U.S. firms to become increasingly insightful about the way successful foreign firms plan for and go about their activities in the U.S. Early in their invasion of the U.S. market, Japanese companies stated they were more insightful about the American consumer than were our own firms. How do foreign companies obtain information and turn their data into effective marketing plans and activities? Becoming better students of foreign firms that are successful in the U.S. should be an item on the checklist of our domestic companies. In fact, acquiring such knowledge will be of paramount importance in becoming more effective in operating in foreign markets.

Europe is on the threshold of becoming a unified or single economic entity. Thus, it will be a major marketplace — and competitor in its own and other markets around the world. Furthermore, at least four out of five persons in the world will live in the lesser and newly developed countries, often with growing economies and resources important to the U.S. And there is the large likelihood that the centrally planned, or socialist, countries will have economics and marketplaces much more like those of the Western world by the year 2000. We simply cannot afford to underplay these other markets.

Demographic Shifts

The population of the U.S. will be older by the year 2000. Much has been written about aging of the U.S. (and the other developed countries) and the new retirees who will comprise a greater and greater percentage of the population. We now have households with two (and in some cases more) individuals having some form of pension or retirement income. The funds available to these retirees, both in terms of income and estates they have acquired, is greater than ever before. There is, however, a characteristic of those who will begin to retire in the mid-1990s that we may have overlooked and that could be highly significant in terms of their lifestyles and spending patterns. Those retiring during the 1990s are those who were born just before or during the great depression of the 1930s. They will be the individuals whose values were set by the economic conditions and political and social actions taken during their formative years. They are the "depression syndrome" children.

Behaviorists have noted that the policies and actions of corporations, government agencies and even nations are a direct function of the values of the persons heading them. It has been stated that those born and who grew up during the depression years of the 1930s are, in many regards, more conservative than either their parents or their children. Do we understand enough about their likely attitudes concerning desired lifestyles and spending patterns in retirement? It is not clear that their actions during their work years will assure that we can be certain about what they will do during retirement. The growing numbers of these age cohorts and their apparently significant affluence demands that we give adequate thought to the likely lifestyles and behavior of these depression syndrome people.

Truth in Marketing and Advertising

Truth in our selling efforts is of growing concern and attention to many public and private sector organizations. Companies are now being taken to task for selling, or attempting to sell, whatever is available as long as a potential profit is seen. Firms are being accused of ignoring the ultimate impacts of their products and services. The publics are expressing concern about impacts on the environment, health, safety and now even about basic values communicated in various advertising and media messages. We see actions to curtail marketing of food additives, pesticides and growth hormones for agricultural purposes, "over the counter" and prescription drugs, alcoholic beverages, etc. Arguments about gun control persist.

Will marketeers choose to accept the assignment no matter what the product or service, and no matter who the potential clients are? Decisions about which product or service to market seem largely to be based on our ability to attain current revenues. Maximization of today's bottom line continues to be the primary ethic. As we age, as we address foreign markets, as we move into the 21st century, what will be the proper mix of attention to today's bottom line versus consideration of the impact of our actions on tomorrow? What was right and proper yesterday does not meet today's standards and certainly will not satisfy tomorrow's. During the 1930s, communities applauded and even demanded the construction of power stations belching smoke since they were visible signs of employment for the community. But those things we previously demanded were damned as we became more affluent and insightful and new concerns arose.

How will we, by the turn of the century, transition effectively to new or modified products when it is decided that the many chemicals we have added (both consciously and unconsciously) to our food chain are causing health and even genetic problems? How will organizations that have become associated with such products appropriately change their image in the marketplace through their marketing efforts (and, through their research and development) and offer products that will be desired and acceptable? Society has a short memory. It damns organizations for producing items it sought previously when it decides that they are no longer acceptable. Clearly, that was the case with the power generating stations noted above.

Insight about such shifts must be developed by industry. And, it probably will be appropriate to conduct programs that educate the public about how new product knowledge impacts on both them and the company, and that should be used in maintaining healthy relationships between the public being served and the companies serving it. I believe the onus rests on the producer for such programs.

Addressing some of these future challenges will be straightforward. In other areas, ways of improving our understanding of, and effectively marketing, the right approaches are not so apparent. Therein lie factors that make involvement in marketing a challenging, demanding and a highly rewarding future endeavour.

Richard N. Cardozo
Curtis L. Carlson Chair in Entrepreneurial Studies
University of Minnesota

As we approach the new millennium, five factors are reshaping marketing institutions and the way marketing is practiced. These changes in institutional structure and practice will open up significant new opportunities and pose challenges for marketers.

The five factors affecting institutional change are *concentration, globalization, technology, politics and labor.*

Concentration is occurring in most manufacturing and distribution industries. In manufacturing, concentration results from declining primary demand in such industries as farm equipment, from shakeouts in evolving industries like micro-computers, and from supplier reduction in a broad range of industries. The fewer, larger firms that remain after consolidation occurs are cutting sharply the number of suppliers from which they buy, in order to reduce their own costs of transactions and of managing diverse inventories. In business markets, these large firms will develop long term contractual and close working relationships with their customers. These formal and informal arrangements will profoundly affect product line and pricing decisions of both parties. They will involve dedicated communications and distribution facilities and service programs. These relationships will enhance the competitive stature of cooperating firms, but may limit the flexibility of those firms in dealing, respectively, with other suppliers or customers.

In distributive industries concentration results from economies of scale. For example, firms like Best Buy Company and Circuit City can purchase home electronics in huge quantities for their chains of super-stores. This buying power allows them quantity discounts that individual appliance and electronics outlets cannot match. The growth of huge, multi-category hypermarkets also moves the institutional structure at all levels toward fewer, larger entities.

Globalization, a process by which firms become multi-national in scope, has an impact similar to concentration. Globalization (the appear-ance in multiple countries of products or institutions originally offered only in one) may result from consolidation and acquisition of firms in one country by those in another. Globalization implies that we must think of markets in worldwide terms, no longer simply in terms of a single domestic economy. Globalization also implies that there are few barriers to the free flow of capital, and that products initially made and used in one country may be made and used in a variety of different countries.

Information *technology* will threaten to overwhelm marketing decision makers with both the sheer volume of information and the variety of computer assisted packages available for processing that information. In this hyper-information environment success will come to those decision makers who understand: (1) what questions to ask, or issues to address, in marketing decisions; (2) what information is really needed, and what is irrelevant or even misleading; and (3) the most efficient and effective means of acquiring, processing and retaining appropriate information.

Communication technology has reduced the need for local or regional entities for communication purposes. Within the United States, we can communicate by telephone across the continent as readily as we can across the city. Time zone differences, rather than lack of communica-tions links, form the greatest barrier to transnational communication among industrialized countries.

Similarly, *political factors* also operate to reduce the need for local and regional entities for delivery and service purposes. For example, the Unit-ed States and Canada are removing barriers to free the flow of goods. In 1992, the European Economic Community (E.E.C.) will have eased its restrictions on free flows of goods and services among member nations.

Although capital and merchandise may flow freely across national boundaries, immigration restrictions may remain in force. Even if those restrictions are moderated, the flow of *labor* typically is slower and less efficient than the flow of goods, services and capital. Thus, by the year 2000 we should still see imbalances of labor supply and demand.

In countries like the United States, where demand for services provided by labor is likely to continue to exceed the supply of labor available, marketing functions will become automated. Automation of purchase transactions is likely to take the form of applying artificial intelligence or expert systems technology. For example, in the purchase of durable goods customers might prefer, over a scarce or unqualified salesperson, a dialogue with an interactive computer system that holds a flexible branching program. Consumers could respond to questions about their tastes, interests, needs and objectives for a particular product. After searching its database, which contains information on the features of many products, the program could recommend particular types of products or specific brands and models. Versions of more primitive systems are already in use in some durable goods retailers.

Transactions themselves have already been automated between, for example, American Hospital Supply and its customers. There is no reason why that kind of automation should not extend to the supermarket. The human cashier performs no functions that a robot, with positioning and vision capabilities, could not perform. Indeed, development of such systems is already under way. Such systems would appear as natural for supermarkets in which customers already bag their own groceries.

Away from the sales and operations sites themselves, marketing planning may take on a different cast. An increasing number of women are entering the managerial ranks in the marketing function, and more and more of them are choosing to take extended periods away from full-time work to raise their children. To accommodate these women, marketers will make arrangements such as providing home work stations, completely flexible hours, and video conferencing hook-ups to replace committee meetings. Although they may initially be reluctant to do so, senior marketing managers will make these provisions for women simply because the most capable women, who can "write their own tickets," will demand them.

Perhaps paradoxically, the emergence of large organizations provides opportunities for new entrepreneurial ventures. As the larger companies increase the quality and variety of products available and reduce their cost, these improvements will raise consumers' levels of aspiration, thus providing opportunities for still more varied, customized, higher quality and lower cost alternatives. Giant companies will be unable to satisfy many of these interests, because the success of the very large companies depends upon their ability to provide standard offerings to mass markets. Thus, opportunities for smaller businesses will arise.

Additional opportunities will come from institutional gaps in the marketplace. The growth of giant institutions with sophisticated marketing management practices will come primarily at the expense of those medium-size organizations that will leave voids for smaller business to fill.

The same technology that helps established organizations facilitates formation of new businesses. Technological advances, such as downsizing of computers and computer-driven equipment, make it possible for businesses to operate on a small scale to fill specialized niches. Entrepreneurs will be available to conceive and operate these new, specialized businesses. As the labor pool shrinks at all levels of profession and skill, costs of labor will rise and available individuals will have to be used at maximum efficiency. These trends argue for deployment of available resources in units that can offer specialized products and services, both directly to customers and to large firms that might not be able to use specialized resources to maximum efficiency. Even if efficient use were possible, individuals whose skills are in short supply may prefer to operate independently, to gain more control over their personal and professional lives.

These entrepreneurial firms will be market driven, that is, they will come into being by virtue of entrepreneurs' recognizing opportunities which may appear as discontinuities or disequilibria in a marketplace. If these opportunities are short lived, the entrepreneurs will not mind. Indeed, many of them may think nothing of establishing a business for five to ten years, then selling it or liquidating it and moving on to another one. As more and more entrepreneurs learn the skill of serial entrepreneurship, we can expect them to fill windows of opportunity more efficiently and more promptly, even though those windows will be open for only a short time.

It will be important, both for the operators of those shorter term businesses and for those that serve them, to understand the processes by which businesses are born, mature, and disappear. By the year 2000, the emerging science of entrepreneurship may well receive more recognition. Because the implications of serving and managing new businesses are so important to marketing, marketing may be the home discipline from which much of this new tradition develops.

Howard V. Perlmutter
Professor of Social Architecture and Management, The Wharton School
University of Pennsylvania

Marketing in the Twenty First Century must be understood in the context of an emerging, unprecedented and apparently irreversible First Global Civilization. The First Global Civilization is based on both shared and conflicting political, economic, socio-cultural-demographic, scientific and technological, and ecological values. And from the point of view of marketing in the year 2000, the direction of shift of these values has major significance. These shared values include a mixture of three value sets described in Table 1.

The first set of values are the values associated with *Industrialization, or "I" values*. These include a concern for efficiency over people, short term profits, without a concern for consequences, a secondary concern with the environment, hierarchical systems as a basis for organizing, competing over cooperating, the dominance dependence mode of relating to others, a male rational, left brain approach to decision making and an ethnocentric or home country approach to the marketing of products and services worldwide.

The second set of values are reactions against industrialism, or *De-industrial* which we call *"D" values*. These values underlie in part a great variety of movement, in greening, in right-brained intuitive thinking, in world wildlife, and concern with species extinction, and strongly doubting the sustainability of the expansive industrialism and its consequences on the planet as in the global warming process, and a preference for self reliance or counter-dependence. "D" values have daily attention in the media and increasingly among legislators around the world, in the right to health care, small is beautiful, feminism, and Islamic Fundamentalism.

The third set of values which we see are *"S" values* or a combination of "I" and "D." "S" stands for *Symbiotic*, in that it seeks a new balance between "I" and "D" values. This approach is marked by both a global and local orientation to problems which we have called geocentric and integrative (or global cooperative–competitive) to distinguish it from the home country oriented or host country oriented or polycentric approach. Other "S" values include: a concern for both people and efficiency, results and consequences, the use of a wide variety of technologies, both hard and soft, the design of environmentally compatible products, and quantity and quality and large scale customization, large and small com-

TABLE 1
THREE VALUE SYSTEMS

"I" VALUES	"D" VALUES	"S" VALUES
Efficiency Primary	People Primary	People & Efficiency
Primacy of Profits Viability Focus	Profits Amoral Legitimacy Focus	Viability & Legitimacy
Results Oriented	Consequence Focus	Results & Consequences
High Tech Best	Appropriate Tech	Wide Tech Variety
Dominance-Dependence	Counter Dependencia-Self-Reliance	Balance Autonomy-Interdependence
Environment Secondary	Environment Primary	Environment Oriented Products
Needs Not Rights	Rights Not Needs	Rights & Responsibilities
Large is Better	Small is Beautiful	Large & Small
Hierarchical Systems	Horizontal Networks	Systems & Networks
Male, Rational, Left Brain	Female, Intuitive Right Brain	Whole Brained, Rational & Intuitive
Ethnocentric MNC	Polycentric MNC	Geocentric Integrative
Quantity Oriented	Quality Oriented	Quantity & Quality
Systems Approach	Network Approach	Systems & Networks
Elitist	Populist	Pluralist
Competition	Cooperation	Competitive-Cooperation
Synthetics is Progress	Natural is Better	Natural-Synthetics
Trickle Down Benefits	Ground Up Self-Reliance	Top-Down, Middle, Horizontal-Bottom Up

panies working together, pluralist values, and seeking a balance between autonomy and interdependence and flatter, flexible, more synarchical as opposed to hierarchical organizations.

Our contention is that despite the very great diversity of cultures on our planet, the level of global interdependence requires more and more shared norms based on "S" values.

Practically speaking, it means that companies and countries have to both cooperate and compete, to find global standards on a great variety of issues from trade to telecommunications, to insider trading, and to international accounting principles and practices. This extends, by the way, to such international problems as how to deal with the global money laundering practices of the drug dealers, diseases like AIDS, terrorism, and world hunger and poverty.

In the year 2000, humankind will still live in at least 200 nations (probably more), will speak at least 3000 different languages, or when dialects are included as many as 10,000, and will still share values of the "I" and "D" variety. But the direction of shift will be towards "S" values.

Many *traditionalists* who now hold mainly "D" values and appear closed to the outside world of change (e.g., Iran), will have evolved into *transitionals and modernists* who see their future as irreversibly locked into a community of nations who hold a variety of Industrial and Symbiotic Values. In our view, Glasnost (openness) and Perestroika (restructuring) are "S" values. Recent and dramatic transitions are taking place in China and the U.S.S.R., where there are different versions of opening and restructuring.

As people of the planet can be thought to belong to the same civilization, it makes sense to talk of global life styles, global life situations, and common experiences at different stages of the life cycle, e.g., the world women's market, the market of one year olds and seventy year olds, those who mow lawns. This global segmentation process is the challenge of Marketing 2000.

We see emerging a Twenty First Century marketing which asks not only what is unique about what is local but also what is universal and will lead to a wide variety of *new global market niches* in almost every business sector from accounting to zippers, in food, fragrances, and fashions.

So marketing in the year 2000 will have a value system in a First Global Civilization which supports both a global-local orientation, and a cooperative-competitive orientation. The direction of this shift is supported by these macro forces:

The irreversible *political* forces towards a more *multi-polar political system*, where by the year 2000, North America, Japan, Western Europe, China and the U.S.S.R. will be the major superpowers.

Along the Triad dimension, Europe, North America, and Japan will deepen their mutual penetration of each others' economies. The current fear in the West is of a Pax Nipponica to replace Pax Americana with the likelihood increasing that some kind of accommodation of being first among equals will be an acceptable outcome by the year 2000.

a) *Along the East-West axis*, transideological-pragmatic approaches are in ascent, in Poland, Hungary and the Soviet Union. These seem irreversible, since the alternatives have already been explored in a Cold War setting; it is possible that a kind of SuperEurope market will develop.

b) *Along the North-South axis*, by the year 2000, Third and Fourth World nations will have moved beyond the post-colonial period of counter-dependencia. They will have given up illusions of autarchic self-reliance by seeking various balances of autonomy and interdependence.

c) *Technological* forces brought about by dramatic changes in transportation, computers and telecommunications will be such that major linguistic barriers will be overcome. A world of instantaneous and simultaneous global information movement and management will come into being.

This Simultaneously Neighboring Functionally Interdependent World (the SNFI World) leads more and more people to experience a series of *world events* on a daily basis, and these are frequently eco-threats.

In the *economic-industrial-commercial* realm, it is clearer that the unprecedented forces that are increasing global economic interdependence are largely irreversible. The emphasis on foreign direct investment being sought from Vietnam to Venezuela, under conditions of host country benefit, will continue while confiscations, national expropriations and nationalizations will become rare.

Both global competition and cooperation will be solidified as a new norm. From the Triad of advanced economies, to those of formerly centrally planned economies, this will mean greater efficiency and sophistication in dealing with world markets, and the development of more *strategic partnerships* to reach global markets. The year 2000 will be marked by a much more interdependent global economy than exists today.

d) *Socio-cultural and demographic shifts* such as an emerging global youth culture will carry into an adult culture. This applies not only to the convergence of tastes and choices (despite continuing diversity) and hybridization of ideas for products and services, but also to the arts, music and dance. Something is happening when *Les Miserables* plays in 40 countries around the world and rock becomes almost universal. By the year 2000, such forms of global entertainment will be commonplace, alongside the individual regional folk and indigenous art and product forms.

Marketing in the year 2000 will, to a large extent, be in the hands of *global networks*, small, medium and large, in advanced and developing countries, in largely private form, along with some that are state owned, in both manufacturing and services. This may be referred to as a corporate galaxy or Global Industrial System Configuration (GISC), global networks linked by mutually beneficial (symbiotic) arrangements in both equity and non-equity relationships. They are already emerging in some industries such as automobiles and semiconductors and financial services. This will increasingly require a mindset that takes both a global and local view at the same time, a *global-local or geocentric- integrative mindset as opposed to an ethnocentric (home country oriented) or polycentric (host country oriented) mindset*. The implication is that the successful enterprises of the Twenty First Century must develop:

1. global cooperative (geocentric-integrative) ways to track the direction and speed of diffusion of ideas for local products and services to global products and services, as well as the reverse for global to become local.

2. multi-directional influence paths inside the organization by involving multi-national (corporate and affiliate) teams in the global design process.

3. global mandates to affiliates in all countries to work inside and outside the firm to reach world markets through co-marketing arrangements to tap global market niches.

References

Howard V. Perlmutter (1984). "Building the Symbiotic Societal Enterprise," *World Futures*, 19, 3-4.

Howard V. Perlmutter and Eric Trist (1986). "Paradigms for Societal Transition" *Human Relations*, Vol. 39, No. 1, 1-27.

Frederick E. Webster, Jr.
E. B. Osborn Professor of Marketing, Amos Tuck School of Business Administration
Dartmouth College:
Five Forces Re-Shaping Marketing

The future for marketing may be very different from the past. Many of the things we take for granted today — things relating to the technical, political, economic, social, and organizational environment — have the potential to change dramatically in the near future. The result will be some exciting new challenges for marketing in the 1990s. Fundamental pressures on marketing as a practice and as a discipline are coming from five key areas: the globalization of markets; information technology; the disintegration of large corporations; the defunctionalization of marketing; and increased awareness of moral and ethical issues, especially those created by the public consequences of private consumption.

Increased Globalization of Markets

Today virtually all markets are by definition global markets, where competitors have global operations and strategic orientations. Consumers and industrial buyers in the information age, with global media and global distribution systems, learn that they have multiple options, and their preferences change continuously based on this information. Purely domestic markets are near extinction. Pick any product or almost any service and you get the picture: automobiles, banking, computers, consumer electronics, chemicals, fashions, hotels, airlines, etc. Changes in the geo-political realm underscore the point: the U.S. - Canadian trade agreement; Europe 1992; the U.S. - Japan agreement to co-develop the FSX fighter plane; etc. Globalization is a totally pervasive aspect of markets and marketing; it is really not a separate issue at all.

Sadly, American firms have been playing a catch-up game for at least the past decade, slowly facing the realization of lost competitiveness. Only in the past few years have we seen American firms making steady and significant progress in such basic areas as reducing costs and improving quality and service in response to global competitors. While a global marketplace was at one time primarily an issue facing multinational corporations, today it is a fact of life for virtually all businesses, large and small.

Much academic research in marketing still ignores the global dimension, using paradigms that are inherently domestic in their orientation, assuming in particular that all competitors are playing by the same rules and that markets are well defined. The real issues for many American firms, those that have had their survival threatened, have come from foreign competitors who have redefined the key success factors in the industry or who have gone to school on their American competitors and learned to beat them at their own game.

There is no such thing as international marketing as opposed to domestic marketing. To treat the globalization of markets as a separate issue is to miss the point: All important questions have a global dimension and to ignore this is to be out of touch with reality.

Information Technology

Slowly, we are sensing how basic and permanent are the changes that are being wrought as a result of information technology — including data processing, communications, expert systems, computer networking, check-out scanners, and a host of new data services. Information technology is collapsing the time frame for decision making to the point where the process itself is changed fundamentally; action must be taken almost instantly based on the instant availability of new "information."   So-called "just-in-time" systems are a good example — products of perfect quality must be shipped in precise quantities upon demand in distribution systems of near perfect reliability.   Inventories, in-coming inspection, returns and rework, lead times, and other time-consuming and slack-producing aspects of the traditional customer-supplier interface have been reduced to zero or very close to it.   Likewise, competitive advertising and sales promotion response time are dramatically reduced in markets where activities are continuously tracked and reported.

Clearly, information technology is having a fundamental impact on the nature of organizations and how they work.   Organizational theorists cannot agree, however, on whether information technology leads to more centralization or more decentralization of decision-making.   We face an urgent research challenge to address this set of issues as they relate to marketing.

The Dis-integration of Large Corporations

Is there a manager whose company has not felt the pressure to downsize, de-layer, become more entrepreneurial, slough off unproductive assets and unrelated businesses, and become more flexible, driven in part by the twin forces of globalization and information technology?   The overwhelming tendency among large corporations today is to try to create autonomous, small, entrepreneurial units to innovate responsive solutions to customer problems in well-defined market niches.   The large, hierarchical, divisionalized, functional, and matrixed organizations that have characterized business for the past century are obsolete in the global marketplace.   The benefits they provided in terms of specialization and control have been offset by their inefficiency and lack of flexibility.

Large corporate structures are being modified by long-term strategic alliances and short-term network organizations focused on specific opportunities.   Many firms have had some experience with strategic alliances in such forms as joint ventures for co-development of technology, entering new markets, or supplying products and services to major customers. Strategic alliances tend to be long-term in their orientation and to represent reasonably permanent commitments by the parties to some common objectives. Recent research in this area suggests that managements often underestimate the complexities and inter-dependencies that have to be managed to make strategic alliances successful, including the issues involved in combining disparate corporate cultures.

Network organizations are more short-term and flexible than true strategic alliances, often created to respond to a specific opportunity such as a major construction project or a clothing fashion fad. Networks are made possible by broad-access information systems. The key roles in the network are the broker, designers, suppliers, producers, and distributors, each entity performing only those functions in which it truly had distinctive competence. The broker is the party who puts together the network, often based on previous experience with the same players, and may have few if any physical or financial assets committed to the project.

There is ample evidence that such flexible, boundary-spanning organization structures are going to become increasingly common in the dynamic, global marketplace. Thus, globalization and disintegration are closely related forces. It is easy to attribute a good amount of the downsizing and de-layering going on in American business to the financial pressures created by takeovers, mergers, deregulation, etc. Clearly, that is a major driver. But equally significant, and even more important, strategically, is the necessity to improve the market responsiveness of the firm.

The De-Functionalization of Marketing

Almost four decades ago, when Peter Drucker first wrote about the marketing concept as a management philosophy, he noted that marketing is really not a separate function at all; it is the whole business seen from the point of view of its final result, that is, from the customer's point of view. In a few firms, especially those in consumer packaged goods, it was possible to make marketing a line management function in a highly functionalized and divisionalized organization. In many other firms, however, the battle has raged ever since over the proper definition of marketing, especially in its relationship to sales. Marketing, among all the so-called management "functions," is the only one that has never been able to define itself satisfactorily.

Some academic thinking, along with management practice, now suggests that marketing should not be a separate function at all, except in the narrow sense of providing specialized services such as marketing research. In fact, even in the case of those services, outside sourcing is increasingly the case.

From a philosophical point of view, marketing, as synonymous with customer orientation, should be a focus for everyone in the organization, not a separate department. Marketing in many companies has been either "pushed out" into the operating units of the business, especially in those companies that are consciously "disintegrating" their organizations, or combined with strategic planning, usually with substantially reduced staffs. In other companies, such as Pillsbury after its takeover by Grand Met, marketing staffs are simply being cut in an effort to reduce costs. Why is "marketing" so easy to cut? Perhaps it is because we still can't agree on what is meant by marketing skills within an organization. Functional organizations per se are becoming obsolete, and more and more companies are becoming aware of the ways in which the functional "chimneys" or "silos" impede timely decision making in a changing competitive environment. Marketing as a stand-alone function in the typical organization will become extremely rare.

The Public Consequences of Private Consumption

In the 1970s, and into the early 1980s, there was a significant amount of research relating marketing management to consumerism, environmentalism, and related questions of public policy. That thrust has largely dissipated in the past decade. The ways in which we commonly think about consumers, customers, and markets are based for the most part on a rather simplistic, uni-dimensional view of buying and consumption. Our traditional models of consumer choice behavior are all built around a simple utility-maximizing model from neo-classical economics. The consumer will do those things which offer the most pleasure or personal gain per unit of expenditure.

But consumers are also members of communities, groups, families, cultures, and subcultures. They are social and moral beings. Not all behavior can be understood or explained by reference to the pleasure motive. In addition to the utility of pleasure, there is also the utility of morality, another reason why people act the way they do. We need to understand that some consumer acts enhance personal satisfaction and others discharge moral commitments. It is too easy to lump them both together under the rubric of "satisfaction" or "preferences," and to treat them both within the economic paradigm of utility maximization, but when we do so we ignore a critical difference.

Marketers need to be aware of the social and political forces at work to deal with the public consequences of private consumption. Smoking in public places, gun control, drunken driving, waste disposal, water pollution, and the destruction of the ozone layer are just a few of the issues that come to mind. What is the connection between our relaxed concern about energy conservation and the massive oil spill in Alaska? How will that event feed back into the public consciousness about the effects of their energy usage patterns? One can expect political, social, and individual actions in response to the oil spill that go well beyond the consumer boycotting of Exxon gas stations that occurred immediately afterwards.

Marketing as a practice and a field of study needs to come back to a central concern for the social, political, ecological, and moral motivation of consumers, and of business buyers as well, that it flirted with too briefly in the mid-1970s. These may be some of the most important issues forced on marketers in the 1990s, and at their core is a recognition that most actions of buyers and sellers have public and moral consequences that go well beyond the simple private pleasure and gain derived from a market-based transaction. Do we really want to leave the discussion and resolution of those issues, and the imposition of solutions, to the public sector and the political process? Do we really believe that it is only a pricing problem, as the economic model would suggest?

These are five concerns that I think are most basic as we try to reinvent marketing to fit the 1990s: globalization; information technology; organizational disintegration; marketing de-functionalization; and the public, moral consequences of private consumption.

William D. Wells
Executive Vice President, Director of Marketing Services
DDB Needham Worldwide, Inc.

1. Over the past eleven years, the single most important influence on marketing has been the impact of the computer. Since the computer's potential has so far been only partly realized, the computer will probably continue to be the single most important influence between the year 1989 and the year 2000.

2. Combined with the retail scanner, computer databases have moved the center of marketing gravity from the manufacturer to the retailer. Because retailers can now tell exactly how profitable every item is, they can dictate which brands, which sizes and which prices will be presented to the consumer.

3. The computer also enables the manufacturer to read short-term consumer response to marketing control variables. This ability has produced a radical shift toward price promotions and away from advertising, with consequent deterioration of brand franchises.

4. The availability of exact response readings has also encouraged a shift in marketing planning from long-term marketing objectives to short-term tactics. When a brand manager's bonus depends upon last quarter's sales increase, said brand manager, not being a fool, will do anything he or she can to produce that increase, however temporary.

5. However, computer data bases are growing larger, and more sophisticated software is becoming available. This software will reveal the long-term impact of short-term marketing planning. The result will be a corrective swing back toward measures designed to maximize long-term, as distinguished from short-term, profits.

6. This new software, and the more complete databases, will also permit manipulation of "stables" of brands, with strategic niche positioning of each member of the stable, and extensive cross-selling. This development will encourage megabrands (e.g., Kraft) which cover a family of related products.

7. As databases proliferate beyond the U.S., marketing planning will increasingly become global. This process will be greatly accelerated by the preparations the multi-nationals are now making for the events that will unfold in Europe after 1992.

8. As marketing planning becomes increasingly portfolio oriented, increasingly long-term, and increasingly multi-national, marketing will increasingly be dominated by a few multi-national competitors in each major category. These few multi-national leaders will be served by a few corresponding multi-national communication companies.

9. Although the ideal of "integrated marketing communication" is now beset by many political difficulties, necessity will force that ideal to become a reality. The present separation of advertising, sales promotion, public relations and direct marketing is grossly inefficient. As soon as one of the multi-nationals begins to overcome the political barriers to integrated marketing communication, others will be forced to follow.

10. Global consumer marketing will run head-on into a world-wide need to protect the environment. This clash will change marketing forever.

11. In the year 2000, people born at the peak of the U.S. post-war baby boom will be 43 years old. In other countries, the people born at the corresponding peaks of their baby booms will be slightly younger. This development will increase disposable income, and it will encourage certain product categories and discourage others. (In 2029, the last of the U.S. baby-boomers will be 65, and most of them will still be alive and in need of support by a much smaller population. This will be a bad year. It will be visible from the year 2000.)

12. In the U.S., Blacks will be a larger segment of the population than they are now, and because of the opportunities provided by the civil rights movement of the 1960s and 70s the Black middle class will have grown substantially. The Hispanic population will also be much larger, and will exercise more influence on marketing. Because of their devotion to learning, Asians will assume leadership roles in many academic and applied marketing environments.

Jerry Wind
Director, SEI Center for Advanced Studies in Management and
The Lauder Professor of Marketing, The Wharton School
University of Pennsylvania

The changes that occurred in marketing in the last 11 years (from 1978 to 1989) are significant. Yet, one can expect much more dramatic changes in the next 11 years. The early indication of these changes are here today but their magnitude, interdependence and impact are likely to drastically change the nature of marketing in the Twenty First Century.

The changing environment includes:

• Rapid and radical technological developments in computers, artificial intelligence, telecommunications, and the information sciences.

• Internationalization of business and the fuller integration of national economies into regional blocks and a global system. Increased international competition and the emergence of global customers and resource markets.

• Continuing pattern of mergers and acquisitions and other domestic and international strategic alliances that alter the competitive structures of increasing numbers of industries.

• Greater complexity of management issues, requiring agility with interdisciplinary skills in both profit and non-profit sectors.

- Growth of entrepreneurship in new and existing businesses.

- Increased scrutiny of business decisions by government and the public, with greater focus on the ethical dimensions of those decisions.

- Increased deregulation and cooperation between business and government.

- The aging of the population, the growth of the Hispanic and other subcultures, and the impact of the changing demographics and life styles on new product and business developments.

- The increased concerns with quality of life and self-fulfillment at work and play and the balancing of the demands of work, family and society.

- Increased importance of the service and knowledge sector.

- Reorganization of work-teams, changes in the traditional staff functions, reduced layers of management and bureaucracy, movement toward global and individually-empowered organizations.

These changes and especially their interdependencies are likely to have significant impact on management in the Twenty First Century and as such are likely to change drastically the nature of marketing. Among the more significant changes we can expect in marketing are:

1. A move away from the traditional mass market to truly segmented approaches including segments of one person. This move is consistent with the dramatic change in consumers' demographics and life styles and is facilitated by the enormous developments in computers and telecommunications. Technology allows the design and utilization of data bases based on a firm's entire customer and prospect list. Developments in innovative specialized media and distribution outlets will also facilitate segmentation. This is already happening in some advanced industrial firms and is likely to move to other industries.

2. A move away from a lopsided emphasis on domestic marketing to global marketing. This globalization of marketing does not mean, however, the development of a standardized worldwide product. It does mean the adoption of a new marketing philosophy focusing on choosing the desired mix of standardization- differentiation strategies, while focusing on both adaptation to local idiosyncratic conditions and to the achievement

of cross-country integration and synergy — "Think Globally - Act Locally."

The globalization of marketing will place new demands on marketing managers requiring understanding/sensitivity to the needs and behavioral pattern of other markets, as well as the ability to deal with the complexity of operating in the rapidly-changing global environment.

3. A move away from a narrow marketing focus on consumers to a broad focus on all the stakeholders of the firm. Increasingly, business success will require close alliances with suppliers, distributors, other research and development organizations, etc. The management of these alliances and the relationships with other key stakeholders of the firm — government, security analysts, the media, etc. — require the development of effective marketing programs for all these stakeholders. A major related development will be the proliferation of co-marketing alliances both within the U.S. and globally.

4. A move toward expanding the scope of marketing from that of a functional department to marketing as a philosophy and perspective that pervades all business functions and decisions.

In fact, introducing marketing concepts and methods to R&D, manufacturing, finance, human resources management, and the management of the Strategic Business Units (SBU) and the corporation will become one of the major roles of marketing.

5. A move away from the sole (and somewhat "imperialistic") focus on marketing as the driving discipline to a truly cross-functional perspective.

Most business decisions involve a fully integrated perspective of marketing, technology, manufacturing, information technology, finance and other key business functions. New roles will be defined for marketing in the management of the various functions of the firm, functions which may focus on innovation, quality, etc.

6. A move away from bureaucratic "command and control" type organizations of marketing activities to flatter organizations, more entrepreneurial in spirit, that are centered on empowered individuals and groups. The organization of the Twenty First Century enterprise and of the marketing activities will be global in nature, based on information technology and designed to capture individual creativity, initiative, loyalty and changing

values. It will be an adaptive learning organization aimed at meeting both the vision of its leaders and the needs of its many internal and external stakeholders.

7. A move toward the increased utilization of information technology and new decision tools including AI based expert systems in all marketing decisions and areas of operations.

Decision support systems augmented with Expert Systems are likely to be the norm rather than the exception. They will be a must for the transformation of the increasing flow of data into information and knowledge, and will encompass all marketing decisions including the most creative, complex and unstructured decisions.

8. Increased attention to the ongoing study and monitoring of consumers and other stakeholders using advanced marketing research and modelling tools. These research methods will provide a better understanding of consumers' and stakeholders' behavior and their likely response to the marketing programs of the firm and its competitors. Research and modelling will be fully integrated, longitudinal analysis and real time analysis of large global databases will be the norm.

9. From a lopsided view of marketing as being the exclusive domain of consumer goods firms to an expanded view that stresses the importance of marketing for all industrial and service firms as well as non-profit organizations including governmental agencies in the U.S. and an increasing number of countries.

10. A change in the nature, scope and operation of marketing institutions. Ad agencies, marketing research firms and other marketing service institutions will offer a wider but yet more specialized array of services. Ad agencies may change to communication firms focusing on all aspects of communication including direct marketing, P.R., promotion, etc. Similarly, marketing research firms will offer integrated modelling and decision support systems. These and other specialized marketing institutions, such as new product development organizations, design groups and others, will offer their services using information technology on a global scale.

In addition, the proliferation of the hollow corporation will see the emergence of innovative new distribution and marketing firms. Overall, these changes and their interdependencies are likely to change the concepts and methods of marketing. Marketing will continue to serve as one of the key functions of all management activities. Its role in the enterprises of the global information age will increase in importance. As a scholarly discipline, the advances in marketing science over the last two decades will continue but with increased concern for the changing needs of the "real world." Thus, marketing will be transformed into a truly cross-disciplinary function and philosophy.

REFERENCES

Salamon, Lester M. (1987), "Of Market Failure, Voluntary Failure, and Third Party Government: Toward a Theory of Government-Nonprofit Relations in the Modern Welfare State," *Journal of Voluntary Action Research*, Vol. 16, No. 1 and 2.

CHAPTER 8

MARKETING: CHANGING PERSPECTIVES AND ROLES

"Managers have no choice but to anticipate the future, to attempt to mold it, and to balance short-range and long-range goals." Peter Drucker

Introduction

A primary marketing management challenge, perhaps the most important challenge in Marketing 2000, will be to manage effectively the impact of the terrific pace of future market changes. That is the inevitable conclusion of the information gathered from this study's participants. All indications are that the forces affecting marketing, particularly the influential external variables that guide and shape markets, will be far less stable in the future. Management will be challenged to deal with marketing in motion. Such an environment will make it much harder than ever before for marketing managers to cope let alone anticipate; more difficult to plan and strategize, let alone carry out marketing operations.

This chapter builds on and extends the ideas presented in the previous chapters. It highlights some of the significant changes they portend for marketing management in the future, focuses on marketers' changing future responsibilities and the implementation of a futures orientation, and describes five new marketing emphases that will likely evolve: proactive marketing, just-in-time marketing, value-based marketing, leading-edge marketing, and network marketing. Marketing's important role as a change agent, and the management of change, are also highlighted.

Futurity and Marketing

As markets veer in new directions, as market turbulence increases, as competition rises in intensity both within and between nations, top-level executives will be directed, as never before, to anticipate, become more keenly aware of future environments, and turn more of their attention outward. They will alter their focus somewhat, moving away from their concentrated emphasis on the day-to-day internal business operations, to paying much greater attention to the external dynamic thrusts of the marketplace.

The ability to think ahead, to anticipate, coupled with flexibility and market adaptability, will become not only guidelines for survival, but hallmarks of leadership. Being able to anticipate, to act rather than react, to adjust organizations from top to bottom in order to capitalize on perceptions of untapped market opportunities, will delineate well-managed companies from those that are not. Futurity will become a major management concern. The caution "that we should all be concerned with the future because we shall have to spend the rest of our lives there" has rich meaning for business directions in Marketing 2000.

Yet, this flies in the face of current management tendencies to focus on past performance and accomplishments, on previous results such as past sales, costs, and profits, on existing company policies and standard operating procedures, and on maintenance of the status quo. Interestingly enough, most companies seem to believe that they are future oriented, and are preparing for future market changes, although our evidence suggests otherwise. In reality most seem to be deluding themselves. They tend to be attuned to the conventional wisdom, bogged down in the present, and are more concerned with the moment and short-run market opportunities, than they are with the future. Figuratively, they turn their backs on the future and look to the past, or at best, see the future through models of the past, which may invite some unpleasant surprises and even disaster.

In Marketing 2000 more explicit credence will be given to the fact that it will be future market developments that ultimately bestow asset value. Companies will come face to face with the reality that they cannot afford the previous postures of treating futurity so haphazardly. Management's stake in futurity will be highlighted as companies address such signal questions as "who is in charge of our future," "whose responsibility is it to anticipate likely developments," "who is charged with considering not only company implications of likely future developments, but equally important, company responses" and "who has the task of keeping in close touch with likely future developments?"

Dealing with the future may, of course, be frustrating and humbling, for its unpredictability haunts marketing decision-makers. Market uncertainties have the potential for increasing management feelings of inadequacy and insecurity. But since uncertainty cannot be eliminated, management cannot neglect or ignore it. Rather it has to be taken into account and dealt with rationally and logically. Regardless of advances in scientific marketing, marketers will have to become ever more comfortable with basing many important decisions on other than scientific data and hard facts; on "future facts," opinions, probabilities, trends, tendencies, guesses, feelings, extrapolations, and sheer judgments. These comprise the substance of futures information.

Enterprises with the capabilities of anticipating, of capitalizing on future marketing trends and developments, of adopting a pro-active stance, may be poised to realize substantial profits. They can be positioned to reap the rich rewards that flow from anticipation, preparation, and adaptability, from making the appropriate changes well ahead of time. Insights and awareness about futurity, the basic ingredients of such preparedness, will become a more valued management asset as market turbulence increases, product life cycles are shortened, risks as well as potential profits multiply, and global competitive responses become more direct and immediate.

Executives will be under increasing pressure to assure that future market implications of rapidly changing environments — technological, socio-economic, competitive, demographic, ecological, and political — are factored into decisions. Such information about "the known future" will form the basis of marketing acumen, the building blocks of strategic marketing planning, budgeting, and effective decision making. More explicit recognition will be given to marketing as a key tool of control. Indeed, the budget itself, sometimes referred to as "the driver of an organization" and the major tool of control, is in reality governed by marketing assessments of the future — by estimates of future sales, revenues, and profits.

Changing Mindset

Figure 1 indicates some of the major general differences in marketing management mindset and operations between the past and what is expected in the future. They were inferred from the information shared by Commission members, other respondents, and the implications of ideas appearing in the literature. They focus on three marketing management dimensions: direction, perspective, and time.

Twenty-First Century Shifts

FIGURE 1

	Twentieth Century	Twenty-First Century
Direction	Hierarchial Superior/Subordinate Top-down Pyramidal Bureaucratic	Participative Consensual Participative Bottom-up Entrepreneurial
Perspective	Single-center Company Nation Centrifugal Process Things	Multi-center Network Changing core Divergent Market Human
Time	Past/Present Discrete Short-run Stability	Past/Present/Future Continuous Longer range Change

Direction in the Twentieth Century took the format of a hierarchial relationship, with the superior/subordinate, pyramidical structure and a top-down flow. It was more bureaucratic in nature. In the Twenty First Century, the direction is expected to utilize a flatter structure, with participative, group consensus decisions, using more of a consultative, bottom-up, and entrepreneurial approach.

The Twentieth Century marketing management perspective has been more of a single center focus, such as the company, the industry or when governments are involved, the state or the nation. It is more of a concentric viewpoint of marketing operations with activities centering around a single core, stressing process, activities and material things rather than people. The Twenty First Century will see the emergence of a more diverse and diffused perspective, with multi-centered focuses, the development of networks, changing cores, greater appreciation and acceptance of divergent views, and marketing approaches that focus more on people and their concerns.

The time orientation in marketing management in the Twentieth Century was firmly focused on the present and heavily anchored in the past. Time was perceived more in terms of discrete periods that were quite stable, changed slowly, and managed for the short run. In the Twenty First Century, the past and present will be folded into the perspective of the future, and marketing management considered from the view of continuous flows, rather than discrete operations. A longer-range view and an acclimation to turbulence and change will be the norm.

Marketing 2000 will see a change in mindset, a transformation in marketing's roles at the most senior level. There will be widespread top-management acceptance of marketing's pivotal position in organizations, whether business or non-profit, consumer or industrial, product or service. Marketing will arrive in the executive suite, its signal role in strategic plans and decisions will be solidified, signifying a new era of marketing in modern management.

Thus, marketing's role will transcend its traditional functional and departmental orientation, and take on the posture of a focal point for the whole enterprise. Top management thinking about marketing will shift from the previous divisional or functional mindset to the perception of marketing as an over-arching corporate philosophy and value system, a way of business life, a means of encouraging continuous adjustments to markets and promoting adaptability, and a vehicle for anticipating and encouraging company-wide change. In the process, some of the widely-held beliefs about markets and marketing will become outmoded, major changes in marketing management operations will occur, and marketers will be motivated to think in new terms, to keep in closer touch with future marketing developments, nationally and globally, and to make major adjustments in marketing, as well as social policies.

Some evidence indicates that executives immersed in a futures perspective change their approaches. They tend to rethink their businesses more regularly, reevaluate priorities, reassess business precepts, and extend their conceptions of valuable marketing information. They appreciate the value of less than factual information — the usefulness of insights about the indefinite future. They are more likely to anticipate and shape changes, act rather than react, and move purposefully in new directions rather than protect the status quo. They do more than merely try to cope; they act before conditions force reactions. They develop greater appreciation for such futures-related activities as the following:

- Scanning emerging market environments;
- Developing and assessing future scenarios;

- Delineating possible future market opportunities and their strategic and operational consequences; and

- Preparing contingency marketing plans and organizational responses.

Marketing Management Postures

As a result of all our deliberations, we have concluded that at least five related and overlapping marketing emphases or postures will emerge. They are: *pro-active marketing, just-in-time marketing, value-based marketing, leading edge marketing,* and *network marketing.*

Pro-active marketing stances embody perceptions of the "knowable future," and are based on management insights and assessments about what will likely happen in markets. This orientation sets out to purposefully manage future market opportunities, to induce changes, and to innovate as contrasted with the conventional reactive postures of the past. It explicitly recognizes the importance of marketing the changes themselves. Pro-active marketing factors futurity into marketing strategies, decisions, and operations so that appropriate actions can be taken well before corporate market positions are threatened.

Just-in-time marketing (JITM), the marketing counterpart of just-in-time production, gears marketing operations and resources more precisely to the time requirements of markets, customers, and consumers. It synchronizes the distribution of products and services with market and channel requirements, and places greater emphasis on having products and services, as well as communications, particularly promotions, available at just the right times for the various market segments and niches. It adds customer value and encourages continuous flow rather than stockpiling of inventories.

JITM matches the timing of company offerings more precisely to the timing of market demand and to the windows of market opportunities, and seeks to prevent problems from arising. It is dependent on good information about future demand, the sharing of cost information, integrated and coordinated action and effective scheduling and precision in meeting needs. Attention is given to generating more satisfaction for consumers, while at the same time holding costs in check by bringing the marketing mix factors on-line just as they are needed, rather than over-investing and over-committing. A requisite is the convenient delivery of products of high quality so that the whole process can flow smoothly.

JITM marketing will result in reducing waste, decreasing costs, making companies more price competitive, and increasing marketing productivity and efficiency. It links suppliers, distributors, and retailers more closely to the marketplace and encourages the integration and coordination of marketing with other activities, cross-relationships among separate entities within the total business system and longer range planning. It keeps a total cost approach rather than a cost per individual activity clearly in mind, and seeks mutually beneficial gains for members of the system. The availability of improved on-line marketing intelligence will provide the information needed for the implementation of flexible marketing approaches and the utilization of contingency planning, which will be backed by flexible production technologies.

Similarly, *value-based marketing* stresses the importance of directing future marketing resources and marketing activities to the creation of added customer and consumer value. Many of those interviewed in this project expressed ideas indicating that "value will be the name of the game" in Marketing 2000. Consumers, who have been exposed to global markets, and have up-to-date and more complete sources of market information, will have higher expectations than ever, and will be more secure, independent, and willing to make themselves heard. They will demand full value in their purchases making sure that marketers live up to their promises.

Future consumers will be the best informed consumers to date. They will have more adequate information, conveniently available, literally at their finger tips, in readily usable form. They will be encouraged to become more discerning shoppers, and will be more demanding. The extensive availability of quality products, coupled with improved shopping capabilities resulting from the variety of media and distribution channels, and such innovations as user-friendly, smart, technically sophisticated products will support value-based marketing. Companies will set out to provide consumers with greater value, with those product and service attributes that enhance the quality of life, and increase customer value while controlling costs.

Leading-edge marketing refers to the development of marketing approaches that are more attuned to emerging markets and the opportunities that they portend. Emphasis is on being on the leading edge of new opportunities and on being innovative, bearing in mind that over time, innovations will in turn be superseded. A basic tenet is that during the time that companies are enjoying the benefits of an innovation, when the innovation is still deemed successful and profitable, preparations must be made to move on to improved products and processes.

Among the requisites of leading-edge marketing are:

1. Seeking innovations, making continuous improvements in products/services and supporting marketing management operations. This implies that companies must be willing and able to innovate continuously in order to generate improvements and enhance consumer value.

2 Developing strategic marketing flexibility so that the marketing mix can be adjusted in short order to meet new competitive offerings and capitalize on recognized shifts in the marketplace.

Leading-edge marketing implies being on the forefront of creative changes by investing continuously in R&D, being well apprised of competitive capabilities, and fostering a culture that encourages change and innovation. It requires a mindset that believes that everything can be improved, that small improvement over time makes a major difference, and that innovation is a key to future profits.

Network marketing extends and leverages the marketing capabilities of companies in order to capitalize on unfolding market opportunities. The process involves combining activities of a variety of independent businesses into an enhanced, coordinated and integrated marketing organization.

Marketing networks are the result of focusing on the effectiveness that can be achieved by utilizing complementary capabilities and combining and synchronizing the talents of numerous organizations, or parts thereof, in a manner that portends benefits for all. It encourages several companies to cooperate and focus on joining together to accomplish what none could do separately.

Future marketing networks will evolve at two levels: internal and external. Internal marketing networks will combine company in-house capabilities with the resources of outside companies to carry out the internal marketing charge more effectively. Examples may include the linkage and integration of the capabilities of independent, specialized marketing research firms and their specialized data banks with in-house talents to develop an effective marketing information system. Similarly, the talents of many different advertising agencies, boutiques, and other merchandising and promotional companies may be used to enhance the capacity of internal advertising and merchandising departments. The resources of independent product research agencies may be combined with company resources to improve the internal product development process.

External or inter-marketing networks refer to linking together a variety of independent businesses, such as different kinds of retailing institutions, or transportation and warehousing companies, to achieve coordinated distribution systems. The development of external networks promotes cooperation among manufacturers, distributors, retailers, and consumers, encouraging the delivery of higher standards of living to consumers.

Networking will be particularly applicable to the global marketplace where U.S. companies seek to operate in many different cultures. Network marketing will provide companies with a wider range of feasible marketing alternatives; it will expand company horizons. It will permit companies with limited resources to compete more effectively in a much broader landscape. The result will be the development of more efficient and effective marketing systems. Effective networking, however, will require a different conception of the company and its capabilities along with new methods of organization, communications, and control.

Marketing Management Implications

These new marketing thrusts call for new approaches to marketing management, including:

- Development of increasing enterprise flexibility in order to cope with market dynamism. This means an organizational willingness and capability to accept and adjust continuously to market changes, including the adjustment and fine tuning of marketing programs and approaches.

- Development of likely market scenarios and their operational implications. This helps incorporate futures thinking into management operations.

- Adoption of entrepreneurial approaches to capitalize on future market opportunities. This promotes innovation and a new venture orientation, can lead to vastly different methods of operation, and tends to limit bureaucratic approaches.

- Development of a business culture that encourages the acceptance of risks — reasonable market risks. This means that managers are expected to make some wrong decisions; they are encouraged to experiment.

- Implementation of changes before current marketing practices become late responses to competitors' actions. This underscores the importance of programming innovations, of continuously seeking new and better ways, of striving for the small gains that overall will add up to major advantages.

- Tracking and using information about competitive developments inside and outside of the firm's core industry. This promotes alertness to environmental changes, as well as to new concepts and ideas, and the opportunities they portend.

- Assessing future management skills that will be required and implementing training programs to achieve them. This implies that marketing training will be an important continuing function.

Marketing as a Change Agent

Respondents to our inquiries have characterized future marketing developments in such terms as increasing market turbulence, shorter product life cycles, instantaneous competitor adjustments, global competition from new industry entrants, radically new innovations, and rising product development costs. These suggest both a compression of market response time and a more costly, dynamic, and less predictable environment. They will heighten the need to be acutely attuned to likely market developments and to be prepared to act rapidly on both perceived threats and opportunities.

Marketing's role in the new environment is that of a change agent — to provide guidance and direction for the kinds of changes that a business must make to meet market needs. As such, marketing will become even more concerned with futurity. Part of the marketing mission will be to:

- Unfreeze organizational perceptions and commitments that are rooted in assumptions of the past and will not be attuned to the future.

- Provide greater customer and consumer value by making continuous adjustments and adaptations in the marketing mix so that there is a better fit with market segments and niches.

- Provide the marketing strategies and programs to capitalize on the opportunities that market estimates portend.

- Limit both future threats and market risks by being better attuned to implications of the changing market topography.

- Develop marketing programs that effectively market the innovations and changes themselves, not only to markets, but to all the publics involved.

External Factors Promoting Flexibility

In the environment of Marketing 2000, flexibility will become a new management watchword, not only for marketing, but for the total business, because:

- Competition for market shares will rapidly become more global in nature, resulting in the emergence of the true global corporation, resulting in much more informed and capable competitors, with sizable asset bases.

- Emerging new technologies will provide opportunities for new firms to gain entrance into well established markets by producing superior, user-friendly, and smart products. The result will be increasing quality at lower costs as is now happening in many industries. The pace will be quickened and the impact heightened.

- The emergence of newly industrialized countries, such as Malaysia, Indonesia, the Philippines, along with the four tigers, Korea, Taiwan, Hong Kong, and Singapore. These countries will rapidly expand their outreach and increase productive capacity in many products. Capacity will greatly exceed market demand and the U.S. could continue as the overflow market.

- The pace of technological change will continue to accelerate resulting in a time compression between the discovery of an invention and its commercial application. This will dramatically shorten product life cycles and reduce the time frame of the "window of opportunity." The syndrome that "he who hesitates is lost" will be underscored. There will be less time in which to garner the advantages of new flexible manufacturing systems. In addition, more effective, competitive intelligence will foster faster and more effective competitor response.

- Foreign exchange rates will become a much more important part of marketing considerations. The marketing/finance interface will take on increasing importance as marketing success becomes intertwined with developments in international finance.

- The retailer/manufacturer power nexus will shift further, as retailers continue to develop greater access to significant information, become larger, and emphasize their own brands.

- Some threats to the environment will become increasingly complex and marketers may be called upon to make sudden adjustments as various product ingredients, and indeed products, may be abandoned.

- Trade will become an even more important marketing concern, and the tendency to erect barriers in order to protect local markets will likely be more prevalent in certain sectors of the world. Government/business cooperation will receive more attention to promote access to international markets.

- Public sector costs in such areas as health care, drug abuse, AIDS, and our aging population will absorb an increasing proportion of public expenditures, and private sector market support will be sought out to aid in the development and delivery of relevant products and services.

- The composition of core and target markets will change significantly as a result of major demographic shifts. Included are the maturing of baby-boomers, increased percentages of senior citizens, changes in racial and ethnic components, increases in the number of deaths, the changing structures of homes and families, added longevity and the changing geographic distribution of people in the U.S. as well as in other industrialized countries.

Preparedness

The above, which are just illustrative of the host of future trends and tendencies, have inherent in them both opportunities and threats. They will offer opportunities for firms that are attuned to emerging developments. They will threaten the existence of those firms that simply respond as they always have, by continuing on their way and trying to "roll with the punches." Organizationally, companies will have to develop ways to monitor such trends and reorient marketing practices accordingly.

Since market trends, and future scenarios, impact on all aspects of company endeavors, the usual tendency is to suggest that they are everyone's business. That posture, however, is no longer acceptable. The well-known adage states "that which is everybody's business becomes nobody's business." Business futures are indeed much too important to be left to individual whims. In Marketing 2000, top management may well benefit by keeping the following guidelines in mind:

1. The development of information about likely trends and future market developments is as important as any information in the firm.

2. The inevitability of changing market environments will require changing marketing thought processes and methods of operation.

3. The development of preparedness and willingness on the part of marketing executives to deal with likely futures is paramount.

4. The restructuring of marketing activities is far easier than restructuring peoples' minds, yet the development of different mindsets is paramount.

Conclusion

The future will see a significant reorientation in marketing management priorities and outlook. There will be a reversal in management perceptions and expectations, with stability being viewed as an anomaly, and ongoing market and business change as normal. Continuous learning, the constant generation of improvements and innovations, and maintenance of flexibility will be underscored. Marketing will be seen as a change agent — a means of continuous adjustment and adaptation.

This, in turn, will foster greater appreciation of futures information, and of programs and activities to improve inputs about future activities. Monitoring and scanning, scenario building, and contingency planning will be given greater attention. The future will occupy a far more prominent position in both management deliberations and research concerns. Futures thinking will become a normal consideration — a basic input — a regular building block for the most critical management activities of tomorrow. Emerging trends, after all, hold the keys to the future. And Marketing 2000 is a door — a not too distant door — waiting to be unlocked.

APPENDIX ON METHODOLOGY

The American Marketing Association futures study, Marketing 2000, was carried out by a core group consisting of Dr. William Lazer, Eminent Scholar in Business Administration, Florida Atlantic University, Director; Dr. Priscilla LaBarbera, Associate Professor, New York University, Associate Director; Dr. James MacLachlan, Associate Professor, Rennselaer Polytechnic Institute, and Dr. Allen Smith, Associate Professor, Florida Atlantic University, members of the Commission on Marketing in the Year 2000.

Others members of the Commission on Marketing in the Year 2000, established by the American Marketing Association to guide the study were: Harold S. Becker, President of New Perspectives; J. Daniel Beckham, President of Health Market Inc.; Stephen J. Custer, Vice President of Marketing Services at Creswell/Munsell/Fultz and Zirbel, Inc.; Jane R. Fitzgibbon, Sr. Vice President and Director of Research Development of Ogilvy & Mather; Jeffrey Hallett, Principal of The PresentFutures Group Ann Ives, President of The Educators Network; Dr. Patrick E. Murphy, Associate Professor, University of Notre Dame; and Dr. H. Paul Root, Division Director of Corporate Marketing Research, E.I. Dupont de Nemoures & Co.

To assure a comprehensive and balanced perspective, the investigation involved several phases. To begin with, an extensive and very deliberate literature review was initiated. The literature review sought to identify a wide variety of perspectives and trends pointing out developments of interest both within marketing and in related business areas, their implications for future marketing developments, research methods, and guidelines for pursuing futures research and improving strategic marketing planning. The findings were carefully sifted and summaries of some of the key contributions from the literature are briefly highlighted in Chapter 5. An extensive annotated bibliography of the periodical literature has been compiled and published separately by the American Marketing Association under the title, *Marketing 2000: Future Perspectives on Marketing, An Annotated Bibliography of Articles.*

The next phase comprised personal, in depth interviews with leading marketing research practitioners who are working on the cutting edge of strategic marketing management and marketing research in corporations in New York, Chicago, and Florida. The respondents were involved with providing inputs for corporate planning and decision-making, and in designing studies dealing with the future. They were invited to offer insights and advice, not only about likely marketing trends and developments, but also about guidelines for the execution of a study on marketing in the future. During these interviews the importance of having the involvement of futures researchers, and of top-level, insightful business practitioners, in addition to leading academicians was underscored.

As a result, a Presidential Advisory Committee (PAC), consisting of the leaders of five key firms actively engaged in major future studies, was appointed. Members of the PAC were: Theodore J. Gordon, Chairman, the Futures Group; William B. Johnston, Senior Research Fellow, the Hudson Institute; Rafael D. Pagan, Jr., Chairman, Pagan International; Florence R. Skelly, President, Yankelovich, Skelly & White, Inc.; and Edith Weiner, President, Weiner-Edrich-Brown, Inc. The specific individuals were chosen on the basis of two criteria: 1) references to them and their work in the literature, and 2) the recommendations of knowledgeable practitioners respected for their own work on the future, and/or their insights regarding future marketing developments.

A workshop was held with the PAC and the project directors of the study. The purpose of the workshop was to clarify project objectives, evaluate alternative methodologies and approaches, identify knowledgeable contacts, highlight environmental factors that will likely shape marketing, and outline anticipated marketing developments. The contributions of the PAC members were particularly valuable and continued throughout the study.

A small press release on the Commission's activities and the PAC meeting was carried in the AMA's *Marketing News*. The article invited interested readers to submit their comments about future marketing developments. Twelve individuals sent comments and over 20 readers expressed a desire to be directly involved with the project. In addition, numerous phone calls and letters were received requesting any information and ideas about future marketing developments that the Commission would share immediately. Requests were also received regularly from various marketing publications desirous of publishing study results. The interest throughout remained at a high level.

Next, an extensive list of names was compiled of people who had either expressed an interest in the study, or who had been identified as knowledgeable about marketing in the future. From this list the AMA president, Mr. Manuel Plotkin, invited the eight individuals already mentioned, three academicians, and five practitioners to participate actively as members of the Commission on Marketing in the Year 2000. Included among their many activities were two full-day Commission workshops.

Working together with the PAC, the Commission identified top executives who are regarded as visionaries in a variety of industries. Members of the PAC and the Commission personally approached these business leaders seeking their cooperation in participating in the study. The executives selected for interviews were then sent a discussion guide outlining the study's areas of concern. A professional interviewer, William Harris, of Consulting Marketing Partners, conducted the interviews in Connecticut, Delaware, Illinois, Michigan, and New York.

These extensive interviews were tape recorded and transcribed. The transcriptions were content analyzed and evaluated by the members of the core group to assess trends, sort out major ideas, select representative quotations, and summarize the thinking of the CEO group as a whole. Although the number of executives interviewed is small, it represents top-level individuals with a wealth of experience and insights. The interviewers probed deeply into a wide variety of marketing topics. The thinking of these CEOs is not deemed to be representative of CEOs in general, nevertheless, they are comprised of leaders who are highly regarded for their insightfulness and represent a variety of business endeavors in the manufacturing, retailing, and service sectors. The highlights of the CEO interview findings which include chairmen of the board, presidents, and executive vice presidents are discussed specifically in Chapter 6.

Some leading marketing scholars and noted futurists were invited to participate in the project by preparing brief idea papers, presenting their insights into future developments and the impact on marketing. The participants were selected on the basis of their long-standing reputations for making continual and significant contributions to the marketing discipline, references to their works in the literature, and successful careers as consultants and educators. The contributors are:

- Hal Becker, President, New Perspectives, Inc.
- Leonard Berry, Foley's Federated Professor of Retailing and Marketing Studies, Texas A & M University.
- Leo Bogart, Executive Vice President/General Manager, Newspaper Advertising Bureau.
- Richard N. Cardozo, Curtis L. Carlson Chair in Entrepreneurial Studies, University of Minnesota
- Fred Danzig, Editor, *Advertising Age*.
- Jane Fitzgibbon, Senior Vice President, Ogilvy & Mather Trendsights and Fred Elkind, Vice President, Ogilvy & Mather Trendsights.
- John Howard, George E. Warren Professor Emeritus of Business, Graduate School of Business, Columbia University.
- Phil Kotler, S.C. Johnson & Son Distinguished Professor of International Marketing, Kellogg Graduate School of Business, Northwestern University.
- Theodore Levitt, Edward W. Carter Professor of Business Administration, Harvard University and former Editor, *Harvard Business Review*
- Sidney Levy, Charles H. Kellstadt Distinguished Professor of Marketing, Chairman, Department of Marketing, School of Business, Northwestern University.
- Burt Nanus, Director, Center for Futures Research, University of Southern California.
- Howard V. Perlmutter, Professor of Social Architecture and Management, The Wharton School, University of Pennsylvania.
- Frederick E. Webster, Jr., Osborn Professor of Marketing, Amos Tuck School of Business Administration, Dartmouth College.
- Edith Weiner, President, Weiner-Edrich-Brown, Inc.
- William D. Wells, Executive Vice President, Director of Marketing Services, DDB Needham Worldwide, Inc.
- Jerry Wind, Director, SEI Center for Advanced Studies in Management and The Lauder Professor of Marketing, The Wharton School of the University of Pennsylvania.

AUTHOR INDEX

SUBJECT INDEX